Relationships and Sex Education 3–11

Relationships and Sex Education 3–11

Supporting Children's Development and Well-being

Sacha Mason and
Richard Woolley

BLOOMSBURY ACADEMIC
LONDON • NEW YORK • OXFORD • NEW DELHI • SYDNEY

BLOOMSBURY ACADEMIC
Bloomsbury Publishing Plc
50 Bedford Square, London, WC1B 3DP, UK
1385 Broadway, New York, NY 10018, USA

BLOOMSBURY, BLOOMSBURY ACADEMIC and the Diana logo are trademarks of
Bloomsbury Publishing Plc

First published in Great Britain in 2011
Second edition published in Great Britain in 2019

Cover image: © BraunS / iStock

A catalogue record for this book is available from the British Library.

A catalog record for this book is available from the Library of Congress.

ISBN: HB: 978-1-3500-8072-0
PB: 978-1-3500-8071-3
ePDF: 978-1-3500-8074-4
eBook: 978-1-3500-8073-7

Typeset by Newgen KnowledgeWorks Pvt. Ltd., Chennai, India
Printed and bound in Great Britain

To find out more about our authors and books visit www.bloomsbury.com
and sign up for our newsletters.

For those we love.

Contents

Acknowledgements

We are grateful to all those who have commented on draft chapters and who have supported us as we planned and developed our ideas for this second edition. We express particular thanks to Alison Baker at Bloomsbury for her support and guidance over recent months, and indeed during the development of the original edition. It goes without saying that all shortcomings in the text are our own. Every effort has been made to contact copyright holders for their permission to reprint material in this book. The publishers would be grateful to hear from any copyright holder who is not acknowledged here and will undertake to rectify any errors or omissions in future editions of this book.

We acknowledge that, at the time of writing, consultation is still underway on draft guidance for Relationships Education in primary schools in England. In places we refer to this draft guidance, and we do not anticipate any major change when the final guidance is agreed. The contents of this book go beyond the requirements of this guidance and also integrate sex education with learning about relationships, as we believe this is the most supportive and effective way to develop learning opportunities for children. We hope that readers will share our ambition for the subject. The name of the subject has developed over time, and in places we refer to Sex and Relationship Education (SRE), Relationships Education, sex education, and Relationships and Sex Education (RSE). What is important are the overarching issues relating to this whole area, and we hope that readers will appreciate that in some contexts the terms are interchangeable. We also believe that sex education should be an integral part of Relationships Education, and for this reason we use the acronym RSE when referring to Relationships Education in primary schools.

Finally, our most sincere thanks are expressed to all the teachers, practitioners, children, students, carers and parents who have shared their insights and experiences with us. Without their input this book would lack much of its reality. In all cases, their contributions have been anonymized.

Introduction

It is more common to hear parents swapping stories about children's first teeth and first steps than it is to hear about a child's sexual development. This is understandable, as it is often seen as a very personal aspect of a person's growth and development. Yet this lack of general knowledge about what is 'normal' sexual development can lead to unnecessary anxiety about children's interest in nudity, 'rude' things and sex.

– Better Health, 2010

Over the past decades, Relationships and Sex Education (RSE) and its predecessors have been addressed by schools in a range of ways in England. Some have focused on the statutory coverage of life cycles, as required by the National Curriculum (DfE, 2014), including changes associated with puberty, with others choosing to include sex education to varying degrees. This can involve the brief coverage of information, sometimes by a healthcare professional brought into school especially for this purpose, towards the end of a child's time in primary school. Other schools have developed a more detailed programme to support children's learning about relationships, sex and sexuality. This provides a *context* for such learning and a supportive environment in which children's questions can be explored. While parents and carers have a right to withdraw children from all or some aspects of sex education, all primary schools are required to have a written policy for mandatory Relationships Education, which is freely available and published on its website (DfE, 2018). It is important to note that children also learn in a range of other structured settings, including after-school and youth clubs, uniformed organizations, with childminders and during sporting activities. Each of these provides an additional context in which to ask questions of adults and to learn more informally from peers.

For some practitioners delivering a programme of RSE will involve exploring issues with children for the first time (either for the child or the adult), and may create a degree of apprehension. While most people are sexual beings, speaking about relationships, sex and sexuality is not always easy. For some, this is a private part of their lives that they will have discussed with few, if any, people. This introduction gives voice to some of the concerns raised by students and teachers and provides a context for the chapters that follow. It sets such issues within the context of the introduction of mandatory Relationships Education in primary schools in England and outlines a range of strategies to support and address children's questions, so that members of the children's workforce are prepared to face a variety of situations.

The Sex Education Forum outlined helpful key elements when learning about sex and relationships, which we extend. It should be

- an integral part of the lifelong learning process, beginning in early childhood and continuing through adult life;
- an entitlement for all boys as well as girls [to which we add those with other gender identities]; those who are heterosexual, lesbian, gay or bisexual [to which we add trans, intersex or asexual]; those with physical, learning or emotional difficulties; and those with a religious or faith tradition – everyone, whatever their background, community or circumstance;
- provided within a holistic context of emotional and social development across all settings. (2005: 1)

The guidelines for RSE in England

In 2000, the Department for Education and Employment published guidance on the provision of Sex and Relationship Education (SRE). This was to last for almost two decades. It defined RSE (or SRE as it then was) as

> lifelong learning about physical, moral and emotional development. It is about the understanding of the importance of marriage for family life, stable and loving relationships, respect, love and care. It is also about the teaching of sex, sexuality, and sexual health. It is not about the promotion of sexual orientation or sexual activity – this would be inappropriate teaching. (DfEE, 2000: 5)

This key document identified three main elements within RSE, namely, attitudes and values; personal and social skills; and knowledge and understanding. These are subdivided into further areas, which are worth noting here in full:

Attitudes and values
- learning the importance of values and individual conscience and moral considerations;
- learning the value of family life, marriage, and stable and loving relationships for the nurture of children;
- learning the value of respect, love and care;
- exploring, considering and understanding moral dilemmas; and
- developing critical thinking as part of decision making.

Personal and social skills

- learning to manage emotions and relationships confidently and sensitively;
- developing self-respect and empathy for others;
- learning to make choices based on an understanding of difference and with an absence of prejudice;
- developing an appreciation of the consequences of choices made;
- managing conflict; and
- learning how to recognize and avoid exploitation and abuse.

Knowledge and understanding

- learning and understanding physical development at appropriate stages;
- understanding human sexuality, reproduction, sexual health, emotions and relationships;
- learning about contraception and the range of local and national sexual health advice, contraception and support services;
- learning the reasons for delaying sexual activity, and the benefits to be gained from such delay; and
- the avoidance of unplanned pregnancy. (DfEE, 2000: 5)

In many senses the guidance was problematic. First its title, Sex and Relationship Education, places sex before relationship. While this may be the reality of some people's experience, the focus on love, care and respect within the guidance suggested that the reverse should be the case. Additionally, it used relationship in the singular. It is our contention that relationships should precede sex in the title of this area of study in schools, and that the plural *relationships* needs to be employed in order (i) to recognize that many people experience more than one sexual relationship in life, and (ii) that a wider range of relationships need to be explored in order to support children's emotional development and well-being. The latter is particularly significant when one considers the areas highlighted above which focus on problem solving, respect, empathy and managing both relationships and conflict. These elements relate to a far wider sphere of relationships than purely sexual ones. The introduction of RSE in England from 2019 addresses these issues to some degree, although in primary schools the subject is entitled Relationships Education, with sex education remaining optional. We suggest that combining the strengths of the guidance from 2000 outlined above (DfEE, 2000) with the guidance under development in 2018 (DfE, 2018) provides the opportunity to schools to design and implement an holistic and supportive curriculum designed to meet the needs of all learners.

The inclusion of the statement that it would be inappropriate to promote any sexual orientation in the guidance from 2000 is interesting. The use of *promote* is reminiscent of section 28 of the Local Government Act (1988) which forbade such bodies promoting homosexuality. While technically there was uncertainty about whether this legislation applied to schools, it caused many teachers some degree of apprehension about discussing sexual orientation with their learners. Here, however, it is used in a wider context, which infers that it is not appropriate to promote *any form* of sexual orientation, whether heterosexual, bisexual, homosexual or other. One may question how such orientations could be promoted in any case, given that they are an implicit part of the make-up of a person. However, the result is that teachers cannot use their own views, beliefs or prejudices to advocate any particular way of being. This is an important principle within RSE.

Defining terms

It is important at this stage to make clear some of the terms that are used throughout this book. First, we often refer to children and learners, rather than to pupils. It is our belief that these are more positive and active words than *pupil* is, which is an archaic term that makes the child an object rather than a participant.

Second, we need to make clear the distinction between the terms sexuality and sexual orientation, which are sometimes employed interchangeably in common usage. *Sexuality* is how one perceives and expresses oneself as a sexual being. This can include a range of behaviours, actions and social interactions: it is thus about both feeling and expression. *Sexual orientation* describes the pattern of emotional, romantic or sexual attraction to other people: it relates to the focus of one's sexuality. This is commonly characterized along a continuum of homosexuality, bisexuality and heterosexuality, although in reality this is an oversimplification (as we discuss in Chapter 8).

The term homosexual is itself contentious, and although we use it in places we acknowledge that for many years it was used to identify a perceived medical disorder (see Chapter 8). The Greek word *homos* means same (not to be confused for the Latin word *homo* meaning man), and so a homosexual is a person attracted to another of the same sex. We acknowledge that may people prefer to use alternative terms, including gay, given the historically tainted nature of the word 'homosexual'.

It is interesting that the guidance for England cited above (DfEE, 2000) and also the new curriculum guidance (DfE, 2018) use the word sex rather than sexuality in their titles. The former is often used either as a synonym for gender, or for sexual intercourse. In contrast, the legal framework for Northern Ireland is entitled Relationships and Sexuality Education, which address some of the concerns raised above (DENI, n.d.). This would be a more progressive title and is perhaps something that schools should consider when exploring the values and ethos they wish to present in a curriculum for their school.

Finally, we use a range of terms for members of the children's workforce including teacher, childcare professional and practitioner. It is not our intention to be exclusive by the use of these terms and we hope that readers will apply ideas and concepts to their own roles, contexts and settings wherever possible. Inevitably, some of our discussion will be Anglo-centric, given our context of new guidance for RSE in schools. Again, we hope that the issues, and the examples that we explore, will be accessible to those in other locations.

The concerns of student teachers

In a survey of student teachers' views on difficult and controversial issues (Woolley, 2009) 64 per cent of respondents identified RSE as being an area where they felt apprehensive. This was also the issue that the greatest number of student teachers taking part in the survey identified as having the potential to be difficult to address with children.

Interestingly, of the issues that the student teachers anticipated encountering in their first teaching post, 6.4 per cent of students expected never to encounter children's developing sexualities. Of these, four were training to work with children aged 3–7 years, two for 5–9 years and two for 3–11 years. Two did not indicate an age range. While it might be anticipated that there would be a correlation between the age of the children being taught and the expectation of encountering developing sexualities, across the sample as a whole this was not the case. However 82.1 per cent (of the 166 respondents to the survey) felt that they viewed addressing children's developing sexualities as an important part of their role as a teacher. There is a tension here, between the number that felt that addressing sexualities is important and the almost as significant number feeling apprehension about doing so.

Comments from a range of student teachers from the eight university providers of initial teacher education surveyed (Woolley, 2009, 2010) revealed the following:

> I have had no college input on this matter [RSE] and have no idea how I would approach it within the primary school.
> (Undergraduate Student, East Midlands, training to teach children aged 3–9 years)

> I think this links in with sexuality as families are so versatile in our society and I have similar apprehensions about contradicting the views children may have taken on from their families about what is the 'norm'. It [is] really that classic thing of children going home having listened to their teacher and repeating it to the parent and the parent replying. 'I don't care what your teacher says this ... is the way it is!'
> (Undergraduate Student, North East, training to teach children aged 3–11 years)

> I would be happy to discuss anything [relating to sexuality] honestly with children, but would worry about how their parents/carers would react.
> (PGCE Student, South East, training to teach children aged 5–11 years)

These insights provide a suggestion that student teachers expect to engage with RSE in schools, whether in formal or informal ways, and are willing to discuss children's questions. However a significant concern is how parents and carers will respond to this information and this, inevitably, will affect teacher confidence both in delivering materials and answering other questions from their learners. It is important therefore to consider strategies for the effective delivery of RSE and also methods to support the effective engagement with carers and parents. Further views from student teachers (using data gathered in 2016) are included in Chapter 8.

Teachers' concerns

It is not only student teachers who have concerns about the delivery of RSE. The following extracts from interviews with practising teachers highlight some of the fears that they express. Further concerns are included in Chapter 5, where a variety of adults express their apprehensions about the delivery of RSE.

> As a newly qualified teacher with a Year 6 class, I am concerned that I am expected to deliver a programme of both sex and relationships education having had no training in this area. I do believe that a class teacher ought to coordinate this provision; I realise that I know my class well and I would rather explore issues with the children than have a stranger come in to the classroom to lead the discussions. However, I am extremely apprehensive about saying the wrong thing, giving inaccurate information or sharing details that are too adult for my learners.
>
> (Simon, Year 6 teacher)

> The curriculum plan for this term states that I am to cover the correct words for body parts with my Year 2 children. I must admit to being nervous about this. Although I think that I know the right words to use, I am not used to using this language in front of other people, yet alone six year olds. I am concerned that I will become embarrassed, will blush and flounder and might say the wrong thing. I want this to be a positive experience for the children. I guess that really what I want is for them to find a confidence that I do not yet possess myself.
>
> (Neesha, Year 2 teacher)

> I am a single woman and although I think I am a lesbian I have never done anything about it. I am extremely worried that in the lessons on sex and relationships I will be asked questions that I know nothing about. I am sure that my colleagues, particularly the married ones, know something about sex and can use this to think of answers to children's questions. But at the moment I have not had sex or a serious relationship of any kind and I am worried that my total lack of experience – particularly with men – will mean that I end up looking foolish in front of my class. As an experienced teacher I think that this is the point where I have to hold my hands up and say 'this is beyond my knowledge'.
>
> (Corinna, Year 5 teacher)

I am a committed Christian and do not believe in sex before marriage. I do not think that children in primary schools should learn about sexual acts: they are too young and their innocence should be protected. I know that some of the children in my class may soon reach puberty. I am torn between thinking that I should support them as their teacher and wondering whether this is something that should really be introduced by their parents. I do not want to talk about erections and wet dreams, menstruation or how men and women have sex. It just does not seem right. This is not why I became a teacher.

(Emma, Year 4 teacher)

These views show some of the apprehensions held by teachers. Some stem from a lack of personal knowledge or experience, others come from firmly held personal views or concerns about how they will be able to tackle sensitive subject matter with children. A key question is whether it is better for children to receive RSE from a known and trusted adult with whom they have a well-established relationship, such as their class teacher, or whether RSE is best delivered by someone coming into their classroom who can offer impartial and informed advice, without knowing the children. Such anonymity might provide learners with a greater chance to ask difficult questions: however, it would not give the opportunity for questions to be asked on an ongoing basis or for learning to be developed over time within a well-established and familiar learning environment. It is important for practitioners to balance such questions with their own concerns about delivering RSE.

Reflecting on the range of issues raised by teachers in the examples above, consider:

- how you respond to each example;
- what advice you might offer to each teacher in order to help to develop their confidence;
- whether you feel that RSE is best delivered by practitioners known well to the children or by those coming into school to offer special provision; and
- what role you feel that other practitioners have, for example, those working with children in more informal settings.

One strength which practitioners possess is the range of generic skills and strategies that they have to use then exploring issues with children. These provide opportunities for teachers to use the methods they know extremely well, adapting them to deal with the subject matter of RSE.

Strategies

In this section a range of strategies for supporting the effective provision of RSE is outlined. This provides a broad introduction to some of the generic methods employed by teachers to promote active learning, which will be developed further in subsequent chapters and extended, with specific examples, in the final chapter.

Mind mapping provides a useful way of recording ideas in a succinct and clear manner. It can be a useful way to begin thinking about an idea or issue and can record an array of thoughts in a relatively brief time. It can be used, for example, to support thinking about relationships or to gauge children's knowledge about puberty.

Persona dolls are characters introduced to the classroom, which have a specific personality or attributes which always remain constant. They provide a useful distancing technique to enable learners to ask questions of an independent 'person' within a lesson. The doll might be used to suggest questions about feelings or behaviours and a teacher can use these to prompt children to suggest advice. Discussing how the character represented by the doll might deal with situations relating to growing up, coping with a friend moving away or dealing with peer pressure can offer an effective means of modelling positive behaviours for children and enabling them to hear constructive advice.

Role play uses children's imagination to consider scenarios from different perspectives. It offers the chance to *stand in the shoes* of another. It is important to make sure that children understand when they are in role and at what point they 'de-role': this can lessen the opportunity for confusion of embarrassment. While it can never be possible to actually stand in another's shoes, role play offers an opportunity to develop empathy and to see things from different viewpoints. This strategy might be particularly useful when exploring difficulties with friendships or addressing issues relating to conflict resolution.

Small group discussions can provide the opportunity for children to air their ideas outside the more pressured setting of a whole-class discussion. It can be useful to begin in pairs, in order to initiate ideas with the support of a peer, before moving on to discuss in a group of four or six. This strategy, often referred to as *snowballing*, can be particularly effective for children reticent about speaking in front of a whole class, and provides the opportunity to rehearse and develop ideas before sharing them with others. In sessions relating to RSE, practitioners will wish to choose pairs carefully so that children are supported and their views encouraged by their working partner.

Communities of enquiry are core to the approach known as *Philosophy for Children*. This approach supports the skills of enquiry, reasoning and evaluation and facilitates information processing and creative thinking. This enables children to explore meanings, beliefs and values within a supportive and secure community of co-learners (for an overview, see DfES, 2005: 56–7). This approach can support a range of considerations relating to relationships at a variety of levels.

Taking a stand provides the opportunity to argue a particular viewpoint with another child who takes the opposing view. Using two concentric circles of chairs, those in the inner circle face those in the outer one. In this method, children may have to justify views that they do not personally hold and this can provide another means of developing empathetic thinking. This can be a particularly effective strategy to use with older children and, again, offers the chance to see things from different perspectives.

Opinion lines provide the chance to express a view along a continuum of variance. Those positioned along the line can explain their views and seek to encourage others in the direction of their argument. It is important to support anyone who finds themselves alone along the continuum and also to ensure that respect is shown for the range of views. This strategy provides a positive means of explaining how reasoned argument is required when justifying opinions and showing that changing one's mind can be a positive part of learning.

Stories and picture books offer opportunities to consider the experience of others, whether through fact or fiction. A range of such resources are available considering a variety of relationships and family types. Discussing the characters in the book gives an opportunity to talk about the issues *one step removed* from personal experience. It is important to remember that picture books are not only for young children and that a wide variety is available for all ages: a range of materials is highlighted in later chapters.

International perspectives on RSE

The Netherlands

Over past decades the Netherlands has been identified as being particularly progressive in its approach to SRE, with outcomes including low rates of teenage pregnancy. One study in particular (Lewis and Knijn, 2001) compared the experiences of young people in the Netherlands and England, concluding that while both systems covered similar topics, Dutch sex education had a much more positive attitude towards sex. The Dutch system is often referred to, in general terms, as being liberal, open, positive and comprehensive (Ferguson et al., 2008), although this does not give specific detail about the nature and content of the curriculum for RSE. Ferguson et al. suggest,

> Sexuality materials that emerge from The Netherlands are characterized by consistent, relationship-oriented messages about sexuality, safe sex, and contraceptives. Although sexuality education in The Netherlands is still primarily focused on reducing risky

sexual behavior, topics are presented in a positive light, thereby normalizing sexual feelings rather than inducing fear and shame in young people. What are often considered taboo or sensitive topics, such as sexual orientation and masturbation, are common themes in Dutch materials. (2008: 104)

Safe-sex materials include not only those relating to the prevention of pregnancy, but also to STDs and HIV. A key message is that if a person is going to have sex then they need to do it safely. There is a combination of learning about sexual practices with a focus on values: establishing personal values and developing the life skills needed to implement and to maintain those values. This supports both those who choose to become sexually active and those who chose to remain abstinent.

This raises some interesting issues for teachers in other contexts to consider. First, whether they acknowledge that young people begin to have sexual intercourse before the legal age of consent and encourage informed and mature choices. Second, how STDs and HIV are discussed in the classroom, and at what stage or age. Third, how sex can be presented within both the context of relationships and enjoyment. Learning and teaching about responsible sexual activity must address more than pregnancy avoidance; it needs to consider health issues on a wider scale (both to maintain one's own physical and mental health and that of others), but also to acknowledge that an implicit part of sex within a relationship is that both parties gain a degree of pleasure and personal fulfilment. Readers of this book will wish to consider how the curriculum for RSE can empower children and young people to make positive life choices that are informed, thoughtful and respectful to both themselves and others. This notion of *empowerment* provides the opportunity to help learners to develop the skills necessary to make a wide range of decisions in a confident and suitably assertive manner.

South Africa

A survey of Britons (Eurobarometer, 2006) found that over half of the population did not use any form of protection to avoid HIV infection and that 22 per cent wrongly believed that HIV could be passed on by kissing; just over half still wrongly believed that it was possible to become infected by sharing a glass. A survey by Ipsos MORI (2014) found that 15 per cent of adults wrongly thought that HIV could be transmitted by kissing, and 16 per cent by spitting, and the Terrence Higgins Trust found that one in three people in Britain would be uncomfortable performing first aid on someone living with HIV (Terrence Higgins Trust, 2018). Such continuing misconceptions are astounding given that the public awareness of HIV was first raised over twenty years ago and the medical advances that have followed subsequently: 'Effective treatment now means that a person living with the virus who is on effective treatment cannot pass it on to another' (Terrence Higgins Trust, 2018: 4). Furthermore, taking pre-exposure prophylaxis (PrEP) prevents infection.

Learning from the South African experience

When visiting primary schools in the Richmond area of KwaZulu Natal it was surprising to see the prominence of materials relating to HIV/AIDS in every classroom (Woolley, 2007). Those of us working in childcare settings may have been involved in addressing challenging issues with children: alcohol and drug misuse, prejudice, stereotypes and bullying. However, we may never have discussed the impact of HIV or the ways in which it is transmitted.

In one classroom in Richmond a whole display area was dedicated to HIV/AIDS. Posters declared Use a Condom, AIDS Kills and a list of key messages had been collected by the children on how to tackle child abuse. For these children, aged between 9 and 11 years, HIV/AIDS was not only an issue to be faced in their families or community, its implications were a daily part of their classroom environments. It was difficult to judge the possible impact of this constant presence on the lives of the children; it was challenging to see the use of contraception presented in a primary school classroom (Woolley, 2007).

The high incidence of HIV in South Africa has an impact upon identity and the sense of the value of one's humanity. The constant presence of illness and death heightens the sense of the transience of life, and this can impact on value that one puts on one's own life. According to the Joint United Nations Programme on HIV/AIDS (UNAIDS, 2004), HIV prevalence among South Africans aged 15 to 49 was 21.5% in 2003. At this point 4.3 to 5.9 million people were living with HIV – the largest number in any country. It was estimated that around 600 people a day were dying of AIDS-related infections (Ruxton, 2004) and eleven teachers died of AIDS-related illnesses each day (MacGregor, 2005). By 2016 this figure was 18.9% of the population, with 56% of adults and 55% of children on antiretroviral treatment and 7.1 million people living with HIV (AVERT, 2017).

(adapted from Adams et al., 2008: 78–9)

Consider:

- how HIV might impact on children of primary school age in your setting;
- whether children need to be aware of HIV and for what reasons; and
- how children can begin to understand that all kinds of bodily fluids are special and personal, and understand how HIV is transmitted and how it is not.

This information about the situation in South Africa suggests that children are capable of considering difficult issues, whether relating to health needs in their local community or those that could impact on their own lives. Many children, in a wide range of settings, will be aware of HIV through the broadcast media, although perhaps in recent years it has received less attention than it did in earlier decades. Some children have this awareness because of needs that exist within their own families. As a part of effective RSE it is necessary to consider, in age- and developmentally appropriate ways, how personal safety can be maintained. This may begin with discussions about how bodily fluids are special: saliva is designed to help digestion; blood is the special substance that maintains our bodies by transporting oxygen and nutrients; and urine is a waste product that we need to dispose of periodically in an appropriate manner. All these fluids serve a special and personal purpose. Children need to understand that each is dealt with sensitively and in personal, and often private, ways. At times some may carry infections of different types; but this is not always the case. As children grow, they can begin to understand that while some bodily fluids may be shared with others, this is usually done within relationships that matter and are appropriate and not in contexts devoid or care, respect or developing commitment.

Having raised some significant issues from a variety of settings, the next section introduces the range of materials that are explored within this book in order to address such issues and develop context-specific practice.

Overview of the book

Key themes thread their way throughout this book. First, there is the need to be brave in the planning and delivery of programmes of RSE and in addressing children's concerns and needs. Second, it is important to consult with children in order that their voice is heard, whether that is through asking questions, commenting on the advice they receive or identifying areas for further learning. Third, there is a focus on the importance of relationships, in the widest sense of the word, which impact significantly on the way in which people live in a wide variety of settings; this theme is a priority within the book and we believe it is one of the most important aspects of a child's development. We address this particularly though the concept of a *pedagogy of listening*. Fourth, there is the need to approach issues and ideas in an open and honest way, which acknowledges that practitioners do not have all the answers but shows a willingness to support children in finding out. This aspect helps children to develop the life skills necessary to deal with a range of situations in a confident and proactive manner, supported by a sense of their own self-worth and by positive self-esteem. Finally, there is the need to acknowledge that every child is entitled to effective RSE. The inclusion of developmentally appropriate sex education is important if children are to have any sense of context for the physical and emotional changes they will encounter, and to appreciate those in others. A failure to provide this will have a significant and lasting impact on children, young people, their families and wider society.

Throughout this book a range of methods are used to encourage both reflection and the development of effective practice. Pause for thought activities, examples from research and small-scale case studies give the opportunity to consider how challenging and sometimes complex issues can be addressed in classrooms. Here, the first case study provides an opportunity to think about how language can be used in appropriate ways with younger children.

Simon is four years old. Soon after he was born his parents engaged in discussions with friends and family members about what word to use when speaking about his genitals. They felt that something simple, positive and pronounceable was needed, which was also age-appropriate. Simon's father recalls,

We considered all kinds of words. Willy seemed too coarse, tail (the word I used when a boy) is commonly used but could cause confusion when speaking about other matters (for example, when our dog wags its tail), and penis seemed too grown up and might cause embarrassment for both peers and teachers once he started school. After a great deal of discussion we decided to use the name Joey.

When we went to visit Simon's uncle one weekend, we were astonished to discover that his pet budgie was called Joey. We asked that he did not mention this to Simon, to save any embarrassment during our visit. Our main worry was that on returning home he would tell his grandparents that he had seen his uncle's Joey, and the possible concern or hilarity that this might cause.

Consider:

- at what age is it appropriate to use the formal words with children for all parts of the body;
- whether formal names are any more difficult to pronounce or use than other names;
- what impact the use of an informal name or colloquial term might have on a child's feelings about their genitals; and
- why it is that many adults find the use of anatomically correct names for body parts embarrassing.

This is one example of the way in which adults seek to protect children from a supposedly adult world by avoiding anatomically correct names for parts of the body. It is interesting to consider whether using the word penis is any more adult than employing another term. It is no harder to say than most of the euphemisms that are used and might encourage a degree of maturity when children start to enquire about their bodies, discuss physical changes or raise questions about sex and sexual relationships. Throughout this book we consider such issues relating to developmental appropriateness, the use of language and attitudes towards answering children's questions. As a point of reference, the following paragraphs include a brief overview of each chapter.

In Chapter 1 an exploration of the historical context of RSE is developed. RSE is currently on the political agenda in England. In 1999, the Social Exclusion Unit reported in the teenage pregnancy paper (1999: 7) that UK teenage pregnancy rates could be attributed to ignorance as one factor, among others. This identified 'lack of knowledge' pointed to social and, in particular, educational deficits in appropriate RSE. The DfEE SRE guidance (2000) set the context for schools to develop an effective policy for almost twenty years. Subsequently, Every Child Matters (DfES, 2004) renewed pressure on schools to review their sex and relationship curriculum and the agenda gathered momentum following an independent review of RSE undertaken by Sir Alasdair Macdonald across all four key stages of schooling in 2008 (Macdonald, 2009). The DCSF accepted all of the recommendations of the Macdonald review and announced that PSHE, of which RSE is an element, would become a statutory part of the National Curriculum for schools in England from 2011. Unfortunately, the General Election of 2010 meant that this did not reach the statute. This chapter explores the historical, political and current context for RSE. The recent shift from the use of 'relationship' in the singular to the plural 'relationships' in some government documentation has significance and is addressed with particular relevance to professionals working with children, including in the new statutory guidance for the subject (DfE, 2018).

Chapter 2 considers the wider context of RSE. It explores some of the influences that can impact upon children's learning about relationships and sexuality, including the family, peers and the media. Whether it is conversations on the playground, information from older siblings, reading teenage magazines or watching soap operas and reality-based programmes on the television, children can gain a range of information about relationships from a wider range of sources than ever before. Some of these sources may provide inappropriate and unrealistic information about relationships and sexual practices which may cause children to develop unrealistic expectations. They can also give false expectations about relationships or sex devoid of any context that involves love, care or respect; they can be a source of stereotypes which influence children's understanding of others. This chapter considers how safe environments can be developed in which children's questions are welcomed and valued. It also explores how heterosexism and homophobia, both prevalent in contemporary society, can be addressed in age-appropriate ways in learning settings in order to combat preconceptions and misconceptions. Importantly, this chapter addresses how to support children so that they use the internet in appropriate ways and maintain personal safety.

Chapter 3 explores the question of relationships. It is our contention that this aspect of RSE is of particular importance and needs to be addressed with a wide variety of understandings in mind. Relationships and relatedness form a fundamental aspect of how a person understands themself. They influence a sense of self-esteem and identity and can affect the ways in which they value and care for themselves. This chapter explores ways of supporting children in developing the emotional literacy necessary to mature into confident individuals. It considers expectations for gendered behaviours and how stereotypes can often lead to bullying. In addition, it explores the importance of friendships on a range of levels. Children need to be supported so that they are able to make positive and thoughtful choices about their bodies and their behaviours. This chapter considers how such independence can be both supported and nurtured so that children have the life skills necessary to support them in a variety of social roles and contexts.

Children's views are explored in Chapter 4. In 1989, the UN Convention on the Rights of the Child (and particularly Articles 12, 17 and 24; UNHCHR, 1989) established the concept of the voice of the child; for children to be heard in matters that affect them. RSE is no different and increasing research (Walker et al., 2003; Crumper, 2004; Measor, 2004; UK Youth Parliament, 2007) suggests that children are entitled to be consulted on the content of their RSE programmes. Indeed, where such opportunities are afforded this denotes best practice, as highlighted in new guidance in England (DfE, 2018). However, the historical picture has been that children's views were not sufficiently sought. Gordon and Ellingston (2006) cite research conducted with teenagers who state the inadequacies of RSE in terms of addressing 'real' information about pleasures, intimacy, logistics and emotions related to sex. This chapter discusses the relevance of seeking the views of children and young people as to what content should be addressed in a programme of RSE and offers strategies to engage in this process. The challenges that schools and teachers face in undertaking this approach are explored in detail and supported by practical examples.

The views of a variety of adult stakeholders in schools are considered in Chapter 5. Here a range of apprehensions is expressed by a breadth of people engaged in working closely with children. Each example is supported by both questions to support the reader in reflecting on the situation and suggested strategies to promote the development of effective practice. This chapter considers what is meant when practitioners talk about relationships and how they do this without being critical of the family relationships experienced by some children. Importantly, it includes a range of personal situations which cause professionals discomfort and the example of a family with a strong religious commitment. Further, it includes a consideration of how RSE can be provided for children with special educational needs, focusing briefly on the autistic spectrum and visual impairment to provide two examples. This is an area that causes adults significant concern. Considering how to tailor provision for all children is an essential aspect of developing the curriculum for RSE: all children have an entitlement to both information and learning, and it is important that adults consider how to communicate messages in clear and appropriate ways.

Chapter 6 explores notions of age- and developmentally appropriate RSE, drawing on areas identified through the 15 Domains of Healthy Sexual Development (developed by the RSE Hub from McKee et al., 2010). It considers the challenges that schools and teachers face in developing a staged approach to RSE, and has a structured, spiral curriculum can be developed from the early years, dovetailing with the curriculum for secondary education.

Chapter 7 outlines a range of children's difficult questions. For example, 'Why does the penis go hard, what's that all about?' Addressing issues concerning sex, sexuality and sexual pleasure can pose challenges for professionals working with children. This chapter explores the pedagogical issues in managing difficult questions from children. The concepts of values relating to RSE – held by individuals and wider society – are discussed, as is the impact on professionals faced with handling sensitive issues, such as same-sex relationships, with children. Research by Mason (2010) shows that children think deeply about issues of sex and relationships, and are inquisitive about the logistics, feelings and practicalities associated with sexual relationships. This chapter offers a variety of pedagogical approaches that provide starting points for professionals working with children. It also provides contexts to help consider how to deal with difficult questions through the exploration of case studies. It is particularly useful for those faced with delivering RSE for the first time and for those in training who are starting to consider the issues. More experienced colleagues will find the case studies useful in providing a comparison with their own views and experiences.

Chapter 8 considers the nature of inclusion, its scope and breadth. While some professionals use the term to mean special educational needs and disabilities, others (including those contributing to Woolley, 2018) use the breadth of the protected characteristics from the Equality Act (Legislation.gov.uk, 2010) and additional elements (e.g. social disadvantage, social class). This chapter explores how Relationships Education can be inclusive in primary schools, acknowledging the range of patterns of family life from which children come, and the different ways of being family and relating to one another. It addresses strategies for the development of anti-bullying approaches, including homophobic and transphobic bullying.

In the final chapter there is an exploration of issues for professional development and a consideration of next steps for RSE. This chapter provides support for both schools and individual practitioners, considering the following:

- issues to think about when developing a policy for RSE;
- working in partnership with carers and parents;
- developing progression throughout the primary phase of schooling;
- linking to learning in the secondary phase;
- working with other agencies and finding support;
- child protection issues and maintaining professional safety; and
- what to do if you don't have answers or strategies to cope with a child's questions.

Drawing together key themes from the rest of the book, it provides both examples of best practice and guidance on how this can be embedded in schools and other learning settings.

Working cooperatively with parents and carers

A key concern for both teachers and student teachers is how parents and carers might react to some issues being raised with their children. Clearly not all carers or parents are confident in discussing matters relating to sex, relationships or puberty with their children, as is suggested in the vignette at the start of this chapter. The need to take the views of children's primary carers into account is particularly relevant when considering the questions and comments that might arise during the teaching of RSE.

Strategies to alleviate these concerns, some proactive and some more reactive, include:

- *Keeping parents/carers informed.* If it is known in advance that an issue will be addressed with a class, consider alerting parents and carers to this through a class newsletter. This brings the opportunity to suggest that if parents/carers have concerns they can make contact with the school to share these. Sometimes, being proactive in this way removes concerns.
- *Sharing the bigger picture.* In the school newsletter and on its website the head teacher can alert parents/carers to the school policy for RSE, PSHE and citizenship and inform them that, at certain times, difficult issues will arise in class and need to be addressed in order to maintain a harmonious atmosphere in the school. They could invite the parents/carers to discuss this at a coffee morning, or have the policy available to read at open evening. Giving parents/carers the opportunity to raise and discuss concerns in advance, and asking for their support, can help to build a sense of partnership. Some parents/carers will be grateful that the school is willing to address issues that they, themselves, find hard to talk about with their children. Certainly when developing materials to use in the teaching of RSE it is essential to alert parents/carers and to create opportunities to consult with them.
- *Checking school policies* to make sure that staff members are aware of any guidance on how to approach issues with learners is very important when delivering RSE. This is a key part of keeping oneself professionally safe and making sure that the aims and ethos of the school are being followed. The best way to develop policy in school is through discussion, not for practitioners to do what they believe to be right despite what policies state. If there is any concern about the nature of any policies

these can be raised with the head teacher or another supportive colleague.

- *Putting oneself in the parent/carer's shoes.* Empathy can be an effective means of diffusing a situation when a parent or carer raises a concern, and an even better means of thinking ahead and anticipating any difficulties.

- *Responding quickly* to any concerns or comments from parents/carers. Leaving issues aside because they feel too challenging is likely to make them grow rather than subside. If a practitioner is concerned about speaking with a parent/carer it is wise to ask a colleague to accompany them or at least to be close by. If it is not possible to address a need immediately, a prompt message asking a parent/carer to call in to have a discussion shows that their views are being taken seriously and acted upon.

- *Building relationships* before issues arise. It is always better to meet a parent/carer for the first time on a positive basis rather than having to make initial introductions when there is a problem or concern. This is not always easy or even possible. However, having an open afternoon or just sending a note home early in the term to make an initial introduction or to make a positive comment about a child's achievement can make a link that establishes a positive relationship.

- *Asking questions* to clarify the situation when you speak with the parent/carer. If a practitioner shows that they are willing to listen and hear the parent's viewpoint, this may help significantly to resolve any difficulties. It is important to try not to launch in on the defensive from the start. Offering a seat and a drink may also ease the start of any meeting.

(adapted from Woolley, 2010)

Consider:

- how these approaches reflect your current practice and experience;
- what other strategies you use to ensure effective communication and good relationships with carers and parents; and
- how you feel personally about discussing issues about RSE with parents and carers.

Developing physical and mental well-being

Schools have a responsibility to promote both physical and mental health within their communities. Physical health involves children and young people being able to respect their own bodies as well as those of others. This includes knowing how to stay safe and to deal with uncomfortable situations (including inappropriate touching) and is explored in Chapter 3. However, good health also includes the need for emotional and cognitive well-being, which necessitates that opportunities are created for questions to be raised and that both information (knowledge) and a focus on emotions and feelings (the affective) are included in the school curriculum. To focus on factual elements without discussions about feelings is to deliver sex education devoid of love, care, respect or emotion. This is a major criticism of RSE identified in surveys of young people. In one UK survey of over 20,000 young people under eighteen years, it was found that

- 40 per cent thought that the RSE they had received was either poor or very poor;
- 70 per cent of girls and 61 per cent of boys reported not having any information about personal relationships in lessons at school;
- 73 per cent felt that RSE should be taught before the age of 13 years. (UK Youth Parliament, 2007)

Other surveys (Health Promotion Agency for Northern Ireland, 1996; Rolston et al., 2005; Ipsos MORI, cited in Campbell, 2006; Sex Education Forum, 2006; UK Youth Parliament, 2007; Brook GFK NOP Survey, 2006 cited in FPA, 2009) show that the majority of young people, parents/carers and the general public believe that emotional issues should be included in RSE in addition to the limited biological requirements included in the National Curriculum (DfE, 2014).

To deliver RSE without appropriate focus on the 'R' is to fail to prepare children and young people for the pleasures and responsibilities of sexual relationships. Relationship without responsibility is a recipe for dissatisfaction, frustration and possibly thoughtless and even abusive behaviour. The new curriculum in England (DfE, 2018) provides opportunities for this to be achieved, subject to creative, supportive and imaginative approaches by those in schools undertaking its design.

Conclusion and summary of key learning points

This introductory chapter has provided an overview of some key issues relating to RSE. While some of its content has a focus on the new guidance for England, and indeed the historical context preceding this, readers will apply issues and concepts to their own settings. More importantly, it has raised some of the issues that will form a fundamental part of the exploration of RSE in this book. Additionally, it has considered some of the wider experiences gained from international perspectives which aid the evaluation of effective RSE and which help practitioners to consider how to develop effective practice.

The major flaws in policy in England over past years have been: the choice of terminology used, including the title of the subject in schools; the lack of statutory provision (given that schools can develop a policy which states that they will only delivery the basics of the science curriculum); and the focus on conception-avoidance as opposed to more fully thought-out approaches to informed and effective choice-based sexual activity with others, or abstinence. While it may not be fashionable to be chaste, it may be more healthy both in physical and emotional terms to wait until a committed relationship before engaging in sexual activity and intercourse. Importantly, primary schools need to be aware of how their provision of RSE fits within the continuum of learning which children will encounter. Links need to be established with secondary education in order that, having been introduced to some significant issues about relationships, respect and puberty when aged 3–11 years, learners progress to explore issues in increasingly deep, thoughtful and mature ways. If school-based sex education remains focused solely on penis–vagina sex, as may be introduced in the science curriculum for primary schools, important sections of the school population will fail to learn anything of any practical use in their own personal practice, pleasure or safety.

It is not the purpose of this book to be judgemental or to propose the most effective approaches to relationships for young people. However, as practitioners with a duty of care for learners, it is important that all teachers and childcare professionals think through their provision of RSE so that children grow into young people capable of making confident choices which show respect to both themselves and others, remain safe and enjoy both relationships and sex in a positive and nurturing context.

Acknowledgement

Acknowledgement is made to *TIDE~ Global Learning*, a resource centre and network for teachers involved in development education, based in Birmingham, UK, for its contribution to the study visit to South Africa. www.tidegloballearning.net/

Signposts and further reading

PSHE Association (2018) *Preparing for Statutory Relationships Education. PSHE Education Lead's Pack: Key Stages 1 and 2*. PSHE Association. www.pshe-association.org.uk/curriculum-and-resources/resources/preparing-statutory-relationships-education-pshe

References

Adams, K., Hyde, B., and Woolley, R. (2008) *The Spiritual Dimension of Childhood*. London: Jessica Kingsley.

AVERT (2017) HIV and AIDS in South Africa. www.avert.org/professionals/hiv-around-world/sub-saharan-africa/south-africa (accessed 2 August 2018).

Better Health (2010) Sex Education – Primary School Children: Fact Sheet. www.betterhealth.vic.gov.au/bhcv2/bhcarticles.nsf/pages/Sex_education_primary_school_children (accessed 5 August 2018).

Campbell, D. (2006) 'No Sex Please until We're at Least 17 Years Old, We're British'. *Observer*.

Crumper, P. (2004) 'Sex Education and Human Rights – A Lawyer's Perspective'. *Sex Education*, 4 (2), 125–36.

DENI (n.d.) *Guidance for Primary Schools: Relationships and Sexuality Education*. Northern Ireland: DfE.

DfE (2014) *National Curriculum in England: Framework for Key Stages 1–4*. www.gov.uk/government/publications/national-curriculum-in-england-framework-for-key-stages-1-to-4/ (accessed 31 March 2018).

DfE (2018) *Relationships Education, Relationships and Sex Education (RSE) and Health Education: Guidance for Governing Bodies, Proprietors, Head Teachers, Principals, Senior Leadership Teams, Teachers*. London: DfE.

DfEE (2000) *Sex and Relationship Education Guidance*. Nottingham: DfEE.

DfES (2004) *Every Child Matters: Change for Children in Schools*. London: DfES.

DfES (2005) *Excellence and Enjoyment: Social and Emotional Aspects of Learning: Guidance*. London: DfES.

Eurobarometer (2006) *'AIDS' Prevention: 240 / Wave 64.1 and 64.3 – TNS Opinion and Social*. http://ec.europa.eu/health/ph_publication/eb_aids_en.pdf (accessed 5 August 2018).

Ferguson, R., VanwesenBeeck, I., and Knijn, T. (2008) 'A Matter of Facts … and More: An Exploratory Analysis of the Content of Sexuality Education in the Netherlands'. *Sex Education*, 8 (1), 93–106.

FPA (2009) *Sex and Relationships Education Factsheet*. London: FPA.

Gordon, L., and Ellingson, L. (2006) 'In the Eyes of the Beholder: Student Interpretations of Sexuality Lessons'. *Sex Education*, 6 (3), 251–64.

Health Promotion Agency for Northern Ireland (1996) *Sex Education in Northern Ireland: Views from Parents and Schools*. Belfast: Health Promotion Agency for Northern Ireland.

Ipsos MORI (2014) *HIV: Public Knowledge and Attitudes in 2014*. www.ipsos.com/ipsos-mori/en-uk/hiv-public-knowledge-and-attitudes-2014 (accessed 4 October 2018).

Legislation.gov.uk (1986) *Local Government Act 1986*. www.legislation.gov.uk/ukpga/1986/10 (accessed 5 August 2018).

Legislation.gov.uk (2010) Equality Act 2010. www.legislation.gov.uk/ukpga/2010/15/contents (accessed 31 March 2018).

Lewis, J., and Knijn, T. (2001) 'A Comparison of English and Dutch Sex Education in the Classroom'. *Education and Health*, 19 (4), 59–64.

Macdonald, A. (2009) *Independent Review of the Proposal to Make Personal, Social, Health and Economic (PSHE) Education Statutory*. London: Department for Children, Schools and Families.

MacGregor, K. (2005) 'Alarm Sounds as AIDS Claims 11 Teachers a Day'. *Times Education Supplement*.

Mason, S. (2010) 'Braving It Out! An Illuminative Evaluation of the Provision of Sex and Relationship Education in Two Primary Schools in England'. *Sex Education*, 10 (2), 157–69.

McKee, A., Albury, K., Dunne, M., Grieshaber, S., Lumby, C., and Matthews, B. (2010) 'Healthy Sexual Development: A Multidisciplinary Framework for Research'. *International Journal of Sexual Health*, 22, 14–19.

Measor, L. (2004) 'Young People's Views of Sex Education: Gender, Information and Knowledge'. *Sex Education*, 4 (2), 153–66.

Rolston B., Schubotz, D., and Simpson, A. (2005) 'Sex Education in Northern Ireland Schools: A Critical Evaluation'. *Sex Education*, 5 (3), 217–34.

Ruxton, S. (ed.) (2004) *Gender Equality and Men: Learning from Practice*. London: Oxfam GB.

Sex Education Forum (2005) *Sex and Relationships Education Framework*. Forum Factsheet 30. London: National Children's Bureau and Sex Education Forum.

Sex Education Forum (2006) *Sex Education Must Go Beyond Biological Basics Says Sex Education Forum*. London: Sex Education Forum.

Social Exclusion Unit (1999) *Teenage Pregnancy Report by the Social Exclusion Unit*. London: The Stationary Office.

Terrence Higgins Trust (2018) 'DFE: Changes to the Teaching of Relationship and Sex Education and PSHE'. www.tht.org.uk/sites/default/files/2018-02/RSE%20 consultation%20submission.pdf (accessed 5 August 2018).

UK Youth Parliament (2007) *Sex and Relationships Education: Are You Getting It?* London: UK Youth Parliament.

UNAIDS (2004) *2004 Report on the Global AIDS Epidemic: 4th Global Report*. Geneva: UNAIDS.

UNHCHR (1989) *Convention on the Rights of the Child*. Office of the High Commissioner for Human Rights. www.unhchr.ch/html/menu3/b/k2crc.htm (accessed 5 August 2018).

Walker, J., Green, J., and Tilford, S. (2003) 'An Evaluation of School Sex Education Team Training'. *Health Education*, 103 (6), 320–29.

Woolley, R. (2007) 'What Makes Men …? Masculinity, Violence and Identity', in *Comparative Education and Global Learning*, ed. C. Harber and J. Serf. Birmingham: TIDE Global Learning.

Woolley, R. (September 2009) 'Controversial Issues: Identifying the Concerns and Priorities of Student Teachers'. Paper presented at the British Educational Research Association Conference, Manchester.

Woolley, R. (2010) *Tackling Controversial Issues in the Primary School: Facing Life's Challenges with Your Learners*. London: Routledge.

Woolley, R. (ed.) (2018) *Understanding Inclusion: Core Concepts, Policy and Practice*. London: Routledge.

1

The historical context for Relationships and Sex Education

Helen, an experienced teacher, recalls her own school days and the sex education that was available:

> *I remember really very little about learning about sex, there was a small bit in the biology lesson about the reproduction of the earth worm and some sessions with the school nurse who talked to us about hygiene. The nurse was a matronly lady and not very approachable so we just giggled a lot when she talked about sanitary towels but to be honest that is all I can remember. I think that most of my sex education came from the playground and seeing pictures stolen from magazines, you know, from the top shelf. I remember being quite shocked at some of them as no one really told me much. They were mostly nude pictures of women in sexy poses, none of men. I lived in a mainly all-female house, with sisters, and my dad was always quite discreet about his body, so the first time I saw a totally nude man was on my wedding night, which was all a bit scary to be honest. I remember my mum telling me a bit about what I might be expected to do once I was married but the whole thing was a bit of a disaster and a disappointment. Luckily my husband and I had a really good relationship and we were able to talk about it and we have had fun finding out about it all since! We were just both so naive and I do think that children today get a much better education about sex, although sometimes I wonder if they know too much.*

Chapter outline

Introduction

This chapter locates the current Relationships and Sex Education (RSE) policy in England in an historical context. It discusses the development of sex education from the early twentieth century to the present day, with reference to social and cultural influences that have impacted on government policymaking. The notion of relationships and values, both societal and personal, are raised in relation to this controversial and sensitive curriculum area. A pedagogical approach that introduces the concept of 'bravery' is also considered.

In England, sex education has been a long-established term for the teaching and learning of the biological aspects of human reproduction. It is only relatively recently (2000) that the inclusion of 'Relationship' in the title of government documentation has been made and very recently that 'Relationships' in the plural has been used (2018). The separation of relationships from sex is a complex process. It is, therefore, challenging for adults, in and out of the school context, when discussing the biology of sex with children and young people to not talk about or to set aside the dynamics of emotions, desire and intimacy in relationships.

The concept of sex education

The concept of sex education is defined by Wyness (1996: 98) as

> the deliberate and intentional handling of knowledge about sexual matters.

This definition fails to acknowledge the links within a value's framework. As Halstead and Reiss (2003: 3) argue, values 'permeate every aspect of sex education in schools'. This claim makes clear that the transmission of values may, or may not, be conscious on the part of the teacher, in that the formal education system, and not exclusively RSE, is the overt and covert transmission of a value system. Therefore, no educational engagement or teacher–student relationship, whatever the subject content, can be value-free. This extends to informal educational settings where children and young people are exposed to a value's framework, and this may, or may not, present different values to those within formal education. Children can experience a range of differing value systems with each attributed to the varied aspects of their lives: home, school and out-of-school. These values may be mixed, sometimes contrasting with those from other families through their peer groups and the wider community. It can be argued, however, that the value system that is transmitted through the school curriculum represents the most prominent influence on societal values with increasing central governmental control through the introduction of a National Curriculum by the Conservative government in 1989 and the continued agenda of centralization by subsequent governments, which is explored further in the chapter. Marxist theorists such as Althusser (cited in Barry, 2002: 164) claim that in an increasingly secular world where previous 'ideologies' were derived from religion, the power of the state has been extended and evolved through formal education. Education through compulsory schooling is a powerful social tool that establishes the framework to which society adheres – an 'ideological state apparatus'.

This notion of the ability of the education system to change, or impose, the views of society places teachers, and those who lead them, in a potentially powerful and manipulative position. The idea of the power of teachers is now also extended to those beyond the school gates who work with children in extended provision: after- school clubs, early-years providers, childminders and the third sector. Increasingly, more parents and carers are working, leaving greater opportunities for children to engage with activities beyond the school day, which means that these potential influences on them widen. The need for a coordinated and consistent pedagogical approach to RSE between professionals working in these diverse sectors is emerging.

Reflect on the curriculum title Sex and Relationship Education used for many years in England.

Consider:

- What views do you have on the word order?
- What are the implications of relationship in the singular?
- What emphasis should be placed on provision in the primary phase of education?

The historical context

The inclusion of sex education and Sex and Relationship Education (SRE) in the school curriculum developed significantly throughout the twentieth and early twenty-first centuries, under the centralized control of governments from across the political spectrum, to address wider societal issues which largely relate to the health of the nation.

1900–50

In the first half of the twentieth century the most prevalent focus within sex education was the hygiene aspects of sex, and this was not an uncommon focus in state-funded schools across the world (Zimmerman, 2015). This was deemed the most effective strategy to improve the 'physical and sexual-moral health of "The Nation"' (Pilcher, 2005: 154). This particular focus of sex education was in response to the prevalence of venereal disease during the First World War, and government funding was made available to the National Council for Combating Venereal Disease for work with parents, youth leaders and teachers on sex education (p. 154). In conjunction with this funding, an initial series of handbooks for teachers (1928, 1933, 1939) were published to guide schools in their sex education programmes, which detailed the aspects of physical health to be taught, although the omission of the 'human sexual and reproductive body [was] conspicuous by its absence' (p. 156). The intention of the handbooks was to engage schools in the wider state agenda of improving and maintaining physical health, with the implicit message that sex education should not be taught. However, formal provision for sex education varied widely, and any programmes with secondary-aged children were addressed through the biology curriculum. Halstead and Reiss (2003: 157) propose an interesting perspective on the approach of not teaching sex education as they argue that a school cannot avoid sex education occurring. The notion of not discussing sexual relationships or reproduction when teaching English literature would be absurd; for example, it is difficult to read the story of Cinderella without stepping into the realms of different kinds of relationships, such as step family and intimate relationships. So too would the teaching of 'geography without population studies, or history without the suffragette movement, or of religious education without consideration of the gender-specific roles of men and women' (p. 157). Each of these aspects of the curriculum holds the potential to address the wider dimensions of sexual relationships beyond the biological basics and, therefore, presents the argument that schools cannot avoid teaching about sex education. This stance adopted by Halstead and Reiss (2003) regarding the formal curriculum also includes wider influences on children and young people, such as the media, families and peers, which present further challenges to those working with children. These issues will be discussed in greater depth in Chapter 2.

1950–80

The variety of provision for sex education largely continued until the 1950s when for the first time within the fourth edition of the Handbook (1956) a whole chapter was dedicated to sex education. This governmental shift heralded a different agenda in so much as the state guidance for addressing issues of human sexual reproduction 'endorsed the instruction of sex as an integral part of health education' (Pilcher, 2005: 160) and suggests that the then Conservative government acted in response to a rapidly changing post-war Britain (p. 160). This change in approach by the government arose from the earlier publication of an advisory pamphlet for schools by the Board of Education in 1943, which had been based on a survey of what school provided as sex education. The pamphlet noted that while parents maintained responsibility for educating their children about sexual matters, many parents felt unable or unwilling to do so and, as such, the responsibility then lay with teachers (p. 158). The historical significance of this pamphlet is worthy of note as it marked the first publication of curriculum advice for schools that included references to sex and reproduction. The government response endeavoured to redress loosening moral and social frameworks, although the 1960s and 1970s saw exceptional medical and social changes that were to stimulate the sex education debate once more (some of which are outlined in Chapter 2).

The advent of the birth control pill in the 1960s enabled greater sexual freedom, and the reference to oral contraception within the 1968 Handbook, along with a chapter on communicable diseases, suggested societal recognition that sexual activity outside the confines of marriage was more prevalent or at least more widely acknowledged. More explicit acknowledgement of the role of the school in addressing these values-based issues emerged through the 1970s when moral dimensions as part of the school curriculum came more sharply into focus (DfES, 1977).

1980–2000

During the timeframe between 1980 and 2000, evidence of a distinct change in the state approach to concerns in society emerged regarding the protection of children and the rights of the child, the health of the nation and the role of teachers as part of sex education in schools.

The notion of the protection of children had resonance in the Gillick case (BBC, 1983) after the House of Lords in 1985 established the legal position in England and Wales of children under sixteen with regard to medical advice and treatment. This flagship case of a mother taking a local health authority to court, on the grounds that contraceptives had been prescribed for her daughter without parental consent, identified a legal shift from parental rights to those of the child. In 1989 the United Nations Convention for the Rights of the Child heightened the increasing tensions between the rights of the state, the parent and the child, which, it could be argued, remain today. The 1980s also saw the escalation of sexually transmitted infections (STIs) such as human immunodeficiency virus (HIV). The World Health Organization in 1985 sought to address the HIV pandemic across the world and to initiate worldwide action. The rapid rise in the levels of infection among gay men in the West caused widespread concern and generated anxiety, particularly through the tabloid press in the UK (AVERT, n.d.), for heterosexual people. Newspaper headlines contributed to the increasing homophobic prejudice that suggested some gay men had brought the disease on themselves through high levels of promiscuity. In March 1986, the government launched a comprehensive public information campaign that featured somewhat sinister 'tombstones' and monochrome imagery intended to prevent cases of infection from rising in the UK. The campaign continued throughout the 1980s.

In 1986 the Education Act legislated that schools did not have to provide sex education at all if they chose not to. For those schools that opted to provide sex education, the 1986 legislation afforded parents/carer the right to withdraw their children from these classes (Pilcher, 2005: 166). Further clarity of the role of teachers in providing sex education was made evident in the government Circular 11/87, which outlined the legislative framework for schools following the Education Act and stipulated that the promotion of homosexuality as a 'norm' would be inappropriate. Shortly after this, in 1988 this was followed by Clause 28, an amendment to the 1986 Local Government Act, which 'banned local authorities from promoting homosexuality' and remained in place until 2003. Although Clause 28 specifically related to local authorities and not school settings, this controversial addition to the law created anxiety for teachers who were unclear about how to address such issues with their learners. Equally, tensions increased when a circular in 1987 explicitly warned teachers that 'giving an individual learner advice [on contraception] without parental knowledge or consent would be an inappropriate exercise of a teacher's professional responsibilities, and could, depending on the circumstances, amount to a criminal offence' (DfES, 1987, para 26). This created an understandable reluctance among teachers to discuss sexual matters with their learners. The challenges for schools within these legislative frameworks to provide sex education remained.

In 1989, the National Curriculum was introduced following the 1988 Education Reform Act and established the statutory entitlement for some subjects. Science became a core and mandatory element of the new curriculum, with human reproduction included at Key Stage 3 (ages 11–14). The National Curriculum placed a statutory duty on teachers to teach about sexual intercourse and contraception at secondary level. The Key Stage 2 (ages 7–11) (revised in 1999 and 2013) for Science requires schools to teach 'that the life processes common to humans and other animals include nutrition, growth and reproduction (1999)'. The use of the word 'reproduction' is worthy of note and largely unchanged in the various iterations of the document. The interpretation of how much knowledge about the act of human reproduction, for example sexual intercourse, should be addressed is interpreted differently within a range of primary schools (Mason, 2010). Further to this, the use of the word 'reproduction' suggests an emphasis on sex for procreation and not recreation. One of the last Education Acts under the Conservative government (1979–97) was introduced in 1996 and consolidated all previous legislation regarding

SRE. This remained the legislative framework for SRE along with the Learning and Skills Act (2000) introduced by the New Labour government for eighteen years. The key points within the Education Act 1996 were the following:

- The sex education elements within the National Curriculum Science order are mandatory in Key Stages 1 and 2.
- Secondary schools are required to provide an SRE programme which includes (as a minimum) information about STIs, including HIV/AIDS.
- All schools must provide an up-to-date SRE policy.
- In primary schools the policy must state the SRE that is provided or include a statement of the decision not to provide it. (Family Planning Association, 2011)

The long-standing, non-statutory status of SRE, and more specifically Relationships Education until 2019 within the National Curriculum, has had serious and long-term societal implications. It is important to note that post 2019, RSE at primary level remains non-statutory, although Relationships Education is a new worthy addition as a statutory element. The option to opt in or opt out of including RSE in the primary curriculum for schools remains. As such, the ambiguity in official documentation makes decisions regarding RSE programmes and in teaching appropriate content challenging for teachers, schools and governors. This results in an understandable reticence to provide a broad and comprehensive RSE programme specifically at primary school level. Since the turn of the twentieth century, specific societal changes have elicited governmental responses to sex education provision within formal schooling. In the mid-1990s, children faced 'restrictions as to the particular "moral framework" of sex education provided by their schools as discussed above, had no right to receive sex education at all if their parents objected to it and no right of confidentiality about their sexual activities from teachers' (Pilcher, 2005: 167). However, some of these restrictions were soon to change with the General Election in 1997 and the rise of New Labour. In 1998 the Teenage Pregnancy Strategy was launched, its remit influenced by a report *Teenage Pregnancy* issued by the Social Exclusion Unit (SEU) in 1999 from a governmental agenda to develop an integrated strategy to cut rates of teenage pregnancy. The SEU identified in their report that the UK had the highest teenage pregnancy rates in Europe. Stronach et al. (2007: 83–4) comment that the political agenda for reducing teenage pregnancy rates is for economic as well as moral concerns. In a society and an economy where skills and knowledge are paramount, a teenage mother, possibly leaving school to look after a baby, becomes an economic burden. Drawing upon wide-scale research, the SEU reports on three broad causes of these high pregnancy rates:

1 Low expectations in educational achievement
2 Ignorance
3 Mixed messages from different information sources e.g. parents, school, media. (1999: 7)

Kiernan (1995) found that girls with low attainment, and whose educational achievement declined between seven and sixteen, were at a greater risk of having a teenage pregnancy than those whose achievement improved or was higher during this age phase. This factor, linked with ignorance and misconceptions about contraception, the report states, contributed to the rate of teenage pregnancies in the UK. Wellings et al. (1996) argue that the likelihood of teenage pregnancy has more than doubled in young women who could not discuss sex easily with their parents/carers. Here a tension emerges between the increased role of the school, or 'edu-care' setting, in addressing matters of sex and sexuality within the primary- and secondary-aged phases and parents relinquishing their role in the discussion of such issues with their children. In recent years, increasing government response to societal issues through the school curriculum, a top-down approach, has the potential to diminish the voice of parents and create difficulties between children and their families. Zimmerman (2015: 146) argues that 'to many people around the world … they want schools to map proper sexual behaviour, not to liberate individuals to explore it on their own'.

The third factor cited in the report (SEU, 1999) arises from mixed messages. In one part of the adult world, teenagers are bombarded with sexually explicit messages, for example, in music videos, which imply that sexual activity and promiscuity is the norm. This is contrasted by many parents and most public institutions that are 'at best embarrassed and at worst silent' (SEU, 1999) on matters of a sexual nature. Research suggests that this continues to be the case (Corteen, 2006; Brook, PSHE Association and Sex Education Forum, 2014; Sex Education Forum, 2015). These factors are interwoven and create a complex problem to be addressed.

2000 onwards

A sharper focus was given to SRE when it became an additional element of the curriculum within personal, social and health education (PSHE) in 2000, although it remained non-statutory. The Learning and Skills Act in 2000 required that

- young people learn about the nature of marriage and its importance for family life and bringing up children;
- young people are protected from teaching and materials that are inappropriate, having regard to the age and religious and cultural background of the learners concerned;
- school governing bodies have regard for the guidance (DfEE, 2000); and
- parents have the right to withdraw their child from all or part of SRE outside of the National Curriculum Science order.

As part of its strategy to reduce the level of teenage pregnancy the New Labour government issued SRE guidance (DfEE, 2000) which denotes the first curriculum guidance to explicitly link sex with relationships. The document identifies that 'sex and relationship education should be firmly rooted in the framework for PSHE' (p. 3), which assists children to 'develop skills and understanding to live confident, healthy and independent lives' and to deal with 'difficult moral and social questions' (p. 3). Halstead and Reiss (2003: 3) extend this view:

> It [sex education] is about human relationships, and therefore includes a central moral dimension. It is about the private, intimate life of the learner and it is intended to contribute to his or her personal development and sense of well-being or fulfilment.

Here acknowledgement is made that sex education is intrinsically linked to relationships and should be taught as such. Much of the curriculum content is focused on addressing the issues of different relationships, staying safe, making appropriate decisions, respect for oneself and others (as outlined in the Introduction to this book). The most interesting aspect of this document is that it refers to 'relationship' in the singular throughout. This implies that the context for sex should be a single, monogamous and enduring relationship; indeed a clear statement is made in the DfEE's (2000) SRE guidance that learners should be taught 'about the nature and importance of marriage for family life and bringing up children' (p. 4). This is closely followed with:

> But the Government recognises … that there are strong and mutually supportive relationships outside marriage.

These two statements are perhaps intended to make clear the moral emphasis on sex within marriage, with a 'catch-all' follow-up. The most significant point appears at the end of this statement:

> Therefore pupils should learn the significance of marriage and stable relationships as key to the building blocks of community and society.

The language used here is emotive and, with the use of words such as 'significance' and 'strong', appears persuasive. It should be remembered that, at this point in history, marriage in England was only available to heterosexual couples. The linking of sex education with relationships is inevitably linking sexual activity with morality and values. The complexity of this link in contemporary society is contentious. Indeed, Zimmerman (2015: 147) echoes the view of Halstead and Reiss in stating that there is 'nothing even nominally neutral about sex education'. The SRE guidance (DfEE, 2000) places the government in an exposed position for lobbying from pro-marriage and family groups, and equally could be criticized for not embracing alternative family structures now more commonly represented in society. The track record of New Labour, particularly from 2000, suggests that this was not their intention, although interestingly the Marriage (Same Sex Couples)

Bill only gained assent in July 2013, with the first gay wedding in 2014, a law passed under the Conservative/Liberal Democrat coalition. As Halstead and Reiss (2003: 3) suggest, where teachers are inherently transmitting values in their presentation of sex education, it is significant which value system they embrace and transmit – their own personal values, the school's espoused values, or indeed a broader framework that reflects multiple systems. It is made explicit by Halstead and Reiss that children may, or may not, accept the values portrayed (2003: 3). This will be explored in greater depth in Chapter 5.

Lewis and Knijn (2002: 669) discuss, through a 'comparative lens', the very different approaches adopted by the Dutch and the British to SRE policy:

> We argue that the conflictual UK debate [of SRE] which is so striking compared to that in the Netherlands, is embedded in very different understandings of the key issues, and that it has an additional problematic effect on policy making in the UK.

These 'different understandings' are identified as having emerged from the varied pressure groups that are 'fighting larger battles about family change' and 'family values'. The tensions in the political debate about SRE in England stand for

> a number of deeper and wider anxieties, particularly family breakdown and the protection of marriage, homosexuality, teenage sex and sexuality and parental rights. (Lewis and Knijn, 2002: 673)

In light of this research, consider:

- how changing patterns of family life should influence the development of SRE; and
- in your view, to what extent should SRE reflect society or seek to shape society?

Lewis and Knijn (2002) argue that the political resistance to accept current changes inhibits effective policy making. The Dutch approach has been to accept the changes that are evident in society regarding SRE and to aim to address the issues arising from them. The promotion of marriage and stable relationships included in the DfEE (2000) guidance appears to be an attempt to utilize the education system, or ideology, to counter family breakdown. The moralizing tone of government policy for SRE is absent in the Netherlands where they have sought to 'address the new social reality' (Lewis and Knijn, 2002: 677). The differing political roles between the English and the Dutch governments is particularly interesting. It establishes a comparative model alongside that in England, and of relevance is that the Netherlands had, similar to England, a rising teenage pregnancy rate, and this has been systematically reduced. However, Zimmerman (2015) argues that from a global perspective there remains little convincing evidence that suggests sex education is the panacea for managing teenage pregnancy and venereal disease. He outlines that in 2009, the three European countries (Italy, Switzerland and the Netherlands) with the lowest teenage pregnancy rates have taken very different approaches to sex education. For example, the more limited approach taken by Italy was haphazard in comparison to the broad and comprehensive RSE curriculum offered in the Netherlands. If Zimmerman's argument is to be considered, perhaps then, the educational, societal, political context for SRE is more complex.

The relatively recent shift in 2000 in England, from sex education to SRE, marks the growing consensus that children are entitled to more than the 'biological basics'. The inclusion of the 'Relationship' aspect of the curriculum is noteworthy. Here, tensions are exposed in the document, and it is pertinent to further examine some of the difficulties relating to curriculum content. The examination of the use, and of the meaning, of the word 'sexuality' in the DfEE's (2000) SRE guidance may cause confusion for teachers and parents/carers. The use of the phrase 'understanding human sexuality' is misleading when there are clear statements that SRE is not 'about the promotion of sexual orientation' (p. 5). A possible interpretation of this statement is that if it is not about the promotion of sexual orientation then it is not about promoting straight, gay or any other (as we argued in the Introduction to this book). It could, therefore, be argued that this is an even-handed approach. However, the 'promotion' of sexual orientation may imply that relationships other than those within a heterosexual partnership, the 'sexual norm', are beyond the remit of SRE. The use of the word 'promotion' echoes the phrase used in the now-repealed section 28 of the Local Government Act 1986. The word 'promotion' in both these government documents, and the implications that may arise from it, namely, whether a sexual orientation can be 'promoted', is relevant. Sexuality, in one sense, encompasses all issues of the giving and receiving of sexual pleasure. In another sense, it could be viewed as the sexual orientation and preferences of a person. These two definitions can cause difficulties in the interpretation of the SRE guidance (DfEE, 2000) (and lead to our clarification of terms in the Introduction to this book and in Chapter 8). Some topics are listed, such as contraception, abortion and sexually transmitted diseases, and addressed with examples of good practice guidance. However, masturbation, oral and anal sex, for example, are not. The complexities for professionals working with children and parents/carers are evident, and the ambiguous use of language does not assist the development of clear ways of thinking about such issues.

Reflect on the historical development of SRE addressed so far in this chapter:

- To what extent does the curriculum seem reactive or proactive?
- Do you feel that SRE, as described here, fits the needs of contemporary society and of children?
- Can you identify the aims of SRE in your current professional setting?

Consider the example of Helen outlined at the opening of this chapter:

- How does Helen's experience of sex education compare with your own?
- How does your memory of sex education that you received affect your hopes and aspirations for SRE with your own learners?

In 2003 the Every Child Matters (ECM) agenda (DfCSF, 2003) provided a sharper focus and targets to reduce teenage pregnancy rates in England and Wales. This wide-reaching and comprehensive reform agenda to improve outcomes for children established five key areas. The 'Be Healthy' strand outlined the government's renewed commitment to reduce the under-18 conception rates and to reduce STIs. The role of the Teenage Pregnancy Strategy (TPS) in meeting the ECM targets has been significant at local and national levels with focused action located within the engagement of delivery partners such as health service, education sector, social services and youth support services, along with the voluntary third sector. The vision of a unified team around children and young people to focus on issues of sex and relationships sought to address the 'ignorance' and 'mixed messages' factors highlighted in the SEU report (1999). This vision also established the role of formal and informal educators in addressing sexual matters to children and young people and the need for professional development in SRE among those working in the wider context of children's services.

Action by the TPS to improve the availability of sexual health services for children and young people has endeavoured to make contraception accessible to young people, intended to encourage safer sex and reduce teenage pregnancies. One national initiative in 2008, the 'C-card' Scheme aimed at children aged thirteen or over, enables children to register and receive a card that entitles them to free condoms. This preventative measure suggests a more pragmatic approach by the then government in reducing teenage pregnancy, but it appeared to be less 'value'- or 'moral'-based. The strategic approach to encompass the safer sex message in social policy is significant as it identifies a shift from the promotion of abstinence, which historically was the case. Despite the C-card Scheme being in place over almost a decade, there remains relatively static rates of STIs in England (Public Health England, 2018) among those in the 15–24 age bracket. Other strategies implemented by the TPS focus on the prioritizing of SRE. This is centred on support for all schools and informal settings through the local authority to deliver comprehensive programmes for SRE. The role of education in providing information to children and young people is highlighted. Following the Macdonald review (2009), an independent review of SRE across all four key stages of schooling, and the Rose review (2009), an independent review of the primary curriculum, the Labour government announced its commitment to establish PSHE and SRE as statutory elements of the new revised National Curriculum in 2011. This announcement was welcomed by the Family Planning Association (FPA) although lobby groups opposing the move, such as the Family Education Trust (FET), were reported (Wells, 2009). The concerns of the FET centred on what was perceived as an undermining of the role of parents/carers in the sex education of their children. Wyness (1996) makes the claim that critics of schooling would argue that parents and carers are experiencing an alleged loss of authority with a parallel increase in parental accountability. It is worthy of note that the rights of parents to withdraw their child from sex education lessons remain unchanged since the 1996 Education Act. Wyness (1996: 98) also comments on parents engaging with their children about issues of sexual morality and suggests

> that the routine business of bringing up children is suffused with everyday talk which contains implicit and explicit sexual codes that generates ideas and values.

The assumption that parents and carers engage in 'everyday talk' with their children is significant. Riches (2004: 71) cites research by Farrell (1987) who claims that sexual experience in young people lessens the importance of parental influence. Here a contradiction emerges where the expectation and understanding is that parents/carers discuss sexual matters with teenagers. However, once the teenager has embarked on a sexual relationship, parental influence is diminished. Perhaps an argument is made for earlier intervention with children in the discussion of sexual matters, because by the time the child is a teenager, it is all 'too little too late' to expect parental influences to alter sexual behaviours particularly, if, as research by UNICEF (2007) reports, over 30 per cent of fifteen-year-olds in the UK claim to already have had sexual intercourse. The evidence presents an argument for either parents/carers, schools, or indeed both, to address issues of sex and relationships before puberty occurs, although research increasingly suggests that many children under eleven do not talk to their parents about sexual matters (Mason, 2010).

Since 1971, the proportion of all people living in 'traditional' family households of heterosexual married couples with dependent children has fallen from 52 per cent to 37 per cent (BBC, 2007). The latest figures from the Office for National Statistics (2017) identifies a rise in co-habiting families which has more than doubled from 1.5 million families in 1996 to 3.3 million families in 2017. While three main family structures exist – married, co-habiting and single-parent families – by far the biggest ratio of families consist of married couples, and this ratio may now include both opposite-sex and same-sex married couples, although the proportion of married couples has not risen significantly over the last two decades. Single parent, same-sex parents and unmarried parents are, therefore, more commonplace than thirty years ago, perhaps deconstructing traditional family structures consisting of mother and father living together with their children, and potentially creating tensions for a society with changing moral codes. The change in moral codes extends into the field of casual sexual behaviours where sexual pleasure and sexuality are explored with partners, or 'mates', in a series of isolated, temporary, or semi-permanent relationships. For example, the UK has the highest percentage of young people living with single-parent families compared with other economically advanced nations (UNICEF, 2007), and the current variety and fluidity of sexual relationships may be viewed as providing children with different relationship role models to those thirty years ago. These changes in family structures along with an increase in the number of hours carers/parents are at work suggest that social changes may reduce the opportunities for discussion about sexual matters. At the same time, with greater freedom of access to the internet, children and young people have increased opportunities to explore a wide range of sexually explicit material from their own homes.

Historically the debate about SRE has focused mainly on the secondary phase of education. The proposed, although never implemented, new curriculum for 2011 reflected a change in thinking to establish a more comprehensive programme in the primary phase, beginning in Key Stage 1. It is unfortunate that this was not implemented before the General Election in 2010. The Education Act of 2010 (Curtis, 2010) failed to include the new primary curriculum, and the newly elected Conservative–Liberal Democrat coalition government removed the new curriculum website and rejected the proposed programme. As previously highlighted, a perpetual debate centres on the effectiveness of RSE in reducing teenage pregnancy, and many claim that education about sex, sexuality and relationships encourages 'precocious sexual activity and may encourage "experimentation" before or beyond marriage' (Aggleton et al., 2005: 303). On the other hand, the view is held that central to the development of mature and responsible attitudes towards relationships and social well-being is the provision of SRE (Halstead and Waite, 2002: 22). The SEU (1999: 36) draws from research evidence (Baldo et al., 1993, Kirby, 1997; Grunseit et al., 1994) to make the claim that

> good, comprehensive SRE does not make young people more likely to start sex. Indeed, it can help them delay starting sex, and make them more likely to use contraceptives when they do.

Current policy and legislation regarding SRE has been under review in recent years. A distinct political shift was observed when the government endorsed the publication of advice to schools as supplementary and updated SRE guidance in 2014 authored by Brook, PSHE Association and Sex Education Forum. The updated guidance was produced collaboratively and was intended to be read alongside the preceding guidance of 2000. Brook, PSHE Association and Sex Education Forum have actively campaigned for a broad and comprehensive RSE programme in schools, and the endorsing of their guidance perhaps signified a change in stance from the Conservative government. However, proposals for SRE to be a statutory aspect of the curriculum were again raised following governmental reviews of SRE provision and were rejected in 2016. In March 2017, Justine Greening, the relatively new Education Secretary, announced her intention to change the legal status of SRE to being a statutory element of the National Curriculum as part of the PSHE provision. There was also a stated need to change the name to Relationships and Sex Education. Interestingly 'Relationships' was articulated as a plural, rather than the singular as in previous years and placed before 'sex' as part of the curriculum title. Contributing factors for this declared intention centred on the outdated previous guidance of 2000, the need for children to stay safe and the influences of the media on children. Equally, the previous context of academy and free schools being exempt from teaching the National Curriculum (2013) triggered a change that all schools in England would be statutorily obliged to teach RSE. In April 2017, the Children and Social Work Act was passed, and the proposed curriculum changes are expected to start being taught in schools in September 2019. A public consultation followed in December 2017 to support the formation and development of the newly proposed RSE curriculum. Importantly, the new curriculum outlined Relationships Education to be mandatory in primary schools and sex education to be optional. In addition there was a call for evidence from young people, asking for their views of their experiences of existing RSE, what they considered to be important and what they would like as part of the newly proposed curriculum. The consultation received an overwhelming 23,000 responses.

In July 2018, draft proposals for the newly outlined Relationships Education, Relationships and Sex Education, and Health Education guidance were published. The proposed guidance outlined a change in term for the rights of parents to withdraw their children from RSE as 'the right to be excused from sex education' (DfE, 2018: 13), which is discussed further in Chapter 4. The government also makes clear the parameters for the mandatory elements of the proposed curriculum as Relationships Education at primary school level; RSE at secondary school and Health Education in all state-funded schools, which includes academies and free schools. Some important statements were made in the draft guidance (2018) that indicated that RSE remains a complex and challenging area of the curriculum to navigate:

> The depth and breadth of views is clear [from the public consultation during 2017/18], and there are understandable and legitimate areas of contention. Our guiding principles have been that compulsory subject content must be age appropriate. It must be taught sensitively and inclusively, with respect for the backgrounds and beliefs of pupils and parents while always with the aim of providing pupils with the knowledge they need of the law.

It lists twelve legislative and guidance documents (DfE, 2018: 5–6) that provide the underpinning framework for the RSE guidance. Interestingly, the proposed guidance outlines that where schools are already providing relationships or sex education with good outcomes and meet the requirements of the 2018 guidance, they can continue to do so. Primary schools will be required to define what content is covered beyond the statutory Relationships Education within their designated school policy.

Being brave in developing practice

The recent changes to the status of RSE within a statutory National Curriculum is significant and raises some compelling questions as to the societal purpose of this. In the Western world, where a significant public investment is made by any society in state education, it is important to stop and consider why this is being implemented and for whom. In regard to RSE, this might arguably be for economic, political, religious reasons and ultimately, therefore, societal benefit. In terms of who may directly benefit, less is known. For those working with children, the curriculum will provide a more robust framework although equally it may well constrain those whose approach is for a more comprehensive RSE programme at an earlier age. Brook, PSHE Association and Sex Education Forum, for example, have actively lobbied for a statutory RSE curriculum, and there is a word of caution that needs to be applied, which is 'be careful what you wish for'. The new curriculum may result in a more statutorily constrained approach than its predecessor. Perhaps, as Zimmerman outlines, whatever RSE curriculum is implemented in the twenty-first century, children and young people will know and understand far more from mass media and their peers than they are taught in a classroom or at home. RSE is a reaction to the context it works within and is 'a mirror, reflecting all the flux and diversity – and the confusion and instability – of sex and youth in our globalised world' (Zimmerman, 2015: 152).

So, perhaps the way forward is to be brave. The concept of 'bravery' in approaching all aspects of the curriculum is emerging as a significant element of current thinking. McGregor and Rowe (2006) (cited by Mason and Woolley, 2012), in a newsletter for leadership teams across all educational phases, urged colleagues to 'be brave' in reviews of their curriculum. Being 'brave' contributes to the development of a creative culture with whom it engages. The notion of 'relevance' in RSE may be specific to the learners' setting, and indeed the historical and social context, in turn, is determined by the children engaged in the RSE provision. Siraj-Blatchford (2007: 1) outlines a pedagogy for the twenty-first century that explicitly prioritizes the three 'C's: communication, collaboration and creativity. Here creativity is interpreted as embedding creative opportunities for children into all curricular, while adopting a creative, flexible pedagogical approach with specific reference to RSE. Creative opportunities in RSE may mean inviting the views of children and young people about how they want to learn about sexual matters – through discussion, media tools, role play or other art forms. This means a more dialogic, discursive pedagogy, and for some practitioners, this may make them feel uncomfortable, indeed, perceived as risky, and require some amount of bravery. A creative strategy requires teachers and practitioners to be flexible in their approach to the content of RSE, strategies for teaching and their own views on sex and relationships. On the other hand, perhaps there are certain aspects of SRE that children do not know that they need to know. In the decisions that teachers make concerning what they feel children need to know about the aspects of RSE, there might also be a necessity to be brave. These decisions should be considered alongside the rights of the child. Corteen (2006: 96) proposes that SRE should be entitled 'Sexualities Education' and comprise a 'radical and inclusive agenda' which is informed by the rights of children. Crumper (2004: 126) contributes to this discussion by suggesting that there has been an increasing recognition of the rights of children in both national and international human rights law. SRE is included in this. Crumper makes clear that children have been accorded the right 'to be consulted on matters that concern them'. This has traditionally not been the case, and schools may be required to consider the impact of the Human Rights Act 1988 (p. 126) with regard to RSE, in particular, learners' right of access to information about RSE. The law stipulates caveats on children's right to information by the restriction of materials in RSE that are deemed inappropriate for the age, maturity, religious and cultural background of the children. There is, therefore, a complex legal framework that professionals working with children must work within to provide that which is based on children's human rights and, conversely, identify that which is not appropriate for the children and young people. The contextualizing of SRE is essential for it to be meaningful.

A small-scale research project conducted by Maxwell (2006: 437) makes recommendations that RSE should take into account the context of young people's actual experiences in relation to classroom and group dynamics. The fifty-two young men and women recruited to the study were sampled from a range of agencies such as a young offenders' institution, supported accommodation units and fee-paying boarding schools. The young people were aged between sixteen to twenty-three years, and many were already sexually active in the period before and during the research project. The research indicated a necessity to contextualize these sexual experiences in terms of the young person's past experiences and behaviours, their current situation and environment, and with their future aspirations. The findings revealed a wide range of factors that seemed to influence the sexual and intimate relationship attitudes and experiences of the participating young people. The factors did not affect the respondents equally or consistently; for example, peer groups seemed to play a role in influencing the experiences of some participants and not others, as well as the impact of early experiences of relationships and the choices they made. The differing contexts within which learners' experiences are found support the view that matching RSE to the needs of individual children and cohorts is necessary for learning to be effective, and is explored in more depth in Chapter 4.

Consider the challenges for practitioners working with children and young people in teaching a programme of RSE that requires a more dialogical, discursive approach:

- What does the notion of flexibility mean for professional vulnerability?
- Does this pedagogical approach make practitioners feel uncomfortable?
- If so, what are the underlying reasons for the feeling of discomfort or vulnerability?
- Do the elements of a 'brave' pedagogy feature in your setting's approach, or in approaches in a setting you are aware of?

Summary of key approaches to support effective practice

In order to develop effective practice it is important to consider the following:

- how the historical development of SRE/RSE contributes to an understanding of the importance of the subject;
- whether personal experience of sex education affects how issues may be delivered;
- how government documents and programmes can be interpreted and implemented in ways that reflect our own philosophies of education;
- what priorities for RSE are required in particular settings;
- how early, or indeed delayed, intervention can impact on the later sexual behaviour of children and young people; and
- the extent to which contextualized learning is possible and appropriate in SRE.

Conclusion and summary of key learning points

Professional awareness of the legislative framework and governmental guidance is essential for the development of an appropriate pedagogy for differing ages and stages of children and young people, along with the need to value the voice of the child, which has increasing resonance. Practitioners working in formal and informal education should explore their own personal beliefs and values that may influence how they may respond to statutory responsibilities. This chapter has explored the historical context and introduced a pedagogical approach that we feel is relevant to a child growing up in the twenty-first century, who increasingly will look for information about sexual matters beyond the biological basics. The child's need for knowledge and understanding about what an intimate relationship is, how it can develop and be mutually satisfying, requires for parents, carers and those working with children and young people to 'be brave' in their responses.

Signposts

The Sex Education Forum, hosted by the National Children's Bureau: advice and resources for practitioners, including guidance on curriculum development. www.ncb.org.uk/about-us/our-specialist-networks/sex-education-forum.
Your C-Card: http://c-card.areyougettingit.com/Default.aspx.

Further reading

Halstead, M., and Reiss, M. (2003) *Values in Sex Education: From Principles to Practice*. London: RoutledgeFalmer.
Woolley, R., and Mason, S. (2009) 'Sex and Relationships Education', in *Education Studies: An Issues-Based Approach* (2nd edn), ed. J. Sharp, S. Ward and L. Hankin. Exeter: Learning Matters.

References

Aggleton, P., and Crewe, M. (2005) 'Effects and Effectiveness in Sex and Relationships Education'. *Sex Education*, 5 (4), 303–6.
AVERT (n.d.) *History of HIV and AIDS Overview*. www.avert.org/professionals/history-hiv-aids/overview (accessed 6 August 2018).
Baldo, M., Aggleton, P., and Slutkin, G. (1993) 'WHO Global Programme on AIDS'. Paper presented at the IX conference on AIDS in Berlin.
Barry, P. (2002) *Beginning Theory: An Introduction to Literary and Cultural Theory* (revised edn). Manchester: Manchester University Press.
BBC (1983) *Mother Loses Contraception Test Case*. http://news.bbc.co.uk/onthisday/hi/dates/stories/july/26/newsid_2499000/2499583.stm (accessed 6 August 2018).
BBC News 24 (2007) *One Parent Families on the Rise*. http://news.bbc.co.uk/1/hi/uk/6542031.stm (accessed 6 August 2018).

Brook, PSHE Association and Sex Education Forum (2014) *Sex and Relationships Education (SRE) for the 21st Century: Supplementary Advice to the Sex and Relationship Education Guidance*. DfEE (0116/2000).

Corteen, K. (2006) 'Schools' Fulfilment of Sex and Relationship Education Documentation: Three School-Based Case Studies'. *Sex Education*, 6 (1), 77–99.

Crumper, P. (2004) 'Sex Education and Human Rights – A Lawyer's Perspective'. *Sex Education*, 4 (2), 125–36.

Curtis, P. (2010) 'Sex Education and Primary Curriculum Reforms Abandoned'. *The Guardian*. www.guardian.co.uk/education/2010/apr/07/primary—reforms—abandoned—labour (accessed 4 October 2018).

Department for Children, Schools and Families (2003) *Every Child Matters*. https://assets.publishing.service.gov.uk/government/uploads/system/uploads/attachment_data/file/272064/5860.pdf (accessed 4 October 2018).

Department for Education (2018) *Relationships Education, Relationships and Sex Education (RSE) and Health Education: Guidance for Governing Bodies, Proprietors, Head Teachers, Principals, Senior Leadership Teams, Teachers*. London: Department for Education.

Department for Education and Employment (2000) *Sex and Relationship Education Guidance*. Nottingham: DfEE.

Department of Education and Science (1977) *Health Education in Schools*. London: Her Majesty's Stationery Office.

Department of Education and Science (1987) *Sex Education at School*. Circular 11/87. London: Department of Education and Science.

Family Planning Association (2011) *Sex and Relationships Education Factsheet*. London: FPA. www.fpa.org.uk/sites/default/files/sex-and-relationships-education-factsheet-january-2011.pdf (accessed 4 October 2018).

Farrell, C. (1987) *My Mother Said*. London: Routledge and Kegan Paul.

Grunseit, A., and Kippax, S. (1994) 'Effects of Sex Education on Young People's Sexual Behaviour'. National Centre for HIV Social Research, Macquarie University, Australia for WHO Global Programme on AIDS.

Halstead, M., and Reiss, M. (2003) *Values in Sex Education: From Principles to Practice*. London: RoutledgeFalmer.

Halstead, M., and Waite, S. (2002) '"Worlds Apart": The Sexual Values of Boys and Girls'. *Education and Health*, 20 (1), 17–23.

Kiernan, K. (1995) 'Transition to Parenthood: Young Mothers, Young Fathers- Associated Factors and Later Life Experiences'. State Programme Discussion Papers, WSP 113, Centre for Analysis of Social Exclusion, The London School of Economics and Political Science, London.

Kirby, D. (1997) 'No Easy Answers, Research Findings on Programmes to Reduce Teen Pregnancy'. National Programme for the Reduction in Teenage Pregnancies.

Lewis, J., and Knijn, T. (2002) 'The Politics of Sex Education in England and Wales and the Netherlands since the 1980s'. *Journal of Social Politics*, 31 (4), 669–94.

Macdonald, A. (2009) *Independent Review of the Proposal to Make Personal, Social, Health and Economic (PSHE) Education Statutory*. London: Department for Children, Schools and Families.

Mason, S. (2010) 'Braving It Out! An Illuminative Evaluation of the Provision of Sex and Relationship Education in Two Primary Schools in England'. *Sex Education*, 10 (2), 157–69.

McGregor, D. and Rowe, S. (2006) 'Leadership Now'. In: Mason and Woolley (2012). *Relationships and Sex Education 5–11: Supporting Children's Development And Well-Being. London: Continuum.*

Maxwell, C. (2006) 'Context and "Contextualisation" in Sex and Relationships Education'. *Sex Education*, 106 (6), 437–49.

Office for National Statistics (2017) *Families and Households: 2017.* www.ons.gov.uk/peoplepopulationandcommunity/birthsdeathsandmarriages/families/bulletins/familiesandhouseholds/2017#number-of-families-in-the-uk-continues-to-grow-with-cohabiting-couple-families-growing-the-fastest (accessed 4 Ocotber 2018).

Pilcher, J. (2005) 'School Sex and Education: Policy and Practice in England 1870 to 2000'. *Sex Education*, 5 (2), 153–70.

Public Health England (2018) 'Sexually Transmitted Infections and Screening for Chlamydia in England, 2017'. Health Protection Report, 12 (208). https://assets.publishing.service.gov.uk/government/uploads/system/uploads/attachment_data/file/713944/hpr2018_AA-STIs_v5.pdf (accessed 4 October 2018).

Riches, V. (2004) *Sex Education or Indoctrination? How Ideology Has Triumphed Over Facts.* Wiltshire: Cromwell Press.

Rose, J. (2009) *Independent Review of the Primary Curriculum: Final Report.* Nottingham: Department for Children. Schools and Families.

Sex Education Forum (2015) *SRE – The Evidence.* London: National Children's Bureau.

Siraj-Blatchford, I. (2007) 'Creativity, Communication and Collaboration: The Identification of Pedagogic Progression in Sustained Shared Thinking'. *Asia-Pacific Journal of Research in Early Childhood Education*, 1 (2), 1–13.

Social Exclusion Unit (1999) *Teenage Pregnancy Report by the Social Exclusion Unit.* London: The Stationary Office.

Stronach, I., Frankham, J., and Stark, S. (2007) 'Sex, Science and Educational Research: The Unholy Trinity', in *Knowledge Production*, ed. B. Somekh and T. A. Schwandt. London: Routledge.

UNICEF (2007) *Child Poverty in Perspective: An Overview of Child Well-being in Rich Countries.* Innocenti Research Centre Report Card 7. www.unicef-irc.org/publications/pdf/rc7_eng.pdf (accessed 6 August 2018).

Wellings, K., Wadsworth, K., Johnson, A., and Field, J. (1996) *Teenage Sexuality, Fertility and Life Chances.* A report prepared for the Department of Health using data from the National Survey of Sexual Attitudes and Lifestyles.

Wells, N. (2009) *Too Much, Too Soon: The Government's Plans for Your Child's Sex Education.* Twickenham: Family Education Trust.

Wyness, M. (1996) *Schooling, Welfare and Parental Responsibility.* London: Falmer Press.

Zimmerman, J. (2015) *Too Hot to Handle: A Global History of Sex Education.* Oxfordshire: Princeton University Press.

2

The wider context

John, aged seven, regularly watches a popular soap opera on the television. In one episode he has seen a young man and woman who have a romantic friendship. He finds it amusing how they struggle to find a time or a place to be on their own. In one episode they have a candlelit dinner and, afterwards, settle down on the sofa. The young man is clearly excited to find that his amorous attentions are well received by the woman and, when she leaves the room for a few moments, he strips to his underwear expecting that they will have sex on her return. When she re-enters the room she is shocked and runs from the house screaming. John asks his mum why the man had to take his clothes off to have a cuddle.

Chapter outline

Introduction

Children learn about relationships and sexuality from a variety of sources, including family members, peers and the media. While parents and carers may consider carefully the detail they present to their children, they cannot be aware of all the information and materials that their children encounter. One only has to watch popular soap operas on mainstream TV channels to come across a wide variety of relationship patterns and sexual practices. Some children will have a greater awareness of sex and sexuality than others, and their playground talk will affect the awareness of other children. In addition, some children will access pornography in the home, through magazines and DVDs owned by parents or siblings and sometimes through the internet. Older children can also aspire to being teenagers and enjoy reading magazines for this age group, which often address relationship issues. These sources can give false expectations about relationships or sex devoid of any context that involves love, care or respect.

This chapter explores how adults can create safe and supportive environments in which children can share questions and concerns as they encounter increasing amounts of information. It includes an exploration of how to avoid both stereotyping and heterosexism (the assumption that everyone is 'straight') and how to combat homophobia. It explores how adults can address children's questions in age-appropriate ways and how they can create an atmosphere in which questions are welcomed and valued. Importantly, it addresses how to support children so that they use the internet in appropriate ways and maintain personal safety. First, it considers the wider context of how society has changed over past decades, to reflect on how societal and cultural change may impact on both the needs and questions of children and the background of their teachers and other adults with whom they interact.

Relationships and cultural change

How have attitudes towards relationships, sexuality and sexual orientation changed during the past half-century? We (the authors) were born in the 1960s, when to be an unmarried mother was frequently frowned upon and where such mothers were sometimes encouraged to put their baby up for adoption; when sex between two men was illegal (even in private between consenting adults); and when the contraception pill was a relatively new phenomenon. As teenagers, we were educated about HIV/ AIDS through a rather chilling advertising campaign which warned us: 'Don't die of ignorance'; sex between two men was legal, but only if you were twenty-one years or over and both consented (but sex involving more than two men, or if others were in the house, or in a hotel room was still illegal); and the divorce rate was rising.

Consider how this contrasts with a twenty-first-century context: worldwide, HIV is found most commonly among heterosexual people; contraception is widely available and easily accessible; pornography is available at the click of a mouse; dating and sex telephone lines and internet sites are advertised widely and publicly. Sexuality has moved from being in the shadows of popular consciousness to being overt.

Have such changes had an impact on children's awareness of, or interest in, matters of sex and sexuality? Or rather, have such changes made it more possible for children to ask questions in a less stifling and more open society? Change has come in a range of forms and on a variety of levels.

First, there has been change in the legal framework relating to sex and relationships. It is worth mapping out briefly some of the milestones from over the lifetime of the authors, which also relate to the experience of many teachers.

Sex and relationships, timeline

1961 The contraceptive pill becomes available. Its launch gives women greater control over how many children they have. Initially, it was only available to married couples, but the rules were relaxed six years later with the swinging sixties in full flow.

1967 Ten years after the recommendations of the Wolfenden Report, the Sexual Offences Bill was introduced. The new Act implemented the Wolfenden proposals, which introduced new privacy restrictions – homosexual acts could not legally take place where a third person was likely to be present, but these were no longer illegal between two consenting men aged twenty-one years or older in private.

1967 Abortion Act, introduced by Liberal MP David Steel and passed by a free vote of MPs, made abortion legal up to twenty-eight weeks if a woman's mental or physical health was at risk.

1973 Matrimonial Causes Act set out the one ground for divorce: that the marriage had broken down irretrievably. This was to be proven by giving evidence to a court of one of five facts: the adultery of the other spouse; the unreasonable behaviour of the other spouse; two years' desertion; the couple living apart for two years and the other spouse consenting to divorce; the couple having lived apart for five years (with no consent needed).

1978 On 25 July, the world's first 'test tube baby' was born shortly before midnight in Oldham District General Hospital. Weighing 5 lb 12 oz (2.61 kg), Louise Brown was delivered by caesarean section.

1980 Criminal Justice (Scotland) Act decriminalized homosexuality on similar terms to the 1967 Act in England, and in 1982 decriminalization was extended to Northern Ireland.

1988 Section 28 of the Local Government Act banned local authorities from promoting homosexuality or publishing any materials that would promote homosexuality. There was significant debate about whether the Act related to schools and other education settings; whether or not this was the case, it caused teachers a great deal of concern.

1990 The Abortion Act in the UK was amended so that abortion is legal up to twenty-four weeks, rather than twenty-eight, except in unusual cases.

1991 The Conservative government undertook to cease criminal prosecutions against gay men in the armed forces.

1994 The age of consent for gay men was reduced to eighteen.

1997 The government introduced a Sex Offenders Bill that required the courts to place certain convicted sex offenders on a register. The 1997 Act was subsequently amended and then re-enacted by the Sexual Offenders Act 2003. The original proposals would have included all men convicted of gross indecency. After fierce protests from Stonewall and many other lesbian and gay groups this was withdrawn, but men convicted of age-of-consent offences, including the younger person, were included.

1999 The New Labour government set up a major review of sexual offences. The review team, including representatives from Stonewall, made a wide range of recommendations to protect children, women and vulnerable groups from sexual abuse and assault. The review states,

A new offence should operate in a gender and sexuality neutral way. A man and a man – or a woman and a woman – kissing and holding hands in public should no more be criminalised than a man and a woman behaving in the same way. (Home Office, 2000)

2000 Stonewall successfully challenged the privacy provisions of the 1967 Act in the European Court of Human Rights in the case of *ADT v. UK*.

2001 The age of consent for gay men was reduced to sixteen.

2003 Section 28 (see above) was repealed in the UK (apart from Scotland where it had been repealed in 2000). As it did not create a criminal offence, no prosecution had ever been brought under the Act. However, it had caused fear within local authorities and educational institutions and caused much caution and self-censorship.

2005 Civil Partnership Act was enacted on 5 December. Subsequently, human rights activist Peter Tatchell campaigned for all couples to have a choice between marriage and civil partnership, whatever their sexual orientation (for more details, see http://www.petertatchell.net/).

2010 Equality Act enshrined nine protected characteristics in the UK law, building upon earlier equalities legislation: age, disability, gender reassignment, marriage and civil partnership, 'race', religion or belief, sex, and sexual orientation. For the most part it did not apply to Northern

Ireland. The revised National Curriculum for England (DfE, 2014) makes reference to these protected characteristics (see also Chapter 8).

2013 Marriage (Same-Sex Couples) Act introduced equal marriage in England and Wales, and was followed by the Marriage and Civil Partnership (Scotland) Act 2014. The situation in Northern Ireland was still under discussion in 2018. At the time of writing, same-sex marriage was legal in around twenty-five countries around the world.

2017 Children and Social Work Act – Sections 34 and 35 stated that schools must have regard to statutory guidance on RSE, which outlines what they should do and what they must do. The guidance can be followed from 2019, and is to be fully implemented by 2020.

2017–18 Tim Loughton, MP, presented a private member's Bill to end the ban on opposite-sex civil partnerships in England and Wales. Civil partnerships have only been available to same-sex couples.

Second, there has been social change. Some of this may have arisen from changes in the law, and some has driven legislative change. However, the law does not necessarily reflect or affect people's attitudes.

Over the past twenty years divorce rates have fluctuated. In 2016 there were 8.9 divorces of opposite-sex couples per 1,000 married men and women ($n = 106,959$), a rate over 20 per cent lower than the peak in 2003 and 2004 (ONS, 2010). There were 112 divorces of same-sex couples in 2016; of these 78 per cent were female couples. The divorce rates were highest for men aged 45–49 and for women aged 30–39 (ONS, 2010). This must be seen within a context in which increasing numbers of people are choosing to marry later or not to marry at all, which inevitably leads to fewer divorces.

Third, there has been a change in the make-up of British society, which is more evident in some regions than others. Cultural and religious diversity has meant that while in some ways society has increasingly become more secular and that the church has had less influence, issues of modesty in dress (particularly for women), discussion about arranged marriages and issues of sexual morality are being raised for different reasons to those traditionally focused upon during much of the twentieth century.

The wider context for RSE inevitably includes the setting into which a person was born, grew up and developed both personal and professional values and attitudes. These experiences – informed by family attitudes, influences from peers and the media, and possibly religious and political views – all contribute to the way in which teachers and other professionals in the children's workforce approach RSE with their learners. Inevitably, teachers, and those training to teach, have had a different cultural experience to that of the children with whom they will work.

Reflect on the culture into which you were born and in which you grew up, and the legal and other milestones outlined above.

Consider:

- how your background and experience have contributed to your attitudes towards sex, sexuality and sexual orientation;
- how the dominant culture of contemporary society (as exemplified by the popular media) reflects the views that you hold and the views that you experienced in past years; and
- how you feel about the ways in which today's society has become more diverse, inclusive and accepting in terms of matters relating to sex and sexuality.

Relationships and the media

While family and close personal relationships may be the main socializing factors affecting children, the media plays a key role in the secondary socialization of children (Marsh, 2005). When surveying commercial breaks in between children's TV programmes it is possible to appraise the messages that are being promoted about clothing, toys and gendered behaviours (Woolley, 2010). Children can access a wide range of information and images about gender and gender roles though television, magazines and the internet. Many children are able to view TV channels where music videos demonstrate a sexualized culture and where reality TV show participants discuss and demonstrate their sexuality and sexual desires. On mainstream television a wide range of soap operas has addressed issues of divorce, sexual orientation, rape, incest and paedophilia (Woolley and Mason, 2009). These storylines appear at prime viewing times when thousands of children are watching. Some children will also be able to access materials with varying degrees of pornographic content, whether through DVDs and magazines owned by their parents or siblings, or via the internet, with or without the knowledge or supervision of their parents and carers. Children thus receive a great deal of information and see a range of role models, without necessarily having the maturity or experience to interpret them. These relate to a range of gendered identities.

Consider the experience of John and his mother outlined at the start of this chapter.

- What relationship issues have you observed in TV programmes (and soap operas in particular) at a time when it would be reasonable to expect children of John's age to be viewing?

- John's mother does not feel that he is at an appropriate age to know information about sexual acts between adults. How might she answer his question in a way that properly satisfies his curiosity?
- John's mother shares her concern about the content of early-evening TV programmes with you as his teacher. She appreciates how much he enjoys the programme and is worried that if she stops him watching he will only hear of its content from friends on the playground. What might you advise?

TV drama, by necessity, involves the portrayal of situations which involve intense emotions stemming from active situations. Many people will find their lives dull in comparison, and perhaps they will be thankful for this. However, if the media presented drama at the pace of everyday life, viewers would find it tedious for the most part. The conventions of the soap opera genre, in particular, necessitate that the action be based in a relatively confined geographical area, be it a street or a small village, and that the issues faced by the members of that local community be condensed into a matter of minutes at a time. This is something that adults take for granted. However, it means that children can access briskly paced, intense, sometimes violent and often gritty accounts of what appear to be people's everyday lives. Such is the range of media products available that it is difficult to maintain the notion of childhood innocence which some adults use as a reason for avoiding discussions with children about relationships or sex:

> An early introduction to education about sex and relationships is sometimes believed to 'destroy children's innocence'. However, children and young people are exposed to sexual imagery in the media and advertising, which can give them a distorted view of sex, relationships and sexuality without any consideration of possible outcomes such as sexually transmitted infections and unwanted pregnancy. A trained and confident teacher will work with parents to give children and young people appropriate and accurate information to help them make sense of the imagery that surrounds them. (NICE, n.d.: 28–9)

One response to John's mother might be to suggest watching the TV programme with her son. This would ensure that she was aware of the issues that he was seeing and that she might provide an opportunity for him to raise questions. If John was embarrassed by watching with his mother this might suggest that he knows that the content is a little beyond his current maturity, and he might resolve the situation by choosing other viewing times or finding alternative activities. Leaving John to watch the programme alone on the TV set in his bedroom will leave the issues unaddressed. The parent/carer has a responsibility for what they allow their child to view.

Relationships and virtual reality

This responsibility extends further, to the materials that are accessible by children in the home. As noted earlier in this chapter, some households will include pornographic materials (e.g. magazines or DVDs) owned by its older members, or access to the internet without parental controls; some children will access materials in the homes of their friends. Such materials come with restrictions on the age for which they are appropriate; allowing children to have access, whether consciously or through carelessness, will inevitably lead to children's questions and possibly behaviours which are not age-appropriate. On a different level, some openly accessible daily newspapers include sexualized images which are taken as commonly acceptable by many people. These will be available to children, and parents/carers and others may not give particular thought to whether the materials are suitable for children to view. Such materials can objectify others (often women) in sexual ways, which, accompanied by parental attitudes, might affect the ways in which children relate to those around them. The internet provides an additional source of material that can be accessible to inquisitive children in an uncensored manner.

Children may consciously or inadvertently access inappropriate or illegal sexual material. Additionally, email, text messages and social media can be used to harass; such bullying is most likely to occur between children and young people. Chat rooms can be used by predatory adults (sometimes posing as children) to groom children. It is important to stress that children should never give personal information to others on the internet. This includes name, address and telephone number, and details about one's family or school. If children are permitted to use chat rooms they need to understand the need to be polite to others and the importance of expecting others to show respect to them. Key to this is their understanding that they must tell an appropriate and trusted adult if they encounter anything scary, rude or threatening, or if another person makes them feel uncomfortable or worried. Children in general have increasingly well-developed skills in the use of technology. They can understand that if they send a photograph to someone then it can be shared with others and/or modified; they also need to understand that, once shared, they lose control of such images. They can also understand that incoming messages can include attachments which, when opened, may introduce viruses that will damage their computer. Developing healthy and safe online relationships is a key aspect of the updated guidance for Relationships Education in England (DfE, 2018).

In schools, despite good levels of internet security, it is still possible for children to come across inappropriate content. One example is of a child in a primary school innocently searching online for robin redbreast in the days leading up to Christmas. The results were unexpected and very embarrassing to them, despite the school's firewall. Teachers have an important role to play in helping children to stay safe, both when they use the internet in school and when they are away from the school environment and may have unlimited and possibly unsupervised online access. In the same way that educators address *stranger danger* with their children in school, teachers need to reinforce the importance of online safety which includes danger associated with online grooming and the need for children to know that they must never meet anyone they initially encountered online:

> Exposure to graphic sexual images and sexually explicit language and content on the internet and TV and in films, magazines and pornography can result in children and young people forming inaccurate views and negatively influence their expectations about sexual behaviour and relationships. Some young people may use mobile phones to send revealing photographs or intimidating messages that can put themselves or others at risk of harm or abuse. SRE [*sic*] can give children and young people the confidence to resist pressures and knowledge about where and how to get help if they feel upset or threatened. (NICE, n.d.: 29)

Computers are not the only electronic gadgets which can be misused. Increasingly, mobile phones are being used to harass or bully others. Children need to understand that they need to look after their phone: a good reason for this is that it is probably the most expensive piece of equipment they carry around with them. They need to understand that if they lose their phone, or if it is stolen, it may be possible for someone else to use it to impersonate them. For this reason it is helpful to use a pin number to lock the phone when it is not in use and to keep the pin number secret. The phone should also be kept in a safe place, and not placed on show in public when not in use.

Children need to know that if they receive text messages or phone calls which make them feel uncomfortable, embarrassed or scared, they *must* tell an adult they trust as soon as possible. If they receive such communications from strangers they should also always report this. While phones can be very helpful in enabling children to stay safe and to maintain contact with home, they also have the potential to be a source of danger. In addition, children need to understand that any photographs that they send using their phone are out of their control and can be misused by others. They should never give their mobile number to a stranger, whether in person or online. Phone safety is an important aspect that must not be missed alongside the coverage of stranger danger and internet safety. It provides the possibility of relating to others in unpleasant ways. Strategies for dealing with such forms of bullying are explored in the next chapter.

Relationships and gender

While work has been done in settings and schools in recent years to address gender stereotyping, this may have more to do with traditional girl/boy roles in play than the ways in which people see each other in terms of more intimate and personal relationships.

It is possible for boys and girls to be friends without any romantic element. This is not always easy, and peer pressure can play a part in undermining such platonic friendships. Similarly, boys who like to play with their female friends may be bullied and have their sexual orientation challenged by peers, as may girls who play with boys. Traditional stereotypes are common and play a fundamental part in how girls and boys discover – and are allowed to discover – their identities, both in positive and negative ways:

> *Becoming somebody* is the primary motivation of boys' and girls' social behaviour at school ... many boys learn that they must establish their position in a hierarchy of masculinities to avoid being positioned as the marginalized. (Meyenn and Parker, 2001: 173)

Supporting children as they relate to one another is an important part of their schooling, for such relationships can be a form of support, pleasure, tension or bullying. This can arise for a range of reasons, some of which are more fully acknowledged than others within school settings. Eighty-six per cent of LGBT pupils regularly hear phrases such as 'that's so gay' and 'you're so gay' in school, with 66 per cent hearing this frequently or often (Stonewall, 2017); 40 per cent of these pupils have skipped school because of homophobic bullying (Stonewall, 2017). While some of these incidents will occur in secondary schools, Stonewall's *School Report* gives a clear indication that this is a matter that needs to be taken seriously in primary schools:

> I have been bullied since Year 2 for being gay. People called me names like 'gay' and 'faggot' before I even knew what they really meant. (Stonewall, 2017: 10)

In recent years it has become statutory to record all racist incidents in schools. A logical next step is to record all incidents of homophobic bullying in order to ensure that its profile and significance are heightened and that a clear message that it is unacceptable is presented to all stakeholders in schools. This is a key strategy in order to safeguard the emotional well-being of children and young people, whatever their awareness or understanding of their own sexual orientation.

Children's picture books (appropriate for several age ranges in primary education) provide a means of enabling children to explore how they relate to one another. Particularly good examples which explore the sometimes complex relationships between boys and girls are:

Jennifer Jones Won't Leave Me Alone (Wishinsky, 2004). As the title suggests, this is the story of a boy who is receiving the unwelcome attentions of Jennifer Jones. His friends tease him that they are a couple. She sends messages and shouts in his ear. He considers that she could be launched in a rocket, be sent to the Arctic and then he discovers that she is moving away. When she leaves, the boy is left with no one to sit with in class: he focuses on his school work and mopes around in the playground. When he receives a letter from Jennifer he is worried that she is having such fun that she may never return, but on hearing that she is coming back to school he runs to the local store to buy her a gift. This is a sweet tale of a boy and a girl who are good friends; it is just that one of them does not realize this until halfway through the story. It raises issues of how boys and girls are friends in primary school. The suggestion of romance is interesting and would provoke lively discussion with children in Upper Key Stage 2.

Ed Loves Sarah Loves Tim (Schreiber-Wicke, 2000) tells the story of Ed, who feels strange every time he sees Sarah: he becomes enthusiastic about going to school, and then Sarah asks him to be her boyfriend! All is well in the world. Then suddenly, things start to go wrong: on the day that he is late for school he finds that Sarah is sitting with Tim. There seems to be no room for Ed. He becomes miserable and feels like he is friendless. One day, when he is late for school again, the strange feeling returns when he meets Hannah. This book explores the making and breaking of friendships. Some readers may feel that the 'romantic' element of the story is inappropriate for younger children, but others will recognize the innocent boyfriend/girlfriend friendships which some children experience. It provides an accessible way for older children to discuss the younger characters, and perhaps to consider how their own feelings might compare.

Oscar and Arabella and Ormsby (Layton, 2007) is a story which presents the adage 'Two's company ... three's a crowd' in a format for children to consider. Oscar and Arabella are the very best of friends, but when Ormsby arrives on the scene, things are not so pleasant. Oscar was not very keen on Ormsby, although Arabella quite liked him. In fact, Ormsby seemed to be seeking to impress Arabella and he and Oscar soon come to blows. Meanwhile, Arabella wanders into danger and the two male characters charge to her rescue, becoming friends along the way. There is a happy ending with all three becoming friends, most of the time. This is a story about how rivals can become friends. While a romantic element may be inferred, this need not be the case. The focus on animal characters (and mammoths, in particular) means that this aspect of the story may be more accessible than those books which consider boyfriend/girlfriend-style relationships involving children.

> Further children's picture books looking at situations of change in children's lives can be accessed in the *Transitions Reading Resource*, details of which are included at the end of this chapter.

Much has been done in recent years to address gender stereotyping, and there is a greater awareness of homophobic bullying in schools than in the past. However, the focus on both gender identity and sexual orientation remains, to a great degree, centred around a binary of female and male identities. Many children can label their own or another person's gender by thirty-six months, and are said to have achieved gender identity (Smith et al., 2003). This is followed by gender stability (at around four years) when children understand that gender is normally stable, and gender constancy (by around seven years) when they realize that biological sex is unchanging, despite changes in appearance (Papalia et al., 2003). However, for some children there will be a sense that the gender assigned to them at birth is not that with which they identify. Hellen suggests that often homophobic bullying arises not out of a child's sexual orientation (or others' perceptions of this) but as a result of gendered behaviours:

> It may be reasonable to argue then that homophobic bullying in schools, especially primary schools, is a result, not of a child's sexual orientation, but of a child's appearance or mannerisms in relation to gender. Indeed it is probable that the only way a potential homophobic bully would have of singling out a victim would be with reference to gender variant appearance or behaviour, so those lesbian, gay and bisexual (but not transgendered) children who still conform to the normative expectations of their gender probably run a greatly reduced risk of homophobic bullying whilst others who are not lesbian, gay or bisexual may suffer from it considerably. (2009: 95)

Hellen argues that teachers need to be aware of the possibility of trans children being within their class. It can be a difference which is hidden, as children learn to conform to the expectations of those around them and have to face the pressure of expectations for gendered behaviours based around a fixed binary of male and female. Further details about trans matters are available in Hellen (2009) and from the Mermaids website, included in the Signposts at the end of this chapter. These are discussed in more detail in Chapter 8.

Relationships and pressures on children

There can be considerable tensions between the different and conflicting pressures experienced by girls. A survey by Girlguiding UK and the Mental Health Foundation found that girls aged 10–14 felt

- compelled to act older than their age;
- sexual pressures from boys on the school playground;
- pressure from magazines and websites concerning what they 'ought to be', for example, thin, trying drugs or having cosmetic surgery; and
- that boredom led to aggression, including the possibility of self-harm. (2008: 13)

It is important to note how many of the girls' concerns relate to appearance and its impact on self-esteem. The survey suggests significant pressure on girls to conform to the expectations of peers, family members and the media. The focus on boredom is interesting and may relate to the significant and sometimes inequitable amount of time that boys demand from teachers. This will have consequences for girls' understanding of both gender and power roles.

Similarly, boys can be pressured to show certain behaviours through media representations and social relationships. Francis identifies that they are expected to show displays of 'hardness' (2000: 100), 'having a laugh' (p. 65), sporting achievement, an interest in pastimes and subjects construed as masculine, showing off and non-studious behaviours (Skelton and Francis, 2003). Masculinities work at different levels: the national and international levels of identifying with heroes and role models, and the local level of finding acceptance and one's place in friendships and community relationships. Sometimes the two conflict, and boys come to understand that what may be acceptable in the media is not as acceptable in their community or family, and vice versa. They also come to understand what is acceptable in school, both from peers and staff (Woolley, 2010).

In England, over recent years, there has been an increasing focus on children's emotional and mental health as well as other aspects of health, including physical well-being. Mental health needs are one of the last remaining taboos in British society, although increasingly they are being faced. It is important that children understand the importance of good mental health, alongside knowing how to keep healthy physically. If educators are to meet the needs of the whole child they need to appreciate the importance of mental health and well-being, and to make these a priority, which necessitates addressing issues of equality directly.

During a lesson on 'Our Futures' with a Year 6 class, I noticed that one of the girls, Lisa, had listed that she wanted to have children later in life. I asked whether she also wanted to include getting married as one of her ambitions (I should probably have asked whether she wanted to have a partner) and whether this might enable them to start a family together. Lisa (aged 11) responded, 'I'm not getting married. It only means you end up arguing lots of the time and I'd end up looking after the baby myself in any case.' When asked further why she would like to have children she replied, 'They give you someone to care for and love. You can look after them and as they get a bit older you can do all sorts of stuff together like me and my mum.'

– Anya (Year 6 teacher)

Consider Lisa's responses:

- Might Anya make any presumptions about Lisa's experience of family life?
- How do you see the role of the family and how might this affect the way in which you teach children about possible future relationships?
- Might Anya's response suggest an assumption that Lisa is heterosexual?
- Should Anya challenge Lisa's viewpoint, affirm it, or let Lisa's feelings and ideas continue to evolve naturally over time?

In the UK, media portrayals of men appear to show that diversity across a spectrum of masculinities is valued. However, when a political figure admits to being gay, this media openness is often revealed as being superficial. It is still relatively rare for a high-profile sports personality to come out as gay, and when they do, the media scrutiny can be intense. In the media, diverse masculinities (and male sexualities) are neither so much welcomed or embraced as tolerated and found to be conveniently interesting. Publicity about one's sexual orientation (and thereby, for some, one's perceived masculinity) can still be an unwelcome intrusion and a perceived threat to one's career. Society has not become as open as it sometimes wishes to appear. It still remains important to boast about sexual activity in order to posture within hegemonic (heterosexual) masculinity, and apparent difference is only accepted against the background of a certain sense of what it means to be a man. Connell defines the leading pattern of masculinity as being hegemonic – in other words that which is 'culturally exalted' or 'idealised' (1990: 83). This male potency derives from traditional stereotypes of the heterosexual man. Despite moves towards greater equality for all men, including (as indicated in the timeline earlier in this chapter) the equalization of the age of consent and the introduction of civil partnerships and equal marriage, there are still dominant expectations for what constitutes maleness within society.

Jason is aged 10 years. During break times he is usually to be found with a group of friends in a quiet corner of the playground playing card games or swapping football cards and stickers. One afternoon a gust of wind caught some of the cards and blew them across the tarmac. When I went to help pick them up I found that this pack of playing cards had photographs of seminaked women on the back. When I asked Jason

> *where they came from he said that he had taken them from a drawer in his older brother's bedroom.*
>
> – Annabelle (Year 5 teacher)
>
> Consider Annabelle's response to this situation:
>
> - Whom does she need to inform about her discovery?
> - What action might need to be taken and whom might she consult with?
> - How might Annabelle, or others, need to address the needs of others (e.g. other children who collected the cards from the playground and their parents/carers).

In Jason's situation, the response will be informed significantly by the teacher's knowledge of him and his maturity. It may be that he has discovered a new pack of cards at home and brought it to add to the wide variety already used in his playtime games. He may or may not be aware that the photographs are mildly pornographic or that they are of a sexual nature. Indeed, it may be the teacher's response that introduces him to such notions. How Jason responds when the teacher speaks with him about the cards and their source should give a good initial indication of his understanding: is he embarrassed; does he try to avoid answering questions; does he find the situation amusing? It may be that Jason is positioning himself within his group of friends, asserting an expected form of masculinity in order to gain popularity or assert a laddish stereotype. It is the culture of a society which exerts most influence in the creation of masculine behaviours:

> You don't have to be the mother of a son to worry about what kind of men we are asking boys to grow into when so many of the old role models are redundant. Male identity has always been built on the subordination of women. If girls are achieving so much more academically, how will boys accommodate women's equality? (Bunting, 2000)

The increasing success of girls in the English school system, reflected in the now annual debate and comparison between genders when end-of-year test and examination results are published, has brought into question how it is possible to engage boys and to encourage them to see learning as being important. Belying this view is the sense that men have traditionally identified themselves in terms of dominance and superiority, but now find themselves achieving at lower rates than their female counterparts. Traditionally male identity has been derived from a sense of power and from power relationships:

> It is important to recognise ... that violence by males against males, which is often interpreted as boys being boys or as bullying, is indeed gender-based. Such violence is often a form of boundary policing, usually with a homophobic edge, which serves

to both normalize particular constructions of masculinity while also determining where a boy is positioned within a hierarchical arrangement of masculinities. (Mills, 2001a: 4)

In a setting where boys and men are finding themselves achieving less than their female peers, it is important to explore how men develop a sense of maleness and a sense of personal identity in a setting where the tradition of dominance is undermined and untenable:

The real boy crisis is a crisis of violence, about the cultural prescriptions that equate masculinity with the capacity for violence. (Foster et al., 2001: 16)

Indeed, Skelton (2002) suggests that what is required is a move away from stereotypical understandings of what constitutes masculine and feminine, in order to transcend the limitations of sex role theory and appreciate that the gender identities commonly enshrined in male and female bodies are restrictive and now discredited. When talking about men it is important to remember that they differ a great deal in 'race', location, age, socialization, family structure and cosmology (Morrell, 2005). Being a man is a diverse, individual and unique experience. The risk of being seen as different exerts a great pressure on men to conform to social norms and expectations. Homophobia works to subordinate those who do not conform to the requirements or expectations of male culture (Mills, 2001a). This can be the case for both heterosexual and gay boys. The fear of this happening can lead to boys establishing power relationships which maintain traditional macho behaviours. The fear of being different can significantly affect behaviour and pressurize males into showing outward behaviours that protect themselves. The threat of being treated differently and of being identified as 'different' causes some boys and men to live within the general confines of society's expectations:

Homophobia and misogyny are two of the most important policing mechanisms of dominant masculinities. (Mills, 2001b: 63)

Men who have a different view of masculinity from the perceived norm can be pressurized into conforming, or at least appearing to conform, to the expectations of those around them. Gender can be used as a form of social control (Baird, 2004) and is perhaps a more important consideration than biology, psychology or spirituality. Teachers are in a position to help children to consider such pressures and to develop a progressive agenda for RSE which appreciates explanations about inequality: they can help to search for the solution rather than being a part of the problem (Claire, 2001). A school can play two roles in the formation of learners' understandings of masculinity: it can provide the setting and physical space where actions and relatedness take place, but it can also affect such understandings through its policies, procedures and practices (Swain, 2006).

Teachers need to be aware of the ways in which children use stereotypes as a source of bullying. Some signs and symptoms of bullying are addressed further in the next chapter. Sometimes those who do not conform to gender norms can face bullying relating to sexuality or sexual orientation. Children's bullying can be particularly unpleasant and it is essential to be sensitive to its occurrence. A girl who loves to play rugby or a boy who attends dance classes, for example, can be susceptible to such bullying. There is a difference between behaviour which is different to the traditional norm for one's gender and behaviour which signifies a stereotype of sexual orientation. Indeed the latter is an inappropriate concept, as any person with any mannerism or behaviour trait can be lesbian, gay, bisexual, heterosexual, curious, questioning or trans. The media does not always help in this regard, for, while people with a variety of sexual orientations have a high profile on the television, there also remain some crude stereotypes which undermine moves towards inclusion and equality.

If the resources and language that teachers and other childcare professionals use present an assumption that all children, their families and friends are heterosexual then they perpetuate heterosexism in other settings. Resources such as the *Family Diversities Reading Resource* (a pack of over 150 high-quality children's picture books) provide one means of introducing a range of models of being a family into the materials available in our schools (Morris and Woolley, 2017).

Consider the discussion on gendered identities of children outlined above:

- How aware are you of the pressures faced by your learners in terms of gender expectations?
- Do you consider that your learners face more pressure than you yourself did at school?
- Is society becoming more open and accepting of a spectrum of gendered identities and, if so, how is this represented in your learning setting?

Creating safe spaces

For many children, schools and settings are the places where they are able to explore issues and ideas in a safe and supportive atmosphere. This is a particular strength in primary schools, where children get to know key adults with whom they spend the majority of their time. It is also a place where there are clear ground rules so that individual privacy and personality are respected.

Teachers are also aware of how children interact with one another. They see their learners on a daily basis for most of the week and can be aware of changes in a child's attitude or temperament. They know something of the child's background and have a professional duty to ensure that values of respect, tolerance and acceptance are nurtured. This places such professionals in a unique position when it comes to tackling issues that are difficult or complex. Teachers are already engaged in the process of helping children to develop a range of life skills. Many of these are transferable to the consideration of RSE. Being able to communicate effectively, considering the views of others in a thoughtful manner, listening, negotiating and asking for advice and assistance are all skills transferable to the subject. Having the assertive skills to say 'no' and to identify and resist pressures from others are common to many situations, including bullying, stealing, engaging in dares, cheating in a test, telling lies or trying out alcohol, tobacco or other drugs. These skills provide a foundation on which to build in RSE.

AVERT (2010) outlines that

school-based sex education can be an important and effective way of enhancing young people's knowledge, attitudes and behaviour. There is widespread agreement that formal education should include sex education and what works has been well-researched. Evidence suggests that effective school programmes will include the following elements:

- A focus on reducing specific risky behaviours.
- A basis in theories which explain what influences people's sexual choices and behaviour.
- A clear, and continuously reinforced message about sexual behaviour and risk reduction.
- Providing accurate information about the risks associated with sexual activity, about contraception and birth control, and about methods of avoiding or deferring intercourse.
- Dealing with peer and other social pressures on young people; providing opportunities to practise communication, negotiation and assertion skills.
- Using a variety of approaches to teaching and learning that involve and engage young people and help them to personalize the information.
- Using approaches to teaching and learning which are appropriate to young people's age, experience and cultural background.
- Involving people who believe in what they are saying and have access to support in the form of training or consultation with other sex educators.

Formal programmes with all these elements have been shown to increase young people's levels of knowledge about sex and sexuality, put back the average age at which they first have sexual intercourse and decrease risk when they do have sex.

Consider:

- which of these elements are most appropriate for children in the primary phase of education;
- how strategies already in use in the primary school can be adapted and applied to the exploration of relationships and sex issues;
- how such strategies apply to a wider range of settings; and
- how a skills-based approach (focusing on communication, making positive choices and being able to form one's own opinions) might help children more than an information-only-based approach.

Drawing on skills and strategies already known to practitioners is one way of helping to develop their confidence to support children in making positive choices, staying healthy and avoiding risky behaviours. Common approaches such as circle time, role playing, visualization, debates and discussions, using picture books and other literature to provide *one-step-removed* stimuli, and the use of visitors are well known to most teachers and provide a firm foundation based in existing practice. Some of these strategies were introduced at the start of this book. In addition, the ground rules associated with some of these strategies (e.g. that what is said in the circle remains in the circle, that participants do not ask or have to answer personal questions and that they take turns to speak and listen) apply well to any consideration of issues pertaining to relationships and sex. This area is addressed further in Chapters 7 and 9.

From the early years, such strategies can help teachers to introduce materials in age-appropriate ways. From initial discussions about staying safe, understanding that one needs to protect oneself and others from germs, appreciating that parts of the body have formal names which can be used with confidence and realizing that personal privacy can be controlled by oneself, it is possible to develop more detailed discussions about how people relate to others; love, romance and commitment; how to tackle bullying and peer pressure; and what will happen to the body as one grows and matures.

Summary of key approaches to support effective practice

In order to develop effective practice it is important to consider the following:

- Children need to know that they can speak with a trusted adult. Explain that this may be their parent/carer, teacher or other childcare professional.
- When faced with innuendo or materials of a sexual nature, questions need to be asked carefully to establish the child's levels of understanding (unless a case

of abuse is suspected, in which case advice must be sought and the professional must not question the child in case they could influence evidence needed later in court).

- Childcare professionals may see children interacting with their peers in a way not encountered by parents/carers. This means that they may be more aware of peer pressure and other social interactions.
- Do the resources and language that teachers use assume that all learners and their families are heterosexual? How can they ensure that their practices are wider and more inclusive?
- It is important to be brave so that issues can be discussed in the classroom, and not left to be explored unsupported on the playground.
- It is essential to stress to children that it is never too late to tell an appropriate and trusted adult if something is worrying them.

Conclusion and summary of key learning points

Teachers and childcare practitioners may not see it as their role to address the sometimes difficult questions that children raise. This may be because they do not feel that the classroom is a place for some issues about relationships, sex and sexuality to be aired; it may also be that they are very aware of the need to bear in mind the wishes of parents/carers. However, whatever their view, they are in a position to help children to understand the strategies they can use when faced with materials that make them feel uncomfortable, which they know to be inappropriate for them to access, or when they have questions or concerns that cause them discomfort. Knowing that they can speak with a caring and responsible adult is of vital importance, but this must be coupled with an understanding that this adult may not always be able to give an immediate or straightforward response (as is exemplified in Chapter 7).

Teachers also have a responsibility to consider how the practices, policies and ethos of their classroom and school maintain or challenge traditional gendered behaviour expectations. They have the opportunity to create safe spaces in which every child matters and where every child is valued. They can celebrate difference and appreciate similarity. Then, when traditional stereotypes are the source of bullying they can explore the need to respect one another and to value the diversity found among the members of their school community. While this is a positive response, it is reactive. Even more positive is the possibility of proactively promoting the values of acceptance and the celebration of diversity so that these become embedded in the school ethos and are the touchstone by which relationships and relatedness are evaluated.

Diversity is not something that should be a surprise; society and the local community are not homogenous, with occasional occurrences of difference. Rather, they should be understood as heterogeneous: difference is not 'other' but is the norm. This provides an important wider context in which to situate the more specific considerations of RSE in the chapters which follow.

Signposts

The *Child Exploitation and Online Protection Command* (CEOP) is the government body dedicated to eradicating abuse of children. Concerns about inappropriate contacts between a child and an adult, including online, can be reported directly to CEOP. www.ceop.police.uk.

The *Internet Watch Foundation* (IWF) works to remove illegal material from the internet. If you have found any material you believe to be illegal, for example, child sex abuse images, other obscene material, or material which incites racial hatred, you can report it to the IWF. www.iwf.org.uk.

Mermaids: a website to support gender-variant children and their families. www.mermaidsuk.org.uk.

Think U Know: the main UK government website with advice for parents on how to keep children safe online. www.thinkuknow.co.uk.

A number of specialist websites contain general advice that may be of help to parents and teachers. These include www.nspcc.org.uk, www.barnardos.org.uk, www.bullying.co.uk and www.childline.co.uk. Other sites can offer parental support on broader issues. These include www.familylives.org.uk.

Family Diversities Reading Resource: over 100 high-quality picture books which include a wide variety of models of family life; freely available to all education and not-for-profit organizations. http://libguides.bishopg.ac.uk/childrensliterature and at: http://libguides.bishopg.ac.uk/ld.php?content_id=31126500.

Transitions Reading Resource: over 100 high-quality children's picture books exploring times of change in children's lives (including relationships, family issues, death and bereavement). http://libguides.bishopg.ac.uk/ld.php?content_id=24544451.

Further reading

Claire, H. (2001) *Not Aliens: Primary School Children and the Citizenship/PSHE Curriculum*. Stoke on Trent: Trentham Books.

Francis, B. (2000) *Boys, Girls and Achievement: Addressing the Classroom Issues*. London: RoutledgeFalmer.

King-Hill, S., and Woolley, R. (2018) 'Sexual Behaviours and Development', in *Understanding Inclusion: Core Concepts, Policy and Practice*, ed. R. Woolley. London: Routledge.

Skelton, C., and Francis, B. (eds) (2003) *Boys and Girls in the Primary Classroom*. Maidenhead: Open University Press.

References

AVERT (2010) *Effective School-Based Sex Education*. www.avert.org/sex—education. htm.

Baird, V. (2004) *Sex, Love and Homophobia: Lesbian, Gay, Bisexual and Transgender Lives*. London: Amnesty International.

Bunting, M. (2000) 'Masculinity in Question'. *Guardian*. www.guardian.co.uk/comment/story/0,376019,00.html (accessed 5 August 2018).

Claire, H. (2001) *Not Aliens: Primary School Children and the Citizenship/PSHE Curriculum*. Stoke on Trent: Trentham.

Connell, R. W. (1990) 'An Iron Man: The Body and Some Contradictions of Hegemonic Masculinity', in *Sport, Men and the Gender Order: Critical Feminist Perspectives*, ed. M. Messner and D. Babo. Champaign, IL: Human Kinetics Books.

DfE (2014) *National Curriculum in England: Framework for Key Stages 1–4*. London: Department for Education. www.gov.uk/government/publications/national-curriculum-in-england-framework-for-key-stages-1-to-4/ (accessed 31 March 2018).

DfE (2018) *Relationships Education, Relationships and Sex Education (RSE) and Health Education: guidance for governing bodies, proprietors, head teachers, principals, senior leadership teams, tenders*. London: Department for Education.

Foster, V., Kimmel, M., and Skelton, C. (2001) 'What about the Boys? An Overview of the Debates', in *What about the Boys? Issues of Masculinity in Schools*, ed. W. Martino and B. Meyenn. Buckingham: Open University Press.

Francis, B. (2000) *Boys, Girls and Achievement: Addressing the Classroom Issues*. London: RoutledgeFalmer.

Girlguiding UK (2008) 'Teenage Mental Health: Girls Shout Out!' www.mentalhealth. org.uk/publications/?EntryId5=62067.

Hellen, M. (2009) 'Transgender Children in Schools'. *Liminalis: Journal for Sex/Gender Emancipation and Resistance*, 81–99. http://eprints.gold.ac.uk/3531/ (accessed 5 August 2018).

Home Office (2000) *Setting the Boundaries: Reforming the Law on Sex Offences: Volume 1*. Home Office Communications Directorate.

Layton, N. (2007) *Oscar and Arabella and Ormsby*. London: Hodder Children's Books.

Marsh, J. (2005) 'Digikinds: Young People, Popular Culture and Media', in *Critical Issues in Early Childhood Education*, ed. N. Yelland. Maidenhead: Open University Press.

Meyenn, B., and Parker, J. (2001) 'Naughty Boys at School: Perspectives on Boys and Discipline', in *What about the Boys? Issues of Masculinity in Schools*, ed. W. Martino and B. Meyenn. Buckingham: Open University Press.

Mills, M. (2001a) *Challenging Violence in Schools: An Issue of Masculinities*. Buckingham: Open University Press.

Mills, M. (2001b) 'Pushing It to the Max: Interrogating the Risky Business of Being a Boy', in *What about the Boys: Issues of Masculinity on Schools*, ed. W. Martino and B. Meyenn. Buckingham: Open University Press.

Morrell, R. (2005) *Masculinity*. Durban: University of KwaZulu Natal.

Morris, J., and Woolley, R. (2017) *Family Diversities Reading Resource* (2nd edn). Lincoln: Bishop Grosseteste University and University of Worcester.

NICE (n.d.) *Personal, Social, Health and Economic Education Focusing on Sex and Relationships and Alcohol Education Consultation Draft*. National Institute for Health and Clinical Excellence.

ONS (2010) *Divorces in England and Wales 2008*. London: Office for National Statistics.

Papalia, D., Gross, D., and Feldman, R. (2003) *Child Development: A Topical Approach*. New York: McGraw-Hill.

Schreiber-Wicke, E. (2000) *Ed Loves Sarah Loves Tim*. London: Cat's Whiskers.

Skelton, C. (2002) 'The "Feminisation of Schooling" or "Re-masculinising" Primary Education?' *International Studies in Sociology of Education*, 12 (1), 77–96.

Skelton, C., and Francis, B. (eds) (2003) *Boys and Girls in the Primary Classroom*. Maidenhead: Open University Press.

Smith, P., Cowie, H., and Blades, M. (2003) *Understanding Children's Development* (revised edn). Malden, MA: Blackwell.

Stonewall (2017) *School Report: The Experience of Lesbian, Gay, Bi and Trans Young People in Britain's Schools in 2017*. London: Stonewall.

Swain, J. (2006) 'Reflections on Patterns of Masculinity in School Settings'. *Men and Masculinities*, 8 (3), 331.

Wishinsky, F. (2004) *Jennifer Jones Won't Leave Me Alone*. London: Picture Corgi.

Woolley, R. (2010) *Tackling Controversial Issues in the Primary School: Facing Life's Challenges with Your Learners*. London: Routledge.

Woolley, R., and Mason, S. (2009) 'Sex and Relationships Education', in *Education Studies: An Issues-Based Approach* (revised edn), ed. J. Sharp, S. Ward and L. Hankin. Exeter: Learning Matters.

3

The question of relationships

Stephen is a child in Year 5. He has been isolated in his year group with no apparent friends, probably as a result of his behavioural difficulties and frequent angry outbursts. His teacher has been concerned for some time that his lack of friendships might be both the cause and the result of his temperament. After consulting local authority support services, she decided to provide Stephen with a reward system. She explained to him that if he met his small-step structured behaviour targets in five lessons during the week he would be able to choose three other children to invite to share tea and cakes during 'Golden Time' on Friday afternoon. She hoped that this would not only provide him with an incentive to work toward the targets, but also create a social opportunity to help to integrate him more fully within his class. The invitation might also help to make him more popular with peers.

Chapter outline

Introduction

Relationships form the bedrock of both human society and personal identity. Who we are is defined to a great extent by the ways in which we relate to those around us; our self-identify, self-esteem and self-image are all shaped by our relationship with the world around us. Developing a positive sense of self is fundamental to respecting oneself and exercising positive self-care. This chapter explores ways of supporting children in developing such emotional literacy so that they mature into confident individuals. It considers the importance of friendships, ways of learning to resolve conflict, coming to appreciate diversity and difference, appreciating gendered identities and challenging stereotypes, and strategies to cope with inappropriate behaviour from others. Key to this is the need to support children where stereotyping or bullying occurs, for whatever reason. Childcare professionals need to support children so that, if faced with inappropriate situations, they are able to keep safe. This includes emotional and physical bullying by other children as well as less frequent examples of abuse by others, including adults. From the early years, children need to understand that their bodies are special and that different levels of intimacy and physical contact are appropriate in different situations. This needs to be addressed in sensitive ways which do not scare children and which present information in ways appropriate to the age and maturity of the child. Being able to make positive choices and having the confidence to say 'no' in situations when they feel pressured are important life skills our children should develop.

A great deal of what takes place in settings and schools can be termed Relationships Education. Both settings and schools play a significant role in the socialization of children: in helping them to understand how to relate to others, what behaviours are appropriate, and to understand the concepts of respect, patience and valuing difference. In the early years of education this is addressed in England through a focus on personal, social and emotional development. Relationships Education includes the breadth of 'friendships, family relationships and relationships with other peers and adults' (DfE, 2018: 14). It is for this reason, among others, that we chose to put relationships first in the title of this book and are very pleased that the new curriculum in England has now done the same (from 2019). It is essential that children learn to form positive and constructive relationships with others, understand that behaviour (and particularly intimacy) differs according to circumstances, and appreciate that they deserve to be shown respect and should value and respect themselves.

Relationships and citizenship

Relationships work on a wide range of levels, and as children grow and mature their sphere of relatedness to others widens. From the early years when their focus is primarily on close friends and family members it increases to include people with whom they have increasingly tenuous and tentative connections. In addition,

> as they grow up young people extend their relationships beyond their immediate family and friends and begin to explore their own sexual identity. This is a normal part of human development. (NICE, n.d.: 27)

As children grow they have increasing independence and autonomy. This needs to be set within a context in which they understand that they still need degrees of accountability to their primary carers. Parents and carers need to know where their children are going in order to make sure that they remain safe and secure. Older children need to appreciate that they have an increasing responsibility for their own safety and well-being and to know what actions to take if they feel uncomfortable, threatened or unsafe in any situation. As the onset of puberty approaches, they also need to understand that while they may begin to feel both physically and emotionally attracted to others, this cannot legally find the most intimate expression through sexual intercourse until they are over the age of consent (sixteen years in England).

Consider the word *relationships*. What does this term mean to you? Note down as many connotations and associations as you can think of immediately.

Reflect on your responses. How many are positive, negative or neutral? How many are factual and how many emotional?

Consider how your response to the word might affect the ways in which you speak with children about relationships in your classroom/setting.

Self-identity and self-esteem

A wide variety of aspects of the self contribute to how people think about themselves: personality, appearance, ability, gender and social or cultural groupings. These may be termed *self-concept* or *identity*. Some aspects of who we are come from comparisons with others; we continually evaluate the things that we feel ourselves to be good or successful in against both our own expectations and the achievements (or perceived achievements) of others (Smith et al., 2003; Dowling, 2005). Psychologists term these evaluations self-esteem.

Aspects which promote the emotional well-being of children include stable childcare arrangements. Education settings and schools share important characteristics that promote such emotional well-being (DfEE, 2000). These include enabling children to work with just a few primary caregivers in any one day, effective use of behaviour management techniques, low staff turnover that enables effective long-term relationships to be established with children and parents/carers, the levels of staff training, and child–staff ratios. All this is augmented and supported by the provision of an effective curriculum that aims to do more than instil knowledge and is concerned with the development of the whole child (Woolley, 2010a). Indeed, early childhood education and schooling may be viewed as effective strategies that affect many risk and protective factors relating to a child's mental health and well-being (Weissberg et al., 1991). Significantly,

> in the early primary school years, education about relationships needs to focus on friendship, bullying and the building of self-esteem. (DfEE, 2000: 9)

Interestingly, the term self-esteem did not feature in the draft guidance for Relationships Education in primary schools (DfE, 2018), and only featured in guidance for secondary education in terms of building confidence to delay sexual activity (p. 19). Schools may wish to enhance this focus within their own policies.

Education professionals have an important role to play in nurturing children's confidence, self-esteem, well-being and mental health. These aspects work together to help children grow into confident and self-assured young people and adults. Children who grow up in loving, caring environments find it easier to learn to care than those brought up in unemotional, aggressive or manipulative settings. The ways in which they treat other people are modelled on the behaviours of those around them. A loving carer or professional may go some way towards compensating for negative parenting (Einon, 2001). Most preschool children are kind, helpful, affectionate and thoughtful, but rivalry and lack of consideration can increase once they enter the more competitive world of the learning setting (Woolley, 2010b). Thus the care that we show and that we encourage between children provides positive role modelling to assist children in developing effective relationships with others.

Using the vignette at the start of this chapter, consider:

- what impact this strategy might have on Stephen;
- how might it affect his relationships with others in the class; and
- whether there will be drawbacks to this approach? Do you feel that these are outweighed by any possible benefits?

Practitioners also have a particular role to play in helping parents and carers to recognize when their child(ren) may be experiencing difficulties outside the norm (DfEE, 2000:15), as in the case of Stephen, outlined at the start of this chapter. It may be that they can help them to access additional support for their children from a variety of agencies and services, can provide advice themselves, or can be supportive and empathetic so that parents and carers do not have to face difficulties in isolation.

How childcare professionals welcome parents and carers in their settings can have a significant impact on the ways in which a child feels that the different spheres of their life are interlinked and mutually supportive. Providing an opportunity for parents/carers to enter the setting at the start of a session to share a book, toy or game with their child not only makes for a smooth daily transition from home to school and helps to settle the child, but also shows that they are welcome in the setting. Similarly, involving parents and carers in the routines associated with leaving school at the end of a session supports transition while also providing an opportunity for them to discover what their child has been learning and doing. This can provide an opportunity for a child to share information and to receive praise and encouragement; it can be done on a daily basis or perhaps in a special way once a week. Such activities also provide an opportunity for parents/carers to show their interest in their child's learning and to reinforce how important and valuable it is. Practitioners need to support parents/carers in these processes and not to assume that they will know how to use the opportunity to develop talk with their children. Stressing their importance, perhaps during the induction process in the setting or classroom, can help parents and carers to understand the need to build such activities into their routines, whenever possible. While teachers appreciate the busyness of life faced by parents and carers, if they can encourage a routine that includes parents spending some time in the setting, even on a periodic basis, parents will have the opportunity to foster positive links across different aspects of the child's life.

This is important in modelling positive relationships with children and in helping them to understand that their teachers appreciate their home backgrounds. In addition,

> the views of parents about what constitutes education that is relevant to their children's age and maturity will differ. Parents may want schools to introduce sensitive topics earlier than some teachers might assume. Children are likely to want information earlier than their parents might consider appropriate. (NICE, n.d.: 30)

Thus it is important to consult with parents/carers to gauge their views on how RSE should be approached with their children and at what age. This consultation may also include explaining to parents/carers that their children are starting to ask questions about relationships, puberty and sex, or that playground conversations between children include such matters, so that they become aware of the need for the school (or parents themselves) to address the issues with their children. One criticism of RSE has been that it undermines the role of the family in bringing up children. In reality, the extent of the discussion between parents/carers and children about matters of sex and relationships is often minimal (Stone and Ingham, 2006: 202).

What is important is that there is effective home–school communication, founded in positive relationships, that enables all parties to understand what the others are doing and minimizes the possibility of misunderstanding or confusion. This area is emphasized in new guidance for Relationships Education in England (DfE, 2018). This is particularly important for those groups of children and young people who face significant inequalities, which can impact upon sexual and emotional health (Blake and Muttock, 2004: 4). These may include

- those looked after by a local authority;
- some from lower socioeconomic groups;
- young gay men; and
- some minority ethnic groups (including asylum seeking and refugee communities).

There are many issues outside learning settings which impact on a child's self-esteem, sense of self-worth and ability to form positive relationships. They may also affect their physical or mental health and development. Examples include the following:

- housing;
- diet;
- unemployment;
- availability of learning resources in the home and the community;
- parental and carer confidence and self-esteem;
- the availability of safe outdoor and green spaces for play; and
- health needs.

Many of these relate to Maslow's hierarchy of needs (1968) and have a significant impact on readiness and capacity to learn. Each can have an impact on the ability to form positive relationships with others and some can be a source of bullying. While several will be beyond the control of a practitioner, they need to ensure that their settings provide safe, warm, supportive and stimulating environments that can compensate for any deficit outside the setting and nurture children's self-esteem as much as possible. It is also important that they do not make judgements based on these needs that cause them to underestimate the capabilities of the children, otherwise they will become a part of any problem rather than part of the solution (Woolley, 2010a).

In addition, particular learning needs may affect the ways in which children are able to develop relationships or understand the changes that their emotions and bodies undergo as they reach puberty. The guidance of 2000 noted,

> Some parents and carers of children with special educational needs may find it difficult to accept their children's developing sexuality. Some children will be more vulnerable to abuse and exploitation than their peers, and others may be confused about what is acceptable public behaviour. These children will need help to develop skills to reduce

the risks of being abused and exploited, and to learn what sorts of behaviour are, and are not, acceptable. (DfEE, 2000: 12)

Supporting such children in the development of skills and giving careful and clear explanations about the changes that we experience as we grow and mature are important aspects of helping some children with special educational needs to develop into confident young people. This area is emphasized within new guidance for RSE:

> Relationships Education, RSE and Health Education must be accessible for all pupils. This is particularly important when planning teaching for pupils with special educational needs and disabilities as they represent a large minority of pupils. High quality teaching that is differentiated and personalised will be the starting point to ensure accessibility. (DfE, 2018: 11)

In its response to the national consultation on developments in RSE, the National Association of Special Educational Needs (NASEN) identified potential changes to the teaching of RSE with a particular focus on children with special educational needs. It suggested that secondary school is too late to begin teaching about puberty, noting that 'this time can be a particular difficult time for some young people with SEND' (NASEN, 2018: 1). It highlights that:

- RSE should not be a one-off event
- Topics need revisiting to develop understanding
- Euphemisms need avoiding, in order to avoid misunderstanding
- An individualized approach will be needed by some young people with SEND. (p. 1)

Significantly, NASEN noted that young people with limited mobility or independence may rely more strongly than others on social media in order to develop friendships, potentially making them at greater risk of child sexual exploitation. Learning how to protect oneself online is particularly important for such individuals. Importantly, it should not be assumed that because an individual has a particular learning need or disability that they are not a sexual being. When asked to name the three most important subject areas that should be taught in RSE, NASEN focused on one: 'Celebrating difference of all kinds, including dis/ability in order to help develop tolerance and openness' (NASEN, 2018: 2). This area is considered further in Chapter 5.

Further, some children will have experienced relationships that are far from positive. For example, a child may be in public care following incidents in their home where they have been harmed physically and/or emotionally. Others may live in a refuge with their parent because they needed to escape from a violent situation. Some will have experienced the acrimonious divorce of their parents and may now face complex relationships where they relate very separately to each parent. In such circumstances, practitioners need to take great care when approaching issues in a programme of Relationships Education in order to ensure that the child is enabled to learn in a safe and supported environment. It will be necessary to acknowledge that not all relationships are positive and that sometimes it is necessary for adults to leave a situation in order to remain safe and healthy. Sometimes children have to be taken away from such a situation in order to provide respite or a more positive family environment. Here, communication with the child's primary carer is essential in order to make sure that the child is supported in their learning, and to consider which elements of a programme for RSE are appropriate for the child in their current situation and emotional state.

At a different level, it is appropriate to acknowledge to children that, like many other relationships, 'special relationships' do not always go smoothly; that much effort is needed by both partners in order to make any relationship work; and to recognize that some relationships will end because difficulties, disagreements or conflicts cannot be resolved. While it is not the intention to scare children or to make them concerned about the fragility of their current family setting, suggesting that relationships are ever ideal or perfect would be to paint an inappropriate picture of family life, and give children unrealistic expectations of how relationships work.

Daniel is twelve years of age but studies in a Year 5 class. His parents asked that he remain at primary school for an additional year as he was very settled and making progress. A plan is in place for him to move to a special school in the next academic year as he has significant learning needs. Daniel's teacher commented,

Things have been going really well. We all felt (Daniel, his parents and staff at the school) that this was the best place for him for an additional year. He has been making steady progress and we all felt that he benefitted from the range of friendships that he had established over a number of years in this school. Recently, Daniel has begun to show sexual behaviours and on three occasions now he has shown his genitals to a girl on the playground. They have been friends for a number of years, but it appears that having reached puberty Daniel does not understand that he cannot express sexual interest.

I spoke with Daniel's mum and she explained that he has been masturbating in indiscrete ways at home. While she understands that this action is perfectly normal for a boy of his age, Daniel does not appreciate that it is something he ought to do in private. Mum has been embarrassed on several occasions and she is concerned about Daniel's lack of modesty. She seemed relieved to be able to speak about this, having been too embarrassed to raise the subject herself.

We agreed that I would speak to Daniel about acceptable behaviour at school and that she would speak to him about his behaviour at home and school. We both felt that we needed to be direct with Daniel, as he needs to be clear about what is socially expected and acceptable and we need to make sure that both he and others avoid embarrassing or inappropriate situations.

I have also spoken with the girl and her parent who are both very understanding about Daniel's situation. However, I have made clear to them that his behaviour is not acceptable and that if they have any concern whatsoever they must speak with me or any other member of staff in the school. I have also contacted the school nurse and am liaising with the special school to seek advice and work on transition arrangements.

Consider this experience:

- How appropriate do you consider the teacher's response?
- On what other sources of advice and support might the teacher or parents draw?
- How would you speak with Daniel to ensure that he (i) appreciates appropriate public behaviour and (ii) understands that this differs from behaviour in private?

Similar issues are discussed further in Chapter 6.

Developing a sense of self

Respect is an attribute that affects a number of dimensions of life and effective Relationships Education. First, there is respect for oneself: understanding that each person is special, unique and precious and that they deserve to be looked after and need to look after themselves. Second, there is respect for others, appreciating that one should treat them as one would wish to be treated. Third, there is respect for the environment: taking care of resources; understanding that some items belong to other people and may not be for one's use or consumption; and ensuring that those in a group get an equitable share by being listened to and allowed to speak, taking a turn on play equipment or each receiving fruit during snack time. Fairness is a useful concept to use when helping children to develop respect, by asking a child whether they felt their actions or words were fair to another child. Using questions can help children to think through the consequence of their words and actions and to begin to internalize an understanding of how to behave towards others in a range of situations (Woolley, 2010b).

Encouraging children to think independently is an important part of supporting their development. Activities such as circle time, role play and using stories and persona dolls to present situations for discussion and questioning each allow opportunities for children to direct and evaluate their own learning (as elaborated in the Introduction to this book). The use of open-ended questions which challenge children to think though their own values, beliefs and judgements and provide a chance for decision making are most likely to engage children with issues about self-respect and respect for others. This leads to more satisfying learning and helps children to internalize ideas which are the more likely to affect their behaviour and self-view than didactic approaches to teaching. There needs to be a distinction between *authoritarian teachers*, who dominate and stifle learning, and *authoritative teaching*, which helps to develop learning environments that support confidence and independence. This helps to develop and manage effective relationships.

Behaviours such as empathy and altruism (helping others without the expectation of reward) are termed prosocial behaviours (Puckett and Black, 2001; Bee and Boyd, 2003). Prosocial behaviours are particularly encouraged where children see such behaviour modelled by others and where they have experienced nurturing themselves. In general their frequency increases throughout the preschool years (Eisenberg and Fabes, 1998), although some behaviours, for example, comforting another child, appear to be more common in preschool and the early years of schooling (Eisenberg, 1988). These behaviours need to be nurtured throughout the primary years of education so that children understand the importance of respect, care, kindness and valuing one another. If this foundation of self-respect and respect for others can be established in children at this age it provides an excellent foundation on which to build other positive relationships in later years.

Key to showing respect is the appreciation of difference. Differences in any setting will be varied. Children will have different patterns of family life including having one or two parents or carers, an extended family, a parent who lives away from them (due to divorce, the requirements of work, military service or imprisonment), some may have same-sex parents, adoptive or foster parents, or be looked after by a different family member. Many differences between children will stem from the relationships that they have experienced or face daily. Children will also live in diverse locations, in houses or flats, in trailers or on boats. They will come from a range of socio-economic backgrounds, have parents/carers or different ages, some will live in families where a member has a disability and others will be from different nationalities or ethnic backgrounds (Charlesworth, 2000; Woolley and Morris, 2009; Morris and Woolley, 2017). At times teachers will be aware of some of these differences, but not always. It is therefore important to seek to make learning settings inclusive to reflect the diversity of the children in one's care (both known and unknown diversity) and to reflect the diversity of the wider community and society in general. At first, this may appear to be a gargantuan task, but with thought and care it is possible to develop approaches to inclusion and diversity in increasing measure (Woolley, 2010b). This is important so that children are enabled to thrive in school settings, developing positive, healthy and respectful relationships.

Valuing difference can be one way of addressing the intolerance or bullying which arises from stereotyping. Stereotypes are a kind of shorthand that judges individuals according to labels that may derive from their gender, ethnicity or some other characteristic. They make a generalization about a person without taking into account the individual character, abilities or other attributes of that person. Common gender stereotypes are that boys show instrumental traits (e.g. competitiveness and assertiveness) and girls show more expressive traits (e.g. care, sensitivity and being considerate) (Williams and Best, 1990). Other stereotypes may include the notion that parents and carers from some backgrounds are more supportive of their children, that some children have shorter attention spans or cause more disruption, that children with poor behaviour have lower ability or that certain traits infer a person's sexual orientation. It is the role of the education professional to develop a setting in which children's interests and personalities are not limited by stereotyping.

Stereotypes can pressurize children who find that they are being inappropriately labelled by others; they can also cause confusion when children identify with a label but do not feel that they conform to the stereotype. Stereotyping is destructive of relationships as it generalizes who a person is, based on a quick and limited judgement, rather than acknowledging them as unique and special. Relationships Education needs to get beyond such limitations so that children appreciate one another as multifaceted individuals with a variety of strengths, similarities and differences:

> Sex and relationship education should contribute to promoting the spiritual, moral, cultural, mental and physical development of pupils at school and of society and preparing pupils for the opportunities, responsibilities and experiences of adult life. (DfEE, 2000: 4)

In addition, the curriculum should enable children

> to embrace the challenges of creating a happy and successful adult life, pupils need knowledge that will enable them to make informed decisions about their wellbeing, health and relationships and to build their self-efficacy. Pupils can also put this knowledge into practice as they develop the capacity to make sound decisions when facing risks, challenges and complex contexts. Everyone faces difficult situations in their lives. These subjects can support young people to develop resilience, to know how and when to ask for help, and to know where to access support. (DfE, 2018: 6)

Friendship

Government guidance for the delivery of Relationships Education (DfE, 2018) indicates that by the end of Key Stage 2 children should have, at least, an appreciation of families and those who care for them; an understanding of caring friendships and respectful relationships; and an awareness of online relationships and how to remain safe. In addition, maintained schools are required to teach the National Curriculum for science which includes teaching about the main external body parts, and changes as the human body grows including through puberty (DfE, 2014). There is no right for parents/carers to withdraw their child from teaching prescribed within the National Curriculum. This baseline for curriculum coverage has significant implications for the ways in which relationships develop, particularly for those children for whom the onset of puberty begins during their time in primary school. For some, particularly girls, this may be as early as eight years of age (and sometimes sooner), while the science curriculum introduces puberty at ages 9–11.

Children need to understand that puberty is a time when emotions can become intense or unpredictable. Feelings towards friends can become heightened, either through attraction or through mood swings, feeling pressured or becoming withdrawn or easily embarrassed. Understanding that this is the case does not take away the intensity of such situations, but might help the child and their peers to understand the reasons for changes in temperament.

It is essential that children understand that whatever feelings they may have for friends, or others, it is illegal to participate in acts of sexual intercourse before the age of sixteen years. Thus, while friendships may sometimes be romantic, there should be limits to physical expression. Teachers can emphasize that this is one way of showing respect to oneself as well as to others in addition to keeping safe and healthy and, for heterosexual couples, avoiding pregnancy.

Annie and Alison have been friends since before they started playgroup. Now in Year 4, they spend more of their time together both in class and on the playground. Having started school together, they have maintained their friendship and have not found the need to widen their circle of friends. Their class teacher, Neal, comments,

I began to notice that both Annie and Alison were becoming quieter than usual. They had been sociable and generally amiable girls, but over a series of weeks they increasingly withdrew into their friendship and began to seem subdued. I asked their parents to speak with the girls at home to see if there was any underlying problem. Alison told her mother that some older children were calling them names and suggesting that they were 'girlfriends'. It turned out that subtle bullying was taking place, of which I had not been aware.

Consider Neal's experience:

- How might he provide support for the two girls in his class?
- What action needs to be taken elsewhere in the school?
- How might the school address such bullying through its teaching about relationships?

Children need to appreciate that they will enjoy different levels of familiarity and friendship with other children. Not all children will want to be their friend, and similarly they will not wish to be friends with all children. Typically they will find common interests with some peers that lead to a degree of friendship or association. While some will have a circle of friends others may have one particular close friend. Some children will enjoy friendships with those of different genders and others will not. Whatever their situation, it is important to help children to appreciate that they are all different and that this makes each person unique and special: this can provide a strong basis from which to challenge bullying.

Bullying and conflict resolution

At times children do not enjoy positive relationships with one another and instances of bullying occur. Bullying can come in a range of forms and be for a variety of reasons: emotional, physical, verbal, cyber, homophobic, sexual, sexist or racist. It is never justified or justifiable and cannot be tolerated in schools. It has been estimated that one in four primary school children will experience bullying at some point (DCSF, 2007), although national data is not collected (for a detailed exploration of definitions of bullying, see Woolley, 2018).

Bullying can be physical, or emotional, or both; it harms all those involved. Types of bullying can include name calling, mocking, ignoring, taking belongings, gossiping, excluding people from groups, spreading rumours, hitting, pushing, kicking, harassing over email or text messages. Indications of bullying may include a deterioration of performance in lessons and schoolwork, loss of money or belongings, a change in behaviour (such as becoming quiet and withdrawn, demanding or resentful), unexplained damage to clothing, bruises or other injuries. In addition parents/carers may notice that children begin to claim they are unwell or find other reasons to avoid going to school, try to avoid going out from their home or avoid contact with previously good friends.

Every school in England has an anti-bullying policy and each teacher needs to be aware of its scope and content. There must be a zero tolerance policy towards bullying of whatever type. Bullying destroys self-confidence and self-esteem; it damages people's ability to relate to others in positive ways and undermines their sense of safety. It can affect people's reputations and the ways in which they are perceived by others, affecting relationships and the ability to relate (Woolley, 2018). The curriculum guidance for Relationships Education includes teaching about the role of being a bystander, and of having a responsibility to speak up when witnessing bullying (DfE, 2018). This is a positive addition to curriculum guidance. A range of resources and sources of support for teachers and children is included at the end of this chapter.

Saying no and respecting one's body

The previous chapter explored briefly the importance of internet safety. Here it is important to consider safety in non-virtual relationships.

From the early years, children need to understand that their bodies are special and unique. They need to know that while it can be fine to be naked with a brother or sister of a similar age in the bath, or when being cared for by their parents/carers, this is not usually the case with other adults or in public places. They also need to understand that physical contact with others is special and that it should only take place with people that are known and trusted. On one level they may kiss or hug an uncle or their grandmother; they may hold hands with a friend. However it is essential to know that this is not behaviour that is shown to strangers. They also need to understand that their body, and the genitals in particular, are private and special to them. The NSPCC (2008: 12) recommends that parents and carers

> help your child understand about sex, about [their] body and about what is sexually healthy. Talking about this may be a little difficult at first, but it can play an important part in protecting your child against abuse and developing your relationship with your child. For example, your child needs to understand about private parts of their body in order to understand what is appropriate touching and what is not. Be as positive as possible – children should feel proud of their bodies and not ashamed. They also need to know that their bodies belong to them alone. These conversations are a normal part of parenting.

The NSPCC also suggests speaking with a teacher or other childcare professional to seek advice on how to address such issues with children. Its PANTS Underwear Rule (NSPCC, 2018) may provide a good starting point (and is outlined in detail in Chapter 6). Identifying abusive relationships is not easy and abusers can go to great lengths to gain the trust of a child and their family. Indeed, it is more likely that the abuser is a close family friend or member of the family than a stranger. It is important that children know that there are different types of secret, and that if a secret makes them feel uncomfortable or scared it is one that should be shared with a trusted adult with whom they feel comfortable and safe. Parents and carers can look out for adults or older children who take a specific interest in their child, offer to take them on trips or holidays, seek opportunities to be alone with the child or who become too generous and overfriendly. It is important that parents and carers understand that if a child shares with them that they are being abused they need to take this seriously, to react in a way that shows that they value having been told and to speak with their doctor, other medical practitioner, the local children's services or to contact one of the national help lines as soon as possible for advice. A teacher or student teacher who receives such a disclosure from a child has no choice but to tell the named person for child protection at the school. There is no need to have a sleepless night agonizing over whether to share the information: it must be passed on.

Helping children to understand situation-appropriateness is an important part of helping them to stay safe and to appreciate some of the norms of society. While one may be naked with others of the same gender when getting changed for a swimming lesson, such behaviour would not be appropriate with the same people in the playground or when playing in the park. Most children will understand this social norm, but some may need an explanation so that they understand that their bodies are special and usually private. Teachers need to be particularly aware of the need for privacy in Key Stage 2, especially when children are getting changed for physical education lessons. Staff members in schools and other settings need to consider at what point it becomes appropriate for children of different genders to get changed separately in order to save any embarrassment, particularly as children start to reach puberty.

It is important to consider what behaviours may be common among children of primary school age in order to identify behaviour which might suggest emotional or physical abuse or an inappropriate awareness of sexual materials of a non-age-appropriate nature. The NSPCC outlines the following:

School-age children (six to 12 years) commonly:

- ask questions about menstruation, pregnancy and sexual behaviour;
- experiment with other children, often during games, kissing, touching, showing and role playing e.g. mums and dads or doctors and nurses;
- masturbate in private;
- older children in this age range are also more likely than pre-school children to use sexual words and discuss sexual acts, particularly with their friends.

They rarely:

- masturbate in public;
- show adult-like sexual behaviour or knowledge. (2008: 15, 16)

Consider your own reaction to these views:

- How do they compare with your own expectations for age-appropriate behaviour?
- What forms of play would you consider appropriate in a school setting?

For further discussion about appropriate forms of play, see Chapter 6.

A taxonomy of relationships

The traditional title for this subject in schools was Sex and Relationship Education (until 2019). As has been noted in the Introduction to this book, such a title failed to acknowledge that children are engaged in a range of relationships at different levels or that such relationships change over time. It is for this reason that we use the plural 'Relationships' in the title of this book, and from 2019 this title has been adopted for the subject in schools (DfE, 2018). Indeed, the curriculum for citizenship acknowledges the need for children to be prepared to engage in different levels of relationship, each with varying degrees of intimacy.

Children need to understand that relationships work on a range of levels, which we summarize as a taxonomy:

Strangers are people that they do not know. Many are nice, but some are unpleasant and may want to hurt children. They should never go anywhere with a stranger, accept things from them, get in their car or give them personal details. Teachers and other adults need to explain that if a stranger tries to touch a child or makes them feel uncomfortable in any way they should shout as loudly as possible ('No!' or 'Stop!'), run and get home or to another safe place (such as school, a friend's house or a police station) as quickly as possible and tell their parent/carer or another trusted adult as soon as possible.

Acquaintances are people that children know a little. They may include, for example, the person who works in the local shop. Some of the friends of children's friends will be known to them a little. These people are not known to children in any significant or deep way. While they are not strangers one would not go to their house or accept gifts from them.

People that help children may not be acquaintances, but children show them respect because they have a special role to play. Such people include police officers, members of the fire and ambulance services and the person who staffs the school crossing patrol. Children will recognize them because of their special uniform.

Some of them will come to the school to visit and to explain what their job involves. Children may see some of them quite regularly and say 'hello'. They can be useful people to recognize if a child needs to find an adult to help them in an emergency. However, they would not accept gifts from them or go with them on their own without telling parents/carers.

Our *friends* are special people who are known well. Most of them will be of a child's own age or be close to their age. Children talk to them about things that are important to them and might visit their homes or play with them after school, making sure that a parent/carer knows where they are. Children will know some friends better than others: some will be people they play with during breaks times at school; others will be friends outside school and they may visit their houses or invite them to their own. Friends can change over time. It is also important to be friendly towards other children, to be kind and polite to them and to include them in games if they look lonely.

Family members are special because children are related to them. While they do not usually choose their family, they have a special link with them. One's closest family members may include a mum and/or dad, brothers and sisters or other carer(s). Children may also have grandparents, uncles and aunts, and cousins. They might show that they care about these special people by hugging them or giving them a kiss when they meet them or say goodbye. Children can do this if they feel comfortable with them, if they care about them a great deal and if their parents/carers know about it. Rarely, family members can make a child feel uncomfortable or the child does not feel that they are being nice to them. If this happens they need to tell an adult that they trust, probably their parents/carers. Whenever an adult makes them feel uncomfortable or embarrassed they must always tell a trusted adult.

Best friends are special people that are trusted a great deal. Often children will have interests in common with their best friends and they will feel comfortable talking to them about things that matter to them. They might have one best friend at school and know them for years. Sometimes a child's best friend changes as they get older and they meet new people or find new interests. As with all friends, sometimes there will be arguments or disagreements. All relationships have difficult times, and it is inevitable that friends will 'fall out' sometimes. Children might also be jealous if their best friend has other friends. This kind of friendship is intimate because of the sharing of many personal thoughts with one another. As children get older, others – and particularly peers – may pressure them to be girlfriend/boyfriend with their best friend, or they may find that their best friend finds a boy/girlfriend and they get to spend less time with them.

As one grows older it may be that there is a *special friend* that is loved very much. Sometimes a person will hope to be with that friend for the rest of their lives and will decide to make a commitment to them, often in a ceremony where friends and family come to offer support. A marriage or civil partnership ceremony is a way of saying in public that one wants to make a commitment to this special person in one's life. Children in the final years of primary school will learn that this often provides a context for sexual intimacy, which, at its best, is enjoyed within a stable, loving and committed relationship. This also provides the setting in which some people start a family of their own.

When speaking with older children about such a partnership commitment it is important not to teach that sexual intercourse is solely for the purpose of starting a family, nor that all those in such a partnership will engage in sexual intercourse. First, children need to understand that within heterosexual relationships it may take some time and effort for conception to take place; and even if a baby is conceived, in the first weeks of pregnancy it is possible that a miscarriage may occur. Second, some heterosexual couples chose not to have children of their own and may use contraception or abstain from sexual intercourse. Third, same-sex couples may wish to start a family and may do this through adoption, donor insemination or other means. Finally, educators need to explain that sex can be fun: in a stable, trusting and loving relationship it can be the expression of the closeness of the two individuals and can be very pleasurable. This is an aspect that young people have repeatedly identified as being missing from educational provision in their schools.

In this sense, sex within a relationship may provide the opportunity for an intimate, sensual, tender and pleasurable experience for both partners. It is for this reason that teachers, and others involved in the delivery of RSE, stress relationships before sex and consider how this can be the focus of the school curriculum.

Finally, this taxonomy must importantly include the relationship with *oneself*. Self-respect and self-value are essential if any of the above relationships are to be of the best quality. Keeping oneself safe, healthy and seeing the good in oneself are all positive ways of promoting well-being, avoiding self-harm and standing up against negativity or abuse from others.

Relationships with the home

The language that is use in classrooms and other learning environments when referring to children's homes and families communicates messages to children about the value that we put on such settings. The children in our care will come from a range of circumstances, with one or two parents, carers, other family members undertaking parental responsibilities, foster carers, and situations where children have more than two people in parental roles due to separation and new partners.

Sometimes, it is possible to hear teachers saying to children 'When you get home, tell your mum and dad'. In the twenty-first century it is not appropriate to presume that children live in a household with two married parents of different genders. Some will live with a grandparent or aunt, others will spend their time between the two homes of their separated or divorced parents. Some children will be separated from a parent because of bereavement, service in the armed forces, other work commitments, a court injunction or imprisonment. In order to have respectful and caring relationships with our learners and to respect their backgrounds it is important to consider the language that is used in the school environment. It is not best practice for children to have to filter our language so that they can understand it in relation to their own primary caregiver. It can be helpful to direct correspondence to the 'Parent/ Carer of ...' and to ask colleagues to 'Give a message to Aaron's mum' rather than to assume that the parent/carer shares the child's surname. This can avoid awkwardness or embarrassment. It also shows children that the child's family background is appreciated and that a variety of ways of being family are positive and accepted:

> For some children and young people, school or college provides an environment in which they have contact with trusted adults and where they can feel safe. Both teaching and non-teaching staff might be unaware of their potential effect as role models and mentors for these children and young people. (NICE, n.d.: 31)

The ways in which teachers and other adults relate to each other as professionals, communicate with children's families and speak about relationships in their classrooms provides key messages for children about the nature of relationships and the value that is attached to them. Some teachers will speak about their home lives with children, which provides an additional model of and source of information about family life. Others choose not to do this and have a right to this privacy. Whatever approach is taken, as teachers it is important to consider what messages are presented to children about the relationships that are special and valued.

Communication with the home is also an essential part of developing an effective policy for Relationships Education. Parents and carers have the right to be consulted about the content of such programmes and also have a right to request that their child be excused any non-statutory aspects the curriculum that involve sex education (i.e. the elements outside the curriculum for science) (DfE, 2018). This area is explored further in Chapter 7.

Summary of key approaches to support effective practice

In order to develop effective practice in the promotion of positive relationships it is important to:

- understand that relationships of myriad kinds are fundamental to who one is;
- help children to appreciate that individuals relate to different people in a variety of ways;

- nurture a sense of the child's respect for themselves and for others;
- state that bullying is never acceptable and cannot be tolerated;
- consider how one's own views about relationships might affect the way in which information is communicated to children;
- promote positive self-esteem and self-confidence among learners;
- develop effective communication with parents and carers;
- challenge stereotypes and value difference; and
- explain to children that some touching is inappropriate and help them to understand what to do in situations where they are uncomfortable or scared.

Conclusion and summary of key learning points

This chapter has explored a variety of levels of relationship. Children relate to a wide variety of people across a range of intensities. Some of their friendships will be fleeting and transitory, others increasingly deep and long lasting. As they grow older, they encounter an ever-increasing range of people and meet more and more individuals who are known in superficial ways. It is essential that those supporting children's learning in school help them to appreciate that there are different ways of knowing those around them and that each has a different level of closeness. Emphasizing the need for personal safety and explaining ways to remain safe and of reacting in uncomfortable situations is fundamental to this.

As professionals there is a key role in both modelling and valuing good relationships. This is done in particular by how one relates to children, their families and one's colleagues. These are the relationships that children see education professionals engaged in the most.

In the later years of primary education it is possible to help children to appreciate the importance of positive, stable and loving relationships which provide a context for physical intimacy and sexual activity. This necessitates that sex is acknowledged as being, at times, for pleasure or possibly for pleasure and procreation. While it is important to make clear to children that sexual intercourse is not legal until the age of sixteen years, it is still important to explain sex within a context that is broader than the mechanics of a physical act.

Finally, it is now key to return to the starting point of this chapter that one's identity is fundamentally defined by the ways in which one relates to others. Whether as a co-worker, friend, lover, helper, family member, fellow-national or consumer people understand themselves, in many ways, through relationships. Helping children to develop affirmative views of themselves – and effective ways of relating to others – both contribute to positive self-esteem. Such positivity leads to self-confidence which provides a sound basis on which to build safe and secure relationships of all kinds.

Signposts

PSHE Association: information and resources to help develop children's personal, social, health and economic education. www.pshe—association.org.uk.
Resources to support those experiencing or encountering bullying are available from the following organizations:

  www.nspcc.org.uk
  www.barnardos.org.uk
  www.bullying.co.uk
  www.there4me.com
  www.gr8asur.com

Further reading

DCSF (2007) *Safe to Learn: Embedding Anti-bullying Work in Schools*. Nottingham: Department for Children, Schools and Families.
NSPCC (2008) *Protecting Children from Sexual Abuse: A Guide for Parents and Carers*. London: NSPCC. www.nspcc.org.uk/Inform/publications/downloads/protectingchil drenfromsexualabuse_wdf48012.pdf.
Woolley, R. (2010) 'Gender, Identity and Acceptance', in *Tackling Controversial Issues in the Primary School: Facing Life's Challenges with Your Learners*, ed. R. Woolley. London: Routledge.

References

Bee, H., and Boyd, D. (2003) *The Developing Child* (revised edn). Boston, MA: Allyn and Bacon.
Blake, S., and Muttock, S. (2004) *Assessment, Evaluation and Sex and Relationships Education: A Practical Toolkit for Education, Health and Community Settings*. London: National Children's Bureau.
Charlesworth, R. (2000) *Understanding Child Development: For Adults Who Work with Young Children* (revised edn). Albany, NY: Delmar.

DCSF (2007) *Safe to Learn: Embedding Anti-bullying Work in Schools*. Nottingham: Department for Children, Schools and Families.

DfE (2018) *Relationships Education, Relationships and Sex Education (RSE) and Health Education: Guidance for Governing Bodies, Proprietors, Head Teachers, Principals, Senior Leadership Teams, Teachers*. London: Department for Education.

DfE (2014) *National Curriculum in England: Framework for Key Stages 1-4*. www.gov. uk/government/publications/national-curriculum-in-england-framework-for-keystages-1-to-4/(accessed 31 March 2018).

DfEE (2000) *Sex and Relationship Education Guidance*. Nottingham: Department for Education and Employment Publications.

Dowling, M. (2005) *Young Children's Personal, Social and Emotional Development* (revised edn). London: Paul Chapman.

Einon, D. (2001) *Dorothy Einon's Complete Book of Childcare and Development: Raising Happy, Health and Confident Vhildren*. London: Marshall.

Eisenberg, N. (1988) 'The Development of Prosocial and Aggressive Behaviour', in *Developmental Psychology: An Advanced Textbook* (revised edn), ed. M. H. Borstein and M. E. Lamb. Hillsdale, NJ: Erlbaum.

Eisenberg, N., and Fabes, R. (1998) 'Prosocial Development', in *Handbook of Child Psychology. Volume 3: Social Emotional and Personality Development* (revised edn), ed. W. Damon and N. Eisenberg. New York: Wiley.

Maslow, A. H. (1968) *Toward a Psychology of Being* (2nd edn). New York: Van Nostrand Reinhold.

Morris, J., and Woolley, R. (2017) *Family Diversities Reading Resource* (2nd edn). Lincoln: Bishop Grosseteste University and University of Worcester.

NASEN (2018) *Changes to the Teaching of Sex and Relationship Education and PSHE*. www.nasen.org.uk/newsviews/nasen-blog.nasen-s-response-to-consultation-changes-to-the-teaching-of-sex-relationship-education-and-pshe.html (accessed 5 August 2018).

NICE (n.d.) *Personal, Social, Health and Economic Education Focusing on Sex and Relationships and Alcohol Education Consultation Draft*. National Institute for Health and Clinical Excellence.

NSPCC (2008) *Protecting Children from Sexual Abuse: A Guide for Parents and Carers*. London: NSPCC. www.nspcc.org.uk/Inform/publications/downloads/protectingchil drenfromsexualabuse_wdf48012.pdf (accessed 5 August 2018).

NSPCC (2018) *PANTS – Resources for Schools and Teachers*. www.nspcc.org.uk/ preventing-abuse/keeping-children-safe/underwear-rule/underwear-rule-schools-teaching-resources/ (accessed 2 August 2018).

Puckett, M., and Black, J. (2001) *The Young Child: Development from Prebirth Through Age Eight* (revised edn). Upper Saddle River, NJ: Prentice Hall.

Smith, P., Cowie, H., and Blades, M. (2003) *Understanding Children's Development* (revised edn). Malden, MA: Blackwell.

Stone, N., and Ingham, R. (2006) 'Young People and Sex and Relationships Education', in *Promoting Young People's Sexual Health: International Perspectives*, ed. R. Ingham and P. Aggleton. London: Routledge, 102–208.

Weissberg, R., Caplan, M., and Harwood, R. (1991) 'Promoting Competent Young People in Competence Enhancing Environments: A Systems-Based Perspective on Primary Prevention'. *Journal of Consulting and Clinical Psychology*, 59, 830–41.

Williams, J. E., and Best, D. L. (1990) *Measuring Sex Stereotypes: A Multi-nation Study*. Newbury Park, CA: Sage.

Woolley, R. (2010a) 'Self-Confidence and Self-Esteem', in *Personal, Social and Emotional Development*, ed. P. Broadhead, J. Johnston, C. Tobbell and R. Woolley. London: Continuum.

Woolley, R. (2010b) 'Communities', in *Knowledge and Understanding of the World*, ed. L. Cooper, J. Johnston, E. Rotchell and R. Woolley. London: Continuum.

Woolley, R. (2018) 'Towards an Inclusive Understanding of Bullying: Identifying Conceptions and Practice in the Primary School Workforce'. *Educational Review*. DOI:10.1080/00131911.2018.1471666.

Woolley, R., and Morris, J. (2009) *Disability Reading Resource*. Lincoln: Bishop Grosseteste University College.

4

Exploring children's views: A pedagogy of listening

As a young, newly qualified teacher working in a school just outside Brighton, a city with a large gay community, I was asked by one of the 7 year old boys who was in my class, how to spell 'ponce'. Going very red and a bit sweaty, I realised that this incident had the potential to be highly controversial and I felt out of my depth. With my mind whirling, I had the forethought to say 'That's an interesting word, could you tell me what sentence you are trying to write?' He looked directly at me and said 'You know Miss, one a ponce a time [once upon a time]'. This experience over twenty years ago formed an interest in controversial issues: **what could** *I have said;* **what would** *I have said to this child;* **what should** *I have said if his request had genuinely been 'ponce'?*

Chapter outline

Introduction

The experience of the teacher outlined in the vignette at the start of this chapter highlights the need to equip teachers and those working with children and young people with the skills and strategies to help enable learners to better understand relationships and sexual matters. The uncertainty of facing such situations with children can mean that adults become nervous of a child requesting information of a sensitive, or perceived sensitive, nature. In Chapter 1, we introduced the notion of 'bravery' as a pedagogical approach. When those working with children have strategies to address situations such as the incident described, these allow for professional confidence. A key feature to a pedagogy of bravery in RSE is in listening to the views of children through a dialogic approach.

A feature of a dialogic pedagogical approach is that of observing the developmental stages of children in order to plan appropriate next steps in learning for the individual as part of the 'plan–do–review' planning cycle (Kolb, 2015; see Chapter 6 for suggested normative developmental stages). This enables the teacher to plan for differentiation and to map the most relevant content to each individual child. Since the foundation of the UN Convention on the Rights of the Child (UNCRC, 1989) there has been substantial educational research which focuses on hearing the voices of children and the use a participatory pedagogical approach (Halstead and Reiss, 2003; Clark et al., 2005), particularly with young children. Mulliner (2007: 75) outlines that an effective RSE programme needs to be mindful of children's early experiences and should be based on their developmental and expressed needs. Children start to learn about relationships before they begin primary school, and so finding out about what young children know and understand is important.

Clark et al. (2005) advocate a 'Mosaic Approach' for listening to the perspectives of young children. The Mosaic Approach encompasses several ways of listening and seeing that assist in forming a 'picture' of the perceptions of the child. These ways of listening and seeing have origins in the Reggio Emilia pedagogy of the 'hundred languages of children'. The Reggio approach views the child as competent, able, creative and critical, and as such the process of listening to and hearing their voice is essential in using an appropriate pedagogy and devising a curriculum that is able to meet the needs of the child. The identification of the specific needs of the child in relation to RSE is often problematic. Halstead and Reiss (2003: 174) argue that there is a necessity to establish that 'needs' in RSE refers to physical health, the development of rational sexual autonomy, and consideration and respect for others. The value in hearing the voice of the child can be, according to Clark et al. (2005: 30), the 'catalyst for change'. The idea of change is central to our purpose of writing this book as, for us, change is essential in the domain of RSE if the needs of children and young people are to be met, although we recognize that change presents challenge and complexity.

Context for listening

The UNCRC (1989) represented the first internationally, legally binding instrument to acknowledge full human rights of the child. The UNCRC lays out fifty-four articles that state the rights of the child relating to four core principles:

1 non-discrimination;
2 devotion to the best interests of the child;
3 the right to life, survival and development; and
4 the respect for the views of the child

The fourth core principle represents the international acknowledgment of the child as an active participant in decisions that affect them and has significance for RSE. The emerging concern for hearing the voice of the child is identified in Article 12:

Article 12 (Respect for the views of the child): When adults are making decisions that affect children, children have the right to say what they think should happen and have their opinions taken into account.

Article 12 was made legally binding in the UK through the Children Act (1989) in relation to hearing the voice of children in matters concerning them, with a particular focus on court action, such as divorce proceedings and residency issues. An important caveat was stipulated outlining that children would only be consulted depending on their age and stage of development, suggesting that children should not be commandeered to make decisions or choices that they are too young to make. An argument can be made here that it is possible that adults may underestimate the capabilities of the child to engage in decision making or that adults may deliberately not seek the views of the child because of their perception that children are unable to offer any. While the Children Act of 1989 focused on seeking the views of the child during court cases, the Children Act of 2002 focused on educational issues and children's views. The Act of 2002 placed a statutory duty on local authorities and governing bodies of maintained schools to consult learners on matters affecting them. This heralded the establishment of school councils where representatives of each class meet to discuss issues affecting them within the setting. While this appears to meet the remit of the Children Act (2002), the reality of children discussing curriculum issues, particularly those in relation to RSE, is probably rare. However, in the most recent RSE guidance (DfE, 2018), there is a strong emphasis on the need to hear the voices of children.

The agenda for hearing the child's voice has continued, and in 2008 the government issued statutory guidance *Working Together: Listening to the Voices of Children and Young People* (DfCSF, 2008) which was an updated version of the guidance issued in 2004 (*Working Together: Giving Children and Young People a Say*). The purpose of this guidance, according to Knight, then Minister for Schools, was to promote best practice in effective pupil participation, 'to develop critical thinking, advocacy and influencing skills, helping every child to fulfil their potential' (DfCSF, 2008: 1). The concept of affording children and young people 'influencing skills' is an interesting one, and research by Mason (2010) suggests that this remains limited in the arena of RSE. One obstacle that may potentially reduce the 'influencing skills' of children and young people is the right of parents and carers to withdraw their child from RSE.

Right to withdraw

The right of parents and carers to withdraw their child from RSE remains unchallenged with the exception in 2009, when the Labour government intended to remove the right of parental withdrawal from the age of fifteen. The move was rejected in parliament, and section 405 of the Education Act (1996) remains as the legislative framework concerning this:

> If the parent of any pupil in attendance at a maintained school requests that he may be wholly or partly excused from receiving sex education at the school, the pupil shall, except so far as such education is comprised in the National Curriculum, be so excused accordingly until the request is withdrawn.

The date of the 1996 Act precedes the introduction of 'Relationships' to the RSE curriculum title, although the rights of parents and carers have been left unchanged. At this time, schools may have found this ambiguity difficult to reconcile as the curriculum did not explicitly separate sex from relationships. Wyness (1996: 108) comments that the introduction of parental veto in 1996 may be seen by the school as a means of power for parents to 'intrude' into the educational process, potentially undermining the school. The word 'requests' used in the Education Act (1996) offers the perception that the parent/carer is active in seeking the withdrawal, rather than accepting it as offered. The process of inviting consent perhaps makes the school an 'active' agent as opposed to the parent. Halstead and Reiss (2003: 155) cite a survey conducted by The Health Authority (1995), which finds strong support in the UK for the provision of RSE in schools. In the Health Authority study, 94 per cent of participating parents said schools should provide RSE, although this fell to 49 per cent among Muslim parents, with 27 per cent unsure and 24 per cent against. In 2009 the *Guardian* reported on a government-commissioned poll of 1,791 adults and 1,661 parents into whether all learners should be taught about sex. 'A fifth of the parents said parents should never be able to withdraw their children from sex education lessons, whatever age the children were. A third said parents should be allowed to exclude their children from sex education classes if they were aged 11 or under' (Shepherd, 2009). Research in the primary sector conducted by Mason (2010) suggests that whether schools seek permission or wait for withdrawal of learners from RSE, the reality of removing their children from RSE provision is unrealized. This was supported by Ofsted in 2002, who state that only 0.04 per cent of children are withdrawn from the non-statutory aspects of SRE. The interim and updated SRE guidance (Brook, PSHE and SEF, 2014) was produced collaboratively and was endorsed by the government as supplementary advice for schools. It draws on research evidence that corroborates with preceding evidence that very few parents exercise their right to withdraw their child from SRE. Perhaps the sensitive nature of RSE has become a perceived potential conflict with parents, which in reality does not necessarily manifest itself. Further reiteration of parental rights is clarified in the 2018 proposed guidance for Relationships Education, which makes the distinction between mandatory Relationships Education and sex education that remains non-statutory at primary level. As outlined in Chapter 1, schools have a duty to disclose their policy regarding the additional sex education content, including the resources teachers intend to use, to parents. Parents can then exercise their right for their child to be excused from specific aspects of the sex education curriculum. The DfE (2018: 18) recommends that primary schools do have a 'graduated, age-appropriate programme of sex education' in order that children are prepared for the 'changes that adolescence brings'. It is made clear that before any request to have their child withdrawn from sex education, a head teacher would discuss with the parent/carer the implications for this action on the child (misinformation, social and emotional effects, for example) as good practice. At primary level, the request must be automatically authorized by the school. However, at secondary level, a key point that is made is that these requests can be made by parents up until three terms before the young person turns sixteen. The school then must put sex education in place and 'after that point, if the child wishes to receive sex education rather than be withdrawn, the school should make arrangements to provide the child with sex education during one of those terms' (DfE, 2018: 13). This statement articulates a shift towards a child's right over and above those of their parents.

However, if the right of parents and carers to withdraw their child remains, although rarely acted on, this may be because of a myriad reasons: stigma for the withdrawn child; the view of the parent as not wanting to be perceived as overly militant; a lack of information concerning RSE content on which to base the withdrawal of the child; or indeed a reluctance to question the perceived professional sex educator. Alternatively, parents and carers may feel relief that the school curriculum addresses issues of a sexual nature and are content to support the school in assuming the role of educator for RSE. The relinquishing of the parental role in discussing sexual matters with their children may leave children in an information void that encourages them to use other information sources, such as those found in the media, which offer them the information they seek. We argue that parents/carers, as do all adults, have an important role to play in talking to children and young people about sexual matters.

In 2007, the Ofsted publication *Time for Change: Personal, Social and Health Education* identified key findings that suggests that 'young people report that many parents and teachers are not very good at talking to them about sensitive issues in PSHE, such as sex and relationships' (2007: 10). A reluctance to discuss issues beyond the biological facts that moves into realms of sexual desire and feelings creates the need for children and young people to seek information from other sources such as pornography which can provide misleading expectations and distorted understandings of a loving relationship in terms of sexual performance, body image and sexual desire. Limmer (2009: 7) identifies six key themes of gendered social norms that present themselves in pornography:

1 Sex is purely a physical act taking place in an emotional vacuum.
2 Heterosexuality is compulsory, for men at least.
3 Male pleasure is paramount – the encounter is complete on male ejaculation and women's pleasure is conceptualized as evidence of male mastery and expertise.
4 Men should take the lead, be the experts and not refuse a sexual opportunity.
5 Women are always willing to have sex – even though sometimes they 'pretend' that they are reluctant.
6 Sex is consequence-free – issues of infection and conception are absent.

Limmer (2009) discusses how boys use pornography for sexual stimulation and masturbation, and also because it provides them with the explicit information about the female body, and the logistics of sexual intercourse and practices. Another key provision of pornography is that watching it demonstrates masculinity and heterosexuality which is commonly a 'powerful preoccupation' (p. 7) in terms of fitting in with peers. RSE can address some of these issues and challenge the perceptions acquired through the use of pornography, for example, using non-exploitative images within RSE, alongside explanation and discussion that can challenge perceptions and misperceptions acquired from pornography. Pornography introduces the notion of sex as pleasure, and it is this dimension of RSE that is rarely addressed with children and young people by adults. Spencer et al. (2008) support Limmer's view that RSE programmes frequently exclude issues of pleasure and intimacy. Halstead and Reiss (2003) also argue

> Sex education in schools should involve much more than the transmission of knowledge. It should include education of the emotions and offer children opportunities to reflect on the nature of love, intimacy and desire.

Further discussion about issues of pleasure within RSE is included in Chapter 6.

Partnership with parents and carers

Walker et al. (2003: 326) outline the importance of building alliances with parents and carers. The involvement of parents and carers in the forming of RSE policies, discussion on content and evaluation of provision assists in breaking down barriers between home and school. The SRE guidance (Brook, PSHE and SEF, 2014) reports that in 2011, 84 per cent of parents surveyed shared that they want to have a shared role in SRE with their child's school. The Macdonald review (2009: 21) states,

> Effective PSHE education, and SRE in particular, is dependent on open dialogue, clear communication and positive and supportive partnerships between schools and parents, and between communities and schools.

This is also reiterated in the 2018 guidance as an essential aspect of RSE is reaching out to all parents through a range of different approaches.

During discussions with children and young people on issues of sex and relationships, consider:

- what are the implications for parents and carers?
- how can you manage these implications sensitively in relation to parental views and values?

A useful approach adopted by some schools is for the school to host a parents' information event that outlines the potential content covered during RSE sessions, including the resources that will be used. This allows for the parents to hear directly from the school and also to ask any questions they may have either in a public or private forum with teachers. In addition to this, a home/school folder with all the materials used as part of the teaching can be an effective shared resource so that parents can continue any conversations at home where relevant. Boundaries can be established around this folder where rules around who can see the folder are created. This may be especially important for parents with younger children where it may be considered as developmentally inappropriate for them to have inadvertent access to the materials. Developing communication with parents will remain essential when developing the curriculum for sex education, but we suggest it is also important to inform them of the curriculum for mandatory Relationships Education so that they understand what is being taught across the 3–11 age range.

What children want in RSE

A wide-reaching survey (2007) was conducted by the UK Youth Parliament to seek the views of young people (n = 21,602) between eleven and eighteen years about SRE. The young people were asked to respond to six questions. When asked about how good SRE was in their school, 40 per cent of those in the sample thought that it was poor or very poor and 33 per cent considered that SRE was of average quality. In 2005, the publication *PSHE & Citizenship* reported a twelve-year-old-girl's view that her sex education is patronizing, she comments, 'We are not as stupid as people think; young people would rather be treated like intelligent people.' She outlines that much of the content addressed during an SRE lesson was what she already knew, with the exception of a few facts concerning contraception. By the time children reach secondary school, many will have reached puberty and perhaps addressing puberty, sexual health and reproduction at this stage of education is all too little too late. Research by Measor (2004) suggests that young people want to know information about the logistics of a sexual relationship, what to do when having sex, issues of intimacy and emotions related to a sexual relationship. The SRE supplementary guidance (Brook, PSHE and SEF, 2014: 6) also reports that children and young people want to learn about issues of body confidence, love and sexual attraction, how to respond to peer pressure and how to behave in a relationship.

The current absence of information and discussion around these issues means that many young people are turning to other sources of information. A YouGov survey of almost 2,000 teens, commissioned by Channel 4 (2007), found that more than half of teens say they rely on getting advice on sex from friends, the internet, magazines and pornography, with nearly three in ten teenagers saying they need more SRE. According to Measor (2004), girls are more likely to seek advice and information from their family, namely their mother, whereas boys are more likely to seek information from pornography. In the YouGov survey, more than a quarter of boys in the survey used porn at least once a week, with 5 per cent of boys looking at porn daily. This might suggest that RSE in schools and that offered to children and young people from their parents is insufficient in providing them with the information they seek beyond the biological basics. Piercy and Haynes (2006: 12) outline that children are constantly exposed to, 'and accumulate information from, a variety of sources which they struggle to make sense of'.

Childhood innocence

The suggestion that children and young people are seeking information, among other things, from alternative, primarily online, sources raises some questions about childhood innocence and why children are not acquiring information from those closest to them: their parents, other adults in school and out-of-school settings. An adult perspective for not discussing matters concerning sex and sexual relationships may concern perceptions of childhood innocence. Childhood innocence is a frequently used term to defend the withholding of information from children. Many parents and teachers say 'they grow up too quickly once you start with sex education', 'they just need to be children' and perhaps this stance is morally unquestionable as it implies the child's best interests are at the heart of this approach. A contrasting view is that in order to prepare the child for their future life, to be a fully rounded, sexual being then an open and honest approach to what is arguably a fundamental aspect of adult life should be adopted. With this approach, knowledge is considered empowering. The two arguments appear to be uninformed versus informed, or ignorance versus knowledge. Whichever approach is taken, it is shaped by a particular notion of childhood.

The concept of childhood is explored by Buckingham (2000: 5) as a social and historical construction. The notion of the child as an active human being capable of making decisions about matters that concern them is a twentieth-century construct. Buckingham argues that childhood is 'subject to a constant process of struggle and negotiation, both in public discourse … and in interpersonal relationships, among peers and in the family', and in sexual matters, we suggest this 'struggle and negotiation' is particularly evident. The struggle and negotiation is attributed, Buckingham outlines, to the perception that the media have 'erased' the boundaries between childhood and adulthood and by doing so have undermined the authority of adults. The constant access to information, concepts and ideas that are beyond the direct control of the parent or adult through the wealth of media that children and young people have surrounding them, makes censorship almost impossible. It could be that the result of this is the perception of the distinct stage of 'childhood', depicted by an innocence that is unsullied by the evils of sexual desires, is diminished and eroded without the endeavours by responsible adults to protect this proposed innocence.

There is a contrasting argument to this stance, posed by Erriker (2003: 4), who outlines the notion of adult control by suggesting that the protection of a 'fantasy childhood innocence legitimates the fantasy of adult power'. This fantasy of adult power stems from the need to control children and young people's values and behaviours to maintain the social norms. It is relevant to consider that the notion of adult power is closely linked with adult fear – fear of being challenged, and fear of changes to social and cultural norms or expectations. This fear can be a hindrance to the development of the child. Erriker (2003: 5) makes clear that the protection of the innocence of childhood affects the development of 'children's capacities to deal effectively with their experiences or reflect critically on their enculturation'. These conflicting viewpoints are somewhat polarized and are positioned in the current context of children's rights agendas which is not without its critics in the UK and beyond. If as outlined earlier in this chapter, a young person at fifteen can override their parents' wishes to be withdrawn from RSE, then a qualitative change towards respecting the agency of the child and their right to information appears.

Consider:

- Is the protection of childhood innocence an aspect of current societies' value systems? If it is, does this present challenges for practitioners?
- To what extent is the notion of childhood innocence a strategy to protect adults form difficult questions?
- Can children remain innocent, given the sexualized nature of a significant proportion of media outputs?

Where the notion of protecting children's innocence is interrelated to adults' perception of power and their fear, it may be critical to explore the source of adult fear of being challenged by children. Adult fears might include being asked about sexual desire, sexual pleasure, sex as recreation and sex for reproduction. These may feel just too difficult to discuss with children and young people as they are highly personal issues, built on individual histories, experiences and values.

Reproduction is a fundamental feature of all known life. Human reproduction involves two sexes, male and female. Humans may be different from other mammals in their use of sexual activity as an expression of an emotional and intimate response beyond the need to reproduce, and/or for personal gratification. The concept of sexual pleasure is, perhaps, a human phenomenon. The complex interplay of relationships with sexual gratification alongside, or separate from, the desire to procreate makes the nature of sex in humans more than a biological function.

The source of a person's arousal is characterized by their own 'sexuality' – the understanding of what, or who, arouses them. It is well documented through history that the sexuality of individuals has been varied. Forrest and Ellis (2006) make reference to the homosexual activities of the Ancient Greeks and Romans, demonstrating that arousal is achieved through same-sex sexual activity. Sexuality cannot be defined as solely heterosexual, or homosexual. Indeed human sexuality is complex, often fluid and unable to be categorized into simple sexual identities.

The impact of individual sexual behaviours raises some important questions within a social and cultural context. Individuals exist at a particular time and in a social framework that defines the acceptability of sexual behaviours. For example, the Victorians criminalized male homosexuality, whereas in twenty-first-century Britain, sex between two consenting adult males is lawful. Forrest and Ellis (2006: 89) describe sexuality as a cultural field which is subject to both construction and deconstruction as part of a historical process.

The International Planned Parenthood Federation (IPPF) in 2010 promotes a model of RSE entitled Comprehensive Sexuality Education which champions an international model 'of sexuality education that considers the various interrelated power dynamics that influence sexual choices and the resulting emotional, mental, physical and social impacts on each young person's development' (2010: 1). The IPPF are specific in their reference to the need to address with children and young people issues about sexual pleasure in order that they understand that sex is much more than intercourse and 'the biology and emotions behind the human sexual response; gender and pleasure; masturbation; love, lust and relationships; interpersonal communication; the diversity of sexuality' (p. 3).

The 'construction' that Forest and Ellis (2006) refer to is a societal framework established to curb individual sexual behaviours that are perhaps not fully understood or do not fit well with the historical, scientific and religious context within which they sit. One reason why male homosexuality in Victorian times might have been considered a crime was because the sexual union did not result in procreation and in an era where large proportions of babies and young children died, homosexual sex was regarded as wasted semen. The need to preserve semen in the Victorian era drives the value system of the time as lesbianism is absent in Victorian legislation, and continues to be less a focus within the law. Where procreation is not as threatened in the twenty-first century, a shift in the values system is possible, to one which regards reproduction as less of an urgency and concepts of sexual pleasure are more enabled.

The different perspectives on matters of religion, morality, society, wealth and politics evolve a framework or frameworks out of which sexual behaviours and, ultimately, relationships are suppressed or more visible. In today's multifaith Britain, it is more difficult to observe a specific value system of sexual behaviours based on religion. For example, in heterosexual relationships, the Christian faith advocates love as the driving force for marriage and allows individuals to select their own 'mate'. The concept of the arranged heterosexual marriage continues to be practiced among some other religious faiths, where parents select the deemed appropriate 'mate' for their children. This is based on the understanding of the union of strong family values, where love is a potential consequence or outcome, rather than a cause or prelude to marriage. Within this heady mix of multiple value systems sits the increasing articulation of secular reasoning which may have originally been influenced by religious values but have subtly altered to reflect contemporary ethical issues, such as abortion or the ethics of the genetic engineering of the gender of children. The notion of sex outside of marriage, including between cohabiting couples, the current changes in family structures and values have challenged accepted religious sexual values.

The expectation of children and young people in the twenty-first century, established through the media and possibly modelled in the home is that sex is linked to pleasure, is recreational and not always within an enduring relationship. In some instances, this may present a complex picture for children where adults are encouraging abstinence or are coy or silent about sexual matters with the behaviours that they model. Therefore, avoidance of discussion with children and young people about sex and relationships becomes an easier approach to ensure that adult morality or values remain unquestioned. The old adage of 'do as I say and not as I do' holds currency in this approach. Pleasure of all kinds is highly individual and personal; sexual pleasure is no different. It is then necessary for practitioners to understand their own sexuality and sexual values in order to support the sexual development of children and young people. Further discussion about notions of pleasure is addressed in Chapter 6.

What children know by age eleven

Little research evidence in the primary sector about RSE makes understanding the needs of children within this age group and stage problematic. A small-scale study conducted by Mason (2010) offers some insight. The research was undertaken in two primary schools in the north-east of England and identifies very different practices and approaches to RSE programmes. One school begins by addressing puberty and develops content through School Years 3–5 (ages seven to ten), then covering a wealth of issues ranging from sexual health, contraception, sexual reproduction, child birth, sexuality and abortion in a six week programme in the final term of Year 6 (age eleven). The other school offers one 'Growing-up Talk' at the end of Year 6 in a single afternoon session which covers puberty, sanitary products, wet dreams and erections. Mason (2010) suggests that where primary-aged children are taught about aspects of sexual intercourse, conception, pregnancy, birth and puberty in a progressive sequence of lessons from School Year 2, children become accustomed to talking freely and easily about sexual matters in an educational setting. However, where RSE is limited to an isolated, one-off session that seeks to inform learners about puberty, learners are afforded only one part of the process; only one piece of the jigsaw and as such it may confuse or mislead children. Mason (2010) suggests that where children are not offered any formal taught content in RSE until they reach Year 5 or 6 (age ten and eleven), learners may be anxious and confused. Bourne (1996: 23) outlines some findings from research conducted with primary-aged children using the Draw and Write technique. One of the findings shows that learners at 10+ years demonstrated some uncertainty about the changes in puberty and how they would feel about them. Only one third projected positive feelings about being fifteen. This corroborates the findings by Mason (2010: 166) that children's responses to their RSE session were mixed.

The voices of these children, drawn from the data, illuminate their perspectives regarding RSE and demonstrates the uncertainties that some children feel towards their bodily changes experienced during puberty. This increased focus on the emotional aspects of puberty and body changes could be attributed to embarrassment where the children were coming 'cold' to the activity having not received any RSE regarding body changes before. This raises questions about the nature of available support for learners during life and body changes. Preparation for this at an earlier age could alleviate children's concerns about change and in addition suggests that embedding RSE into School Years 2, 3 and 4 allows the gradual acquisition of knowledge to develop and is corroborated by the DfE guidance for RSE (2018). Mason (2010: 166) suggests that a one-off 'Growing-up Talk' may sensationalize the content and the expression of the mixed emotions from the learners in the study could be an indication of this:

> ... angry that I haven't been told before ... puzzled ... curious ... cautious ...
> ... changed ... angry ... new beginning ... happy ... sad

The frequent appearance of the word 'angry' is particularly relevant, especially from the child who expresses her anger at not having been told before. Is this directed at the school or her parents? One pupil said to the researcher, following the session, 'Is that it? Is that all we are doing?' It appeared that this child had anticipated greater content in the session and a sense of disappointment that it was limited to puberty which might suggest that the child knew that there was more information to acquire and was ready to address it.

In the study by Mason (2010: 164) many of the children in both settings referred to 'love' or a 'feeling of being ready' to indicate when they were ready to have sex and a relationship. Children's comments included the following:

- ... they were in love;
- ... they were mentally ready;
- ... they might really love each other;
- ... they might just feel ready from the inside;
- ... they would have thought it through and they would feel it in their hearts;
- ... when they're deep in love. (p. 164)

These findings may tentatively suggest that many children, at the age of ten and eleven, do understand the link between sexual activity and loving relationships, although not specifically linked to marriage. Further responses suggested understanding that being mature, or grown-up, is a sign of knowing when to have sex:

> ... averagely [sic] over 18;
> ... when they have left home and have a driving license;
> ... by their age and when puberty has ended. (p. 164)

With the majority of children claiming maturity or a relationship as a way of knowing when to have sex, significance may be placed on the absence of comments stating that being married was a way of knowing when to have sex. These omissions might indicate a moral framework where sexual relationships for these children are not necessarily solely linked to marriage. The limited references to marriage were relevant in the data. The twenty-first-century concept of family structures potentially makes the association of sexual relationships solely within marriage challenging for children. The reasons for this are complex. Perhaps children do not associate sexual relationships with marriage because the role models that surround them and the influences from the media do not actively make the link. Halstead and Reiss (2003: 114) comment that the traditional Christian view of the 'nuclear family' where the parents are married is not the 'fixed' reality for many children:

> Knowledge and values are constructed by children through interaction between their existing knowledge and the new situations, experiences and ideas they encounter at home, in the media, at school or among peers.

Children bring to schools and informal educational settings wide and varying conceptions of what a family is. This is reflected in the findings from this study and suggests that the curriculum should reflect the diversity of human sexual relationships, in addition to the wider breadth of relationships between people.

Children in this study primarily suggested that sex was for procreation. Only one child articulated the understanding of the two functions of a sexual relationship that are not mutually exclusive: procreation and pleasure. The ten-year-old boy said, 'when they love that person, loves the other person so much they produce new life, or shares [sic] their body' (Mason, 2010: 165). The notion of sexual pleasure is a fundamental aspect of adult life for most people and to exclude this aspect from RSE, we argue, is a serious omission. Sex and relationships are deeply personal, and it may be considered that discussions with children and young people regarding sexual pleasure might promote early sexual debut in the pursuit of sexual pleasure or it might elicit questions that practitioners might be uncomfortable answering for a raft of reasons. A comprehensive RSE programme does not lead to an earlier sexual debut; interestingly Averting HIV and AIDS (AVERT, 2010) points to a wealth of research suggesting that it can delay it. The issue of children's questions is highly relevant and will be discussed in Chapter 7. Developmentally relevant RSE is also addressed further in Chapter 6.

Pedagogy of listening

In most other areas of the curriculum, the teacher will broadly focus on determining the developmental stage of the child and building a programme of learning that maps to that individual. The process of ascertaining the child's developmental stage may be through formative assessment such as observation of and discussion with the child during their learning or through some form of summative task that elicits the child's knowledge and understanding. This becomes challenging with RSE as it may be viewed as an intrusion of privacy, or venturing into the realms of parental responsibilities. However, the need to establish the knowledge and understanding of children is essential for developing a relevant programme of RSE, as with any other curriculum area.

To develop a listening pedagogy, it is necessary to adopt a flexible approach to working with children in order that children may piece together and make sense of the different aspects of information they have received from the variety of influences that surround them: parents, peers, school, out-of-school setting and the media. Where misconceptions are found to exist, the factual and biological knowledge is somewhat easier to correct, however, the understanding of values is a more complex concept to manage. Halstead and Waite (2002: 22) advocate an approach to RSE that helps 'children to reflect critically on the sexual values, attitudes and understanding that they have already started to pick up on in the course of their everyday lives', especially where these may be conflicted. The notion of encouraging the development of critical reflection skills is highly relevant because it affords children and young people the opportunity to challenge the values, views and perceptions of those around them. The process of critical reflection, argue Halstead and Waite (2002), 'makes the activity of sex education genuinely educational rather simply a matter of instruction or training or the transmission of knowledge' (suggestions for practice are explored in Chapter 9). A difficult aspect of a listening approach, however, is that practitioners may feel vulnerable when being challenged which may leave them exposed and result in avoidance in responding honestly and openly to children's and young people's reflections. A dichotomy, therefore, exists between the needs, wants, and rights of the child and the concerns and insecurities of the adult.

Consider:

- How might you respond to a child who challenges the sexual values that you hold?
- What might you say in response?
- How can you openly respond without influencing the child inappropriately?
- Is such influence unavoidable?

Summary of key approaches to support effective practice

In order to develop effective practice it is important to consider the following:

- the need to check and clarify children's use of language;
- the importance of assessing children's prior knowledge and taking this into account;
- how the child's voice can be heard in the process of planning for provision in RSE;
- whether the parental/carer right to withdraw a child from RSE is counterproductive;
- the impact of pornography, particularly on the understandings that young boys and men have of sex and relationships;
- how open dialogue can be developed with parents and carers;
- strategies to taking into account the needs and wants of children in relation to their own learning;
- how adult concerns and children's needs can be balanced;
- the dangers of a mechanics-only approach to sexual practices;
- the need to consider why people have sexual intercourse (and why they do not); and
- the essential need to develop a pedagogy of listening to children's voices.

Conclusion and summary of key learning points

A pedagogy of listening for RSE may require the adoption of different teaching strategies. One useful and well-researched approach is the draw-and-write technique established by Wetton et al. (1989). The 'Draw and Write' technique was pioneered by Wetton et al. who used it to ascertain children's perceptions of healthy living for a research project 'A Way In: Five Key Areas of Health Education' in 1989. Reporting on their choice of investigative technique for their project, which followed extensive pilots, they commented that this research technique was able to adapt to the children's growing communication skills and, therefore, enabled the 'rich response' of the children (1989: 115). This technique has been described by Pridmore and Bendelow (1995) as an 'innovative method' and able to provide researchers with data of a 'sophisticated nature' from young children as it invites the responses of 'children to use their own language and other communication skills freely' as well as maintaining the child and parental rights to privacy. Typically during a Draw and Write session, children are asked to draw and write a response to a question asked of them. In the context of RSE, Mason (2010) used the outline of a non-gendered person and asked the children to draw and/or write all the changes that they might see or know which happen during puberty. This enabled an unprompted response from the children. However, critics of the technique argue that 'picture making requires both knowledge and skill' (Backett-Milburn and KcKie, 1999: 390) and questions what these will tell the researcher about the 'social world and context of the person producing the drawing'. It might be considered that a child's perceptions are misinterpreted from the drawing through the lack of the child's competence or visual communication. This is, of course, possible in the way that any response through any method may be misinterpreted. The strength of the Draw and Write technique is that it can be inclusive of a wide range of abilities and enables children to express their perceptions and understandings of sex and relationships more freely and as such is a valuable tool in hearing the voices of children and young people. This process of 'listening' assists in developing a differentiated and dialogic approach to RSE which enables the teacher to adjust the taught content accordingly.

The use of small group discussions may enable practitioners to 'listen' to children for the purposes of developing an appropriate RSE programme, along with spontaneous and unplanned moments when children may open a discussion about sexual matters. These are opportunities that allow the adult to 'hear' the needs of the child and respond accordingly. Moments such as these should be capitalized upon and used as a springboard to discuss further issues. Family events and changes such as marriages, divorces, arrival of siblings and new relationships provide ideal opportunities to hear the views of children and young people. The media and literature frequently provide moments to talk about relationships and sexuality; popular soaps operas, reality TV shows and films often evoke questions that concern feelings, values and logistics of a wide variety of relationships (as was explored in Chapter 2). RSE should be addressed through a cross-curricular approach in order that all aspects are developed.

Further aspects of a listening pedagogy should incorporate the listening of the views of parents and carers. The involvement of parents and carers enables a shared approach to the teaching about sexual matters to children and young people: this will be discussed further in Chapters 6 and 7. The IPPF (2010: 3) support an RSE that 'seeks to equip young people with the knowledge, skills, attitudes and values they need to determine and enjoy their sexuality – physically and emotionally'. We advocate that this can only be achieved through the construction of a pedagogy of listening that seeks to respond to the needs of individuals. In Chapter 1, we introduced the concept of 'bravery' as a pedagogical approach and a fundamental aspect of this is to listen to the views of the child. The complex context in which RSE is located creates tensions and ambiguities to which teachers in schools and adults outside of formal education have to respond. Pilcher (2005: 168) describes RSE as an 'inherently contentious character' that straddles issues between local and central government, public and private, teachers and parents, health and education, social and moral and finally 'established and "rising" generations':

> In England in the early twenty-first century, as throughout the twentieth, teaching sex education to children in publicly funded schools continues to expose deep rooted ambiguities, about sexuality, about the condition of childhood and about children and young people themselves. (p. 168)

The context and complexities that Pilcher (2005) outlines are indisputable, however, to avoid issues that are contentious with children would be equally as challenging as illustrated in the vignette at the beginning of the chapter. We propose that adults working with children in the primary phase need the tools to deal with these incidents. For adults to have a *toolkit* of strategies and approaches that supports a well-informed and pedagogically appropriate content is essential and the chapters within the book are aimed at providing such as toolkit (for a summary of strategies, see the Introduction, which elucidates generic approaches, and Chapter 9, which exemplifies further teaching methods).

Signposts and further reading

International Planned Parenthood Federation (2010) *Framework for Comprehensive Sexuality Education*. www.ippf.org/sites/default/files/ippf_framework_for_ comprehensive_sexuality_education.pdf.
PSHE Association (2018) *Preparing for Statutory Relationships Education. PSHE Education Lead's Pack: Key Stages 1 and 2*. PSHE Association. www.pshe-association.org.uk/curriculum-and-resources/resources/ preparing-statutory-relationships-education-pshe.

References

AVERT (2010) *Effective School-Based Sex Education*. www.avert.org/sex-education.htm.
Backett-Milburn, K., and KcKie, L. (1999) 'A Critical Appraisal of the Draw and Write Technique'. *Health Education Research*, 14 (3), 387–98.
Bourne, S. (1996) *Girls Have Long Hair: What Do Key Stage 2 Pupils Know about Sex*. Cambridge: Daniels Folens.
Brook, PSHE and SEF (2014) *Sex and Relationships Education (SRE) for the 21st Century: Supplementary Advice to the Sex and Relationship Education Guidance*. DfEE (0116/2000).

Buckingham, D. (2000) *After the Death of Childhood: Growing Up in the Age of Electronic Media.* Oxford. Blackwell.

Children Act (1989) www.legislation.gov.uk/ukpga/1989/41/contents (accessed 6 August 2018).

Clark, A., Kjørholt, A., and Moss, P. (2005) *Beyond Listening: Children's Perspectives on Early Childhood Services.* Bristol: Policy Press.

Department for Children, Schools and Families (2008) *Working Together: Listening to the Voices of Children and Young People.* http://publications.education.gov.uk/default.aspx?PageFunction=productdetails&PageMode=publications&ProductId=DCSF-00410-2008 (accessed 8 August 2018).

Department for Education (2018) *Relationships Education, Relationships and Sex Education (RSE) and Health Education: Guidance for Governing Bodies, Proprietors, Head Teachers, Principals, Senior Leadership Teams, Teachers.* London: Department for Education.

DfES (2003) *Working Together: Giving Children and Young People a Say.* London: Department for Education and Skills.

Erriker, C. (2003) 'Against the Protection of Childhood Innocence'. *International Journal of Children's Spirituality*, 8 (1), 3–7.

Forrest, S., and Ellis, V. (2006) 'The Making of Sexualities: Sexuality, Identity and Equality', in *Education, Equality and Human Rights: Issues of Gender, 'Race', Sexuality, Disability and Social Class* (revised edn), ed. M. Cole. London: Routledge.

Halstead, M., and Reiss, M. (2003) *Values in Sex Education: From Principles to Practice.* London: RoutledgeFalmer.

Halstead, M., and Waite, S. (2002) ' "Worlds Apart": The Sexual Values of Boys and Girls'. *Education and Health*, 20 (1), 17–23.

International Planned Parenthood Federation (2010) *Framework for Comprehensive Sexuality Education.* www.ippf.org/sites/default/files/ippf_framework_for_comprehensive_sexuality_education.pdf (accessed 6 August 2018).

Kolb, D. (2015) *Experiential Learning: Experience as the Source of Learning and Development.* Englewood Cliffs, NJ: Pearson.

Limmer, M. (2009) 'Young Men and Pornography: Meeting the Challenge Through Sex and Relationships Education'. *Education and Health*, 27 (1), 6–8.

Macdonald, A. (2009) *Independent Review of the Proposal to Make Personal, Social, Health and Economic (PSHE) Education Statutory.* London: Department for Children, Schools and Families.

Mason, S. (2010) 'Braving It Out! An Illuminative Evaluation of the Provision of Sex and Relationship Education in Two Primary Schools in England'. *Sex Education*, 10 (2), 157–69.

Measor, L. (2004) 'Young People's Views of Sex Education: Gender, Information and Knowledge'. *Sex Education*, 4 (2), 153–66.

Mulliner, G. (2007) 'Sex and Relationships – We'll Tell You What We Want, What We Really, Really Want!' *Education Review*, 20 (1), 74–81.

Ofsted (2002) *Sex and Relationships.* London: HMI 433.

Ofsted (2007) *Time for Change? Personal, Social and Health Education.* London: Ofsted.

Piercy, H., and Haynes, G. (2006) 'Coherant, Comprehensive and Continuous: Developing a Curriculum for Effective Sex and Relationship Education in an English Primary School'. *Education and Health*, 25 (1), 12–15.

Pilcher, J. (2005) 'School Sex and Education: Policy and Practice in England 1870 to 2000'. *Sex Education*, 5 (2), 153–70.

Pridmore, P., and Bendelow, G. (1995) 'Images of Health: Exploring Beliefs of Children Using "Draw and Write" Technique'. *Health Education Journal*, 54, 473–88.

Shepherd, J. (2009) *Children Under 15 Can Be Withdrawn from Sex Education. The Guardian.* www.guardian.co.uk/education/2009/nov/05/sex-education-lessons (accessed 8 August 2018).

Spencer, G., Maxwell, C., and Aggleton, P. (2008) 'What Does "Empowerment" Mean in School-Based Sex and Relationships Education?' *Sex Education*, 8 (3), 345–56.

UK Youth Parliament (2007) *Sex and Relationships Education: Are You Getting It?* London: UK Youth Parliament.

UNHCHR (1989) *Convention on the Rights of the Child.* Office of the High Commissioner for Human Rights. www.unhchr.ch/html/menu3/b/k2crc.htm (accessed 6 August 2018).

Walker, J., Green, J., and Tilford, S. (2003) 'An Evaluation of School Sex Education Team Training'. *Health Education*, 103 (6), 320–29.

Wellings, K., Wadsworth, J., Johnson, A., Field, J., Whitaker, L., and Field, B. (1995) 'Provision of Sex Education and Early Sexual Experience: The Relation Examined'. *British Medical Journal*, 311, 417–20.

Wetton, N., Williams, T., and Moon, A. (1989) *A Way In: Five Key Areas of Health Education.* London: Health Education Authority.

Wyness, M. (1996) *Schooling, Welfare and Parental Responsibility.* London: Falmer Press.

YouGov (2007) *No Sexperience Necessary.* http://sexperienceuk.channel4.com/teen—sex—survey (accessed 6 August 2018).

Adult concerns about Relationships and Sex Education

Christina is a teaching assistant working in an infant school in a city suburb. At the end of the last term she married her fiancé of three years and invited children to attend the ceremony:

> *I asked the children to attend my wedding as it was held in the local church and I thought it would be special for them to be a part of my day. I love working at the school so much and although we have talked about weddings in class, most children had not seen a real ceremony take place. It seemed to be an ideal learning opportunity and a way to share my celebration with those I work with most closely. My nieces are both in my Year 2 class, and they served as my bridesmaids. I think that some of their classmates would happily have joined them and there were some lovely comments about their dresses. The children sang for the congregation during the signing of the register. After the ceremony we had refreshments for all those attending, partly to use the time while the photographs were taken and partly because I could not invite all the children and their parents to the reception. I received some lovely cards from the children and it was delightful to see the time and care they had put into making them.*

Chapter outline

Introduction

This chapter outlines short case studies of teachers and parents/carers who are apprehensive about addressing RSE with children, with a particular focus on the different dimensions of relationships, accompanied by questions for reflection/discussion and strategies to develop practice. It considers what is meant when talking about relationships and how this can be done without being critical of the family relationships experienced by some children (as already highlighted in Chapter 3). It explores whether there are ideal relationships and how it is possible to be realistic when talking to children about relationships. This chapter examines how practitioners can cope with religious (and other) sensibilities or views about relationships from different stakeholders in schools and others in wider society. It also explores how RSE can be personalized in mainstream schools to meet the needs of children with special educational needs (SENs) or disabilities.

Talking to children about relationships

In Chapter 3 a general overview of the nature of relationships was explored. Now the discussion turns to specific examples and situations where relationships and relatedness are considered in a range of settings, and particularly *special friendship* relationships (as described in the taxonomy in Chapter 3). These are approached using the views and concerns of a range of adults associated with schools. Questions and issues raised by children themselves are considered in the next chapter.

Angela is a teacher with a Year 3 class. As a part of the statutory Relationships Education curriculum (DfE, 2018) she has to explore the special relationships that people form, focusing on marriage and civil partnerships. Angela is not married and has a three-year-old daughter:

My concern is that the children will ask personal questions about my home life. Normally I am very open with them and I often tell stories about what my daughter has been doing. Sometimes I do this to show that even when she is naughty I still love her and at other times I use the stories to give a context when we discuss aspects of behaviour like telling lies or owning up to making a mistake. However, now that I am planning for this term I am worried that the children will ask why I am not married and how I can have a daughter without having a husband or partner. While this is not an issue for me personally – and I chose to have IVF using a sperm donor because I do not want a long-term relationship with a man – I am not going to share this information with seven- and eight-year-olds and I do not want to face embarrassing questions. Of course they may not arise, as the children seem to have taken my situation in their stride so far.

Consider:

- how a teacher's personal situation might cause them concern when planning to teach RSE;
- how you feel that Angela might prepare to answer any difficult or personal questions that the children raise; and
- whether you feel it would be appropriate for Angela to share her personal experience with children in her class.

Angela's situation highlights an important aspect of preparing for RSE with children. Practitioners need to consider their own boundaries in terms of what personal information they are willing to share with children. They may wish to talk about their partner or families, but not all would wish to bring their personal lives into the classroom. This should not be required or expected. Key to this area is the setting of clear guidelines prior to the commencement of sessions on RSE; indeed, most classes have a set of guidelines or rules which inform good relationships and encourage respectful behaviour. In many cases these will prove sufficient to ensure that any discussions in RSE are both positive and constructive for all concerned. This may include the need to be polite and respectful to others, an expectation that the genuine views and questions of all are valued and welcomed, and that no personal remarks or questions are introduced – each provide for the creation of a safe and secure learning environment. These could form the basis of good practice on a day-to-day basis in the classroom, or practitioners may choose to have a specific set of guidelines to make sure that the content of RSE sessions has a particular focus on respectful attitudes which promote openness and deeper learning.

In Angela's case, she might choose to decline to answer any personal questions. This would be wholly appropriate and in line with her classroom guidelines. Alternatively, she could explain that all members of the class, and indeed the school, come from different kinds of families with one or more parents/carers, members of an extended family and others. Highlighting shared differences would provide a sufficient answer without any need for her to share other personal information.

John is the coordinator of a Foundation Stage Unit in a large primary school, working with children aged 3–5 years. He has two children, both of whom attend Key Stage 2 classes in the same school. They live with his ex-wife, and he now lives with his partner, Jack. John knows that older children in the school are aware that he is gay and, as far as he can tell, his own children do not receive any adverse comments about this. Parents, carers, staff and governors in the school know that John has a civil partner and several attended the ceremony two years ago.

This term, the children have been exploring the topic of 'Our Homes'. John has spoken about how his children stay with him and with Jack each weekend and sometimes during school holidays. Several children in the class also visit a parent at the weekends because their birth parents have separated.

Consider:

- how it is possible to discuss the topic of Our Homes or Our Families in an inclusive way, which recognizes that there are many patterns of family relationship;
- whether children in a Foundation Stage Unit will be aware of same-sex relationships to help them appreciate John's home life; and
- to what extent should practitioners share their own life experiences and circumstances with children in their classes.

The topic of Our Homes has been a staple in primary schools for many years, particularly with younger children. It is essential for practitioners to ensure that they do not give stereotypical representations relating to this topic, and to consider carefully how their own home backgrounds might colour their presentation of the materials. As already noted in this chapter, children come from a wide variety of models of family life. It is important to ensure that this variety is represented in the stories, picture books and other materials that are included in the classroom. Children will be aware of a variety of types of family from the broadcast media, including soap operas, and so practitioners will not be introducing new ideas to children; rather, they will be including representations of the world that would seem strange to omit. One means of identifying materials to support this approach can be found in the *Family Diversities Reading Resource*, details of which are included at the end of this chapter. This collection of over 150 high-quality children's picture books, for learners across all ages in primary schools, provides a comprehensive sample of some of the resources available to schools.

If John chooses to speak to the children about his partner, doing this in the same matter-of-fact way that other colleagues may speak about their partners should not cause any issue. It is more likely that several of the children are aware of John's partner and his children and that they may find it unusual if he does not speak about them. Once again, the choice is John's, and his personal comfort and his own boundaries of privacy should be the guiding factor. The fact that his children have more than two parents will be a fact appreciated and understood by some of the children in his class, as will the experience of living between two homes.

Using the case of Christina, outlined at the beginning of this chapter, consider:

- whether it is appropriate for a practitioner working with children to cross the boundary between the personal and the professional;
- how Christina and her colleagues might work with children to build on this experience or use it in the future with others; and
- how a real-life context can enhance the learning and understanding of children.

Experiential learning can be a very effective way for children to develop and to deepen their knowledge and understanding: it can offer a real-life context which builds on an introduction provided in the classroom. The children who attended Christina's wedding were able to put into context one example of how a marriage ceremony is conducted, which moved their discussions in the classroom from the abstract level of role play and using books to actually seeing, hearing and feeling the real event. The fact that the children sang during the signing of the marriage register added to their involvement and made the event all the more special. It is interesting to note that Christina included the children in the public ceremony but not in the more personal wedding reception, which was a celebration for family and friends. This maintained a personal–professional balance with which both she and her partner were comfortable. This case study offers one example, and is certainly not intended to suggest that teachers should invite children to attend out of school events. Although, in this instance, Christina was able to follow up the event by showing the children a selection of photographs from the wedding, some of which included themselves, and discussing their feelings and what they had learned from attending. She did this sensitively in order to make sure that all her learners were included, as not all were able to attend.

Jennifer has recently returned to school following a period of compassionate leave. Her husband died suddenly, aged thirty-seven, after ten years of marriage:

> I was not looking forward to coming back to school. I needed some time off after the funeral in order to sort some things out and to begin to come to terms with Rakesh's death. It had all been so sudden and it was such a shock that I did not feel in any fit state to be in charge of a class. Returning to work was a huge step. I was worried that there would be questions from both children and colleagues and that the expressions of sympathy, particularly from the children, would be too much for me to bear.

Consider:

- how colleagues could help to make Jenny's return to work smooth and help the children to respond appropriately;
- how she might respond to children's questions about her husband's death, including those in relationships lessons where children might ask about her feelings; and
- how the school might best support Jenny in the coming weeks when she should be leading the delivery of a series of lessons on Relationships Education.

Jenny's situation may provide some children with their first encounter with loss and grief. While they may not have known her husband, they may feel some sense of sadness for the loss she has experienced. Some of these children may not know how to respond, and will not have any past experience upon which to draw. It can be possible for them to overreact, showing behaviours that they feel should be exhibited, possibly influenced by media representations of grief (Woolley, 2010). Other children will react because the loss makes them think of their own family and brings the implication that they too could lose a parent or sibling at some point. This latter aspect may be one of the first times that a child has encountered the fact that relationships can end suddenly and sometimes unexpectedly.

Practitioners can create the opportunity to reflect on ideas and to feel the sense of the moment. At times, words are inadequate and feelings are too complex and immediate to express. Allowing space for silence – and sharing silence together – can help both adults and children to gain a sense of being together which brings a sense of security and wholeness in difficult times (Woolley, 2010). These times also provide the opportunity for adults to model the sharing of feelings and to acknowledge that they do not have all the answers (Adams et al., 2008). Such times need careful structuring, with an introduction to explain to children what they are for, a focus (e.g.

lighting a candle or listening to music) and a clear ending with the possibility of an opportunity to respond in some way (by making a card, writing thoughts to share in a 'feelings box' or planting bulbs as a memorial) (Jewett, 1984). These strategies can work in a variety of settings, and are by no means exhaustive. It may be appropriate to provide such a structured opportunity as making a card or a small gift a vehicle for any children who wish to express their feelings to Jenny in some way. Practitioners can then explain that having made this gesture it is important to allow Jenny to return to work with as much of a sense of the normal routine of the classroom as possible, and to help the children to consider how they will support this.

Janine reflects on her own experience of growing up and how this affects the ways in which she can relate to the children in her Year 4 class:

> I did not have a particularly happy childhood myself. My parents used to argue a great deal and latterly their anger turned into physical aggression. I used to lay awake at night listening to them and occasionally I saw them hitting each other. Eventually I was taken into public care and stayed with various families before my grandparents agreed to take care of me. I stayed with them in the holidays between terms at a boarding school from the ages of nine to eighteen. I find it very difficult to talk about home life and families with the children in my Year 4 class, because I cannot identify with the experiences that the children share. They talk about family holidays, days out and special birthdays and celebrations and I feel that I missed out on all of that myself. I do have a wonderful partner and we have a lovely home, but until I have children of my own I am not sure that I can empathize with the children's experiences of family life.

Consider:

- whether Janine's past experience need impact on her teaching;
- how she might focus on her current happy experience as a source of stories to share with the children, as she feels appropriate; and
- whether Janine's experience might help her to empathize with other children whose home life is not idyllic.

Janine's situation is distinctive in many ways, but it highlights some key issues for consideration. All practitioners bring a degree of what might be termed *baggage* to the teaching of RSE. This is an inevitable part of how life's experiences shape our views and values. The significant factor here is that she is aware of this fact and therefore more likely to take her own feelings into account when trying to deliver ideas in a balanced an open way. This is a stronger position to be in than if she was not so self-aware. There is no need for Janine to share personal experiences with the class; rather she can be open to listen to the children's ideas and stories and can use her expertise in asking questions in order to develop discussion. It may be that, in fact, this provides her with the opportunity to ensure that the focus is on child-focused talk rather than teacher talk.

Janine's concerns also highlight another significant issue. If the discussion of homes and families in a classroom always include idyllic tales of daily life, children whose experience does not reflect this may wonder why their home life does not live up to the model shared in the classroom. Indeed, to discuss family relationships without acknowledging that sometimes all people disagree, argue or find one another frustrating would be to paint a false picture that lacks realism. This area of relationships has already been highlighted in Chapter 3. The logical conclusion from Janine's concerns is that one cannot teach anything that one has not experienced personally. Clearly this is not the case, and with a focus on enabling the children to discuss, to learn from one another and to find out from a variety of sources she will ensure that the emphasis is on the children's learning rather than her teaching. This is a model for good practice.

Reflecting on the range of situations outlined in this chapter so far, consider:

- how your experiences, whether as a practitioner, student or previously as a child, affect your views on the ways in which RSE should be approached;
- what other issues and areas you think it will be useful to consider with colleagues before embarking on a series of lessons focusing on RSE; and
- what sources of advice you will draw on before tackling issues which cause you some concern or apprehension.

Having effective resources supports effective RSE and can assist in providing a relevant framework to discuss relationships and sex. One resource which will support children's discussions about conception, pregnancy and birth is Babette Cole's *Mummy Laid an Egg* (1995), to which we will return in the final chapter. This amusing book shows two parents explaining to their twins where children come from, including being found under a stone, being made from sugar and spice and exploding out of an egg! The twins are amused by their parents' misconceptions and begin to elaborate the real way in which they came into being. Using characteristically humorous illustrations, the children show that they know about sexual intercourse and are aware that it can be great fun.

This book would provoke discussion with children about where babies come from. The fact that it shows children who know this information, apparently teaching parents who do not, offers an unusual and accessible way into the subject. The simple drawings outline the mechanics of sexual intercourse to add information within a broader context of a loving and caring relationship. The content can be adapted and interpreted by practitioners in order to develop its age-appropriateness.

Accounting for the views of parents/carers and other stakeholders

Parents and carers have the right to withdraw their children from sex education in England. This is not a right for the child, but for their primary carer(s). It need not be for the entire programme being delivered by the school; the parent/carer can, for example, ask that the child attend lessons about conception but not about contraception.

This opt-out provides an interesting situation for the child. They will be excluded from all or part of an experience that is available to their peers and will, no doubt, learn about what they have missed through conversations with friends and with others on the playground as discussed further in Chapter 4. Parents and carers may have the ability and the right to withdraw their child(ren) from formal lessons, but more informal learning is much more difficult – and perhaps impossible – to control.

Maria and Stuart have a daughter in a Year 6 class. Recently the school invited parents and carers to an open evening to view materials that were going to be used in relationships and sex lessons. Some of the materials included information about the use of various means of contraception and some accounts from young men and women about their feelings on becoming parents aged fourteen and fifteen years. As practising Roman Catholics, Maria and Stuart do not use contraception and they do not want their daughter to be taught about this issue:

We might be seen as having quite traditional views, but the Church is about tradition and it is important that some of the more promiscuous and permissive aspects of modern day society do not undermine the traditional teachings of the Church. We appreciate that some people use

> *contraception and that it can help to avoid unwanted pregnancy and even stop the transmission of sexually transmitted diseases. But our faith tell us that sex is to be enjoyed by a man and a woman who are married, and our hope for our daughter is that she will wait to enjoy that special first time with her husband and that they will only ever have sexual intercourse with one another. We know that this is not the norm in society today, but for us it is the only option and the one that our religion tells us is the best.*

Consider:

- how a teacher might speak with Maria and Stuart to consider whether withdrawing their daughter from parts of the RSE provision is the most effective way;
- how a school's RSE provision might help children to consider a variety of approaches to relationships and sex, including abstinence from sexual intercourse, an informed choice to use/not to use contraception and about waiting for a committed relationship before sexual debut; and
- how Maria and Stuart might speak with their daughter prior to and after the delivery of RSE in school (whether or not she attends) to make sure that her learning is supported and that she does not receive misinformation on the playground.

Maria and Stuart's concerns are very genuine and stem from deeply held convictions. It is important for practitioners to emphasize that their views and wishes are understood and appreciated. It is important to explain to them that they have the right to request that their daughter be excused from some or all aspects of sex education provision. However, they also need to consider how they will explain this to their daughter in a way that means that she understands that their decision is meant to be a positive one. They also need to consider what alternative explanations they will provide, and how they will prepare her for the post-lesson conversations that will inevitably take place on the school playground.

An alternative approach might be for their daughter to attend the lessons in school, with Maria and Stuart being fully aware of the content of the materials having viewed them at the open evening, and for them then to speak with her that evening to explain that some people have different views. The school might also acknowledge in the lesson that different views about the use of contraception exist and that people make choices based on their beliefs and values. Significantly, it will be useful to discuss how children gain the information they need in order to make informed personal choices as they grow and mature. While Maria and Stuart will hope that their daughter will grow up in the faith which they hold dear, she also needs wider perspectives and understandings in order to make her own choices. It is also important that teaching about contraception is realistic and makes clear that it is not a fail-safe way of avoiding pregnancy; to infer otherwise would be to misinform children.

The Sex Education Forum suggests that in effective consultation with parents and carers on matters relating to RSE, practitioners should

- not expect reciprocated respect until trust is established;
- be prepared to use the skills of professional empathy;
- be prepared to listen to contradictory and hostile opinions and attitudes without feeling personally challenged;
- be prepared with a coherent explanation of your value's framework and how these relate to the wider context of the school mission and ethos;
- recognise that discussion of core values can support positive dialogue and be proactive in exploring values and their meaning;
- feel confident enough to explain that faith perspectives will be included as a part of the continuum of perspectives which also contain the teaching of equality, freedom from discrimination and individual rights. (2004: 3)

These points provide an effective basis on which to develop dialogue with parents and carers, governors and colleagues where religious beliefs and values are a significant consideration. It is important to avoid hostility and to understand that consensus is not always possible. Disagreement is not a sign of failure and ideally all parties will come away from consultations feeling that their views have been heard and appreciated.

One aspect of RSE which Maria and Stuart's concerns highlight is the relationship between the sexual and the spiritual development of children. This is a neglected area of discussion. A primary aim of the National Curriculum in England (DfE, 2014: 5) is to promote the 'spiritual, moral, cultural, mental and physical' development of children. There was a single reference to the contribution of RSE to the first two of these aspects in the SRE guidance (DfEE, 2000), although interestingly to all aspects in the RSE guidance (DfE, 2018). Spirituality is difficult to define and can be dismissed as being vague, ethereal or unquantifiable. However, for many people the interconnectedness between people is a spiritual aspect of life. This can include connections relating to sexuality. Indeed, it involves a consideration of the whole person, rather than separating them into elements such as body, mind and spirit. Part of a child's development as a whole person is a growing sense of their own sexuality and sexual identity. This involves a deepening understanding of self as well as an awareness of, and relationship to, others. For some readers this is implicit to spiritual development as another facet of the development of the whole person.

Gemma returned to school after the summer break as Miss Morrison. Having engaged in protracted but positive discussions with both the head teacher and chair of governors over several months, she felt able to begin to live as a woman full time in order to start the process of gender reassignment. The head agreed that, in due course, time off could be arranged for surgery to take place, although some of it would need to be taken as unpaid leave. The main thing for Gemma was to begin to live as the woman she knew she had been for the past twenty-nine years:

My main concern was how the parents would react to me. I had considered changing school in order to have a fresh start, but I have been very happy in this school for several years and felt that starting again might leave me more isolated. I think I have been a popular teacher and my results certainly show that my work is effective. Having sounded out a couple of colleagues, who are close friends, I felt that members of staff would be generally supportive of me. The main obstacle was to face any prejudice or opposition from parents and carers. While telling my own parents of the change had been a major event in my life, the thought of telling those without a close and loving link to me was daunting to put it mildly.

Consider:

- what, if anything, teachers might say to their classes in order to make Miss Morrison's experience positive and welcoming;
- how colleagues can show their support for and acceptance of their colleague; and
- what strategies might be used in order to address any questions from children, without making an issue of, or intruding into, Gemma's situation.

First, it is important to assert Gemma's legal position. The Gender Recognition Act (2004) came into force in April 2005 and allowed trans people to seek full legal recognition of their gender identity. It allowed trans people to apply, through the Gender Recognition Panel, for a gender recognition certificate. This meant that they had the same legal rights and responsibilities as associated with their gender identity. In addition, the Equality Bill (2009)

requires public authorities to make attempts to improve the equality of opportunities between transsexuals and non-transsexuals; and to eliminate transphobic discrimination and harassment towards, not only transsexuals, but those associated with them such as friends and family, those who might have a different type of transgender or intersex identity and those who are perceived to be transsexual. (Barry, 2002)

The subsequent Equality Act (2010) ensures that employers must be more explicit in their promotion of fair practice for trans people.

Second, the school needs to consider how it will ensure that Gemma's continuing employment is supported. Practitioners can play a key role by modelling fair and accepting behaviours and by making sure that any negative attitudes or comments from adults or children are addressed both promptly and clearly. Should Gemma or her employer need advice or support they can access a range of organizations, including the Equality and Human Rights Commission (www.equalityhumanrights. com). It is likely that the children in Gemma's school will be the most accepting and adaptable stakeholders, and that the concerns of others about how they will respond to her situation will be relatively unfounded. Explaining to learners that some people identify with a gender different to that assigned at birth and change their identity in order to address this can provide a clear and concise way of acknowledging the change without needing to provide extended or detailed information. Children will be aware of other situations when teachers return to school with a new name or identity. They may have had to get used to calling a teacher by their married name, or have encountered a change of name following divorce or for other reasons. The fact that identities can change for a variety of reasons may help teachers to explain Miss Morrison's new name. Linking to children's existing experience in this way can help to develop understanding in an age-appropriate way.

Difficult questions from children often come at unexpected moments about the complexities and dimensions of different relationships, including those with self. This is possible on the school playground, in the sports or youth club or in an informal moment when attending a uniformed organization. Outside of a formal learning setting, such as a school, a child's language may be more colloquial and, perhaps, their question will be expressed in a more direct manner. Sometimes children can find the school setting restrictive and, while understanding the protocols of formal education, find that this is not quite the right place to ask the question most on their mind.

Jason is a youth worker, leading a club for 7–12-year-olds in a small town in the East Midlands of England. He recounts a recent experience:

I have been working in the youth club for about three years, having started here after a youth work degree at university. Although I have had a range of training including the safeguarding of children, child protection and child development, I was totally thrown when Jacob (aged 10) initiated a conversation a few weeks ago.

We were washing plates and cups after supper and I could tell that Jacob was not his normal humorous self. When I asked what was on his mind he said, 'It is so embarrassing, but I guess I have got to tell someone. My mind is totally buzzing with what my brother, Reuben, said last week. He is always lying to me. But this time it has got in my head. He said that if I wank too much [a colloquial word for masturbation] I will go blind, and if I don't go blind I will use up all my sperm and not be able to have children if I get married. And he said that if I do get married I will probably not be able to have sex with my wife anyway because I prefer doing it by myself.'

Consider:

- how Jason might respond to Jacob's question;
- how common myths about masturbation might worry boys and young men and how such myths can be addressed; and
- how peer pressure from older children can introduce misconceptions and concerns for those who are younger.

Jason reflects on his own response to Jacob's worries:

I have been thinking how I handled the conversation with Jacob. On reflection, I am not sure that I used the right language. He talked about 'wanking' and I used that word when I talked to him about how it is not harmful. Well, I told him that it does not do any physical harm but explained that if he gets into it too much it might affect how he enjoys being with a partner in the future: he might like things the way he does them rather than how it is with them. I am now worried that I should have used more formal language, but that would have felt odd to me because I used the same words that he did. I never use the proper words when I am talking to friends, but I know that he was talking to me as a professional and not a friend. I also wish I had told him that his brother is probably making up stories: Reuben (aged 12) was probably trying to make Jacob embarrassed, and it worked.

Consider:

- how you respond to Jason's use of familiar and colloquial language when responding to Jacob;
- whether you feel his response was supportive and collegial, or inappropriate and unprofessional; and
- whether Jason should follow up the conversation in order to develop a more professional tone.

Jason's case, above, shows how an informal situation can prove to be difficult. He has mirrored a child's language in his response, which has probably been comprehensible to the child and has reflected his own culture. To use more formal language might have caused confusion and would have felt uncomfortable for both parties. However, Jason also has a professional role to maintain and this adds an extra dimension to the scenario. It is important to consider whether it is his role to introduce, explain and use formal terms (such as *masturbation*). Jason will need to consider whether to raise this matter again with Jacob, and what tone to take if he does. He explained that he does not wish to speak to their parents, as this would cause embarrassment for both boys. However, he is uncomfortable about his use of informal language.

Consider:

- whether Jason should speak to the parents of Jacob and Reuben;
- if this is a private matter between Jacob and Jason which should go no further;
- whether Jason should develop a more formal/professional discussion with Jacob; and
- how Jason could offer guidance and support to either boy.

In the next section there is a consideration of a range of matters relating to RSE with children who have SENs and disabilities. This can be a particular area of concern for adults, whether parents/carers or professionals, as there can be a clear and significant need to consider age-appropriateness and also very clear and direct language in order to make sure that learning is effective.

Approaching RSE with children with special educational needs and disabilities

Discussing issues about growing up, sexuality and sexual practices with children who have special educational needs (SEN) or disabilities requires sensitivity and sometimes necessitates that parents, carers and practitioners are very clear in their use of language and in the detail which they present (Sex Education Forum, 2004). This can cause some concern for such adults as they seek to provide clear information which will help to support the child or young person. This concern is the reason why this material is included in a chapter which focuses on the views and approaches of adults.

The Special Educational Needs Code of Practice (DfE and DfH, 2015) stresses the need to consult children with learning difficulties and SEN. This is true of all aspects of their learning, including RSE. Practitioners need to consider carefully how they will elicit the views and questions of children with particular needs so that these can be accounted for when planning programmes of study (for ideas to support such developments, see DfES, 2003; and National Healthy School Standard, 2004). While it is impossible here to explore a wide variety of issues, two key examples serve to illustrate how RSE may be approached with children who have a variety of needs and to suggest aspects of good practice that can be applied to other situations.

Children on the autistic spectrum

Children and young people on the autistic spectrum can have a variety of needs which relate to relationships and communication. At times, this can cause adults some anxiety about their isolation from others, as they are mainly concerned with their own interests (which some may term as *obsessions*) and do not have well developed skills in relating to others. While this may be a familiar scenario for those experienced with children on the autistic spectrum, those children reaching puberty can sometimes begin to focus on their own sexual needs and desires without the people skills to understand that place, time and location are key elements of exploring oneself and one's ideas.

For example, a child in one class was fascinated with superhero comics. His teacher themed his work so that she could maintain his interest in a range of curriculum areas and classroom activities. Such an approach is common and capitalizes on the young person's interest in order to engage them with learning. However, as he began to mature physically and to reach puberty, his interest began to change and to focus very significantly on masturbation. It proved necessary to speak with him in clear terms to make sure that he understood that this was something to be undertaken in private and not in the classroom. While it was important to explain that masturbation can be enjoyable and is engaged in by most boys and young men before and during puberty, and beyond, the personal and private nature of the pleasure had to be emphasized in order to avoid embarrassing other children, staff and other adults. This is important in order to encourage social behaviour which would avoid any other inappropriate public activity.

Preparing for change is a critical part of supporting a child or young person on the autistic spectrum. This includes preparing for the onset of puberty, which for any young person can be an unsettling, confusing and emotionally stressful time. Explaining the changes that will begin, outlining that they are a normal and healthy part of growing up and being willing to address a significant number of *why* questions are all a part of supporting this process. For practitioners it is important to speak with parents and carers to ensure that a collaborative approach is being taken. It is also key to address a child's questions, perhaps making clear when one does not have the answers or when the setting in which the question is asked necessitates that it is returned to later. The content of lessons needs to be considered carefully so that information overload is avoided. It may also be necessary to return to information, perhaps on several occasions, in order for it to be processed by the child. Using visual or interactive materials may also help to support learning (e.g. online materials provided by the BBC are highlighted at the end of this chapter). The consolidation of learning, its pace, allowing plenty of opportunity for questions and including visual elements within the learning will all be aspects to consider when planning for the appropriate provision of RSE. These strategies will also help to enhance the quality of provision for all children.

Children with a visual impairment

A great deal of a child's understanding about sexuality is derived from visual sources, for example, the broadcast and print media and observing those around them. For a child with a visual impairment these avenues may not be available. It may be that they learn about their developing sexuality through the feelings within their own body, which at times may happen in inappropriate locations. Privacy is an abstract concept for someone who cannot see. Thus it is important to stress that personal touch, including masturbation, is kept for the privacy of one's own room (or perhaps the bathroom at home if the child shares with a brother or sister).

Responding sensitively to inappropriate non-private expressions of sexuality is important in order to maintain a child's sense of self-esteem. It is not that the child is exploring in any way different to or more frequent than their peers, it is just that they are less aware of the need for privacy.

Materials developed by the Scottish Sensory Centre (Sweeting, 1998) provide an overview of some of the enduring key elements to consider when exploring RSE with children who are visually impaired:

- The responsibility for gradual, appropriate teaching of human sexuality for pupils who are visually impaired must be shared between parents, teachers and other key workers.
- Programmes of study designed for sighted children often assume that a large amount of visual information has been received. Pupils who are visually impaired may require specific information taught by appropriate, well informed, well prepared professionals.
- A pupil who is visually impaired needs to experience a programme of study which is conceptually orientated. Misconceptions can arise because of the lack of opportunity to reinforce and/or modify initial understanding with a variety of visual experiences. Careful discussion will often reveal a lack of basic understanding as a result of incomplete

or misinterpreted information, in young people who converse using sophisticated terminology.

- The pupil who is visually impaired has a right to the programme of study designed for the whole school population. Certain adaptations may have to be made to ensure the pupil who is visually impaired benefits to the full from those curriculum experiences. This could include the provision of alternatives to visual media as well as opportunities for sensitive discussion.
- It is very important that the attitudes and emotions surrounding the pupils' sexuality at all stages of their development, are taken into account.
- Gender identity, reproduction processes, sexual and social issues, including health and safety, must be included, in relation to individual pupil need and local authority [and school] policy.

Consider:

- what additional needs and provision do these points identify;
- to what extent does sexuality use visual stimuli and body language;
- how might a person with a visual impairment be enabled to develop other skills;
- how can a sense of both place and privacy be nurtured so that behaviours are appropriate;
- what alternatives to visual materials might be developed; and
- what elements do these guidelines provide to support best practice for all children.

Children with a visual impairment will need particular support to develop independence as they mature. They need to understand the difference between appropriate and inappropriate touching by others especially, for example, as they may not be able to identify from whom the touch comes. A visual impairment can give a sense of isolation at times, and this can be compounded in uncomfortable or unpleasant circumstances. Providing clear strategies to deal with stranger danger and situations which cause discomfort is essential.

On a practical level, girls will need to have sanitary products that are accessible (e.g. it may be useful to have a draw-string bag rather than a packet which needs to be torn open), to know where an appropriate place is to use them and where to dispose of them. Both boys and girls will need clear guidelines so that they know the appropriate places to change for PE and how to get changed (as they do not necessarily have visual cues from others on what to take off and what to wear). Such planning will help to develop independence; readers will want to consider the ways in which they can help to promote this with children with particular needs in their settings.

Developing a positive sense of self is an essential part of effective RSE. It is important that the information, advice and support offered by adults enable the development of self-confidence and self-esteem. This is true for all children and particularly for those with a visual impairment. Schools have a duty to 'ensure that there are no barriers to every pupil achieving' (DfE, 2014: 8). This necessitates that where RSE is delivered, it is tailored to the particular needs of individual learners.

What about childhood innocence?

Finally, we now turn to a major concern expressed by adults: that RSE will take away children's innocence. This was introduced in the previous chapter. However, the question may not be whether children are too innocent to consider such issues, or whether they need to be protected from life's challenges, but whether adults seek to protect children in order to protect themselves. Do adults avoid discussing complex issues in order to protect their own sensibilities or hide their lack of knowledge (Adams et al., 2008)? This is an aspect of RSE that warrants careful consideration and personal reflection.

As outlined in Chapter 4, the idea that children are innocent and must be protected from difficult issues is hard to maintain (Erricker, 2003), particularly given the influence of the media and the banter of the playground or school yard (Adams et al., 2008). In addition, as is explored in several places within this book, the fear that early RSE will encourage young people to start exploring their sexuality prematurely appears to be unwarranted (Sandford et al., 1998). On the contrary, as was explored in Chapter 4, studies have shown that sex education seems to have a slight delaying effect on the age at first intercourse (Mellanby et al., 1995; Wellings et al., 1995) and to increase the rate of contraceptive use at first intercourse markedly (Aggleton et al., 1993; Greydanus et al., 1995).

This emphasizes the importance of good RSE in primary schools, for if children are enabled to explore issues of sexuality before puberty, or at its onset, they are supported in making effective and positive choices affecting their own behaviours once they have the ability to be sexually active. To leave such matters until later in their development may be too late. Leaving children's questions unanswered fails to support or nurture their knowledge, skills or understanding of such matters. To replace concerns about childhood innocence with childhood ignorance is counter intuitive and can result in teenage regret.

Summary of key approaches to support effective practice

In order to develop effective practice it is important to

- support parents and carers and to provide opportunities for them to discuss the scope and content of RSE provision with practitioners in the learning setting;
- ensure that school policies are clear, positive, inclusive and in line with current legislation;
- consider how to address issues arising from particular learning needs, religious beliefs and other personal factors when planning for RSE;
- explore how RSE can enable children and young people to explore a variety of choices and to make informed decisions based on high-quality information;
- acknowledge that RSE is an area which raises genuinely felt concerns, which need to be explored with sensitivity;
- appreciate people's misapprehensions and nervousness about RSE (whether colleagues, parents/carers or other stakeholders in the school) and be prepared to invest time in exploring these and offering support.

Conclusion and summary of key learning points

This chapter has explored a range of difficult issues related to the multiple dimensions of intimate relationships encountered by practitioners and others involved in and with schools. It has raised some concerns that may be felt by parents and carers. While the exploration of issues is not exhaustive, it has provided some strategies to help to support the development of positive, caring and fair settings which create supportive and safe learning environments for both staff and children.

A recurring issue throughout the chapter has been the balance between the professional and the personal. Inevitably this is a matter for personal consideration, but this can only be achieved when a school supports the decisions of its members. There should be no requirement to answer personal questions and no expectation that one's own experience will contribute overtly to teaching. This said, who one is, one's past experiences and one's past and current circumstances will all inform how RSE is managed. Being self-aware can help to foster a balanced and positive approach to learning. As professionals, the development of an open and enquiring attitude to the RSE is fundamental to supporting the future well-being of learners.

Signposts

How It Is: an image vocabulary for children, called 'Howitis', about feelings, rights and safety, personal care and sexuality developed by the NSPCC and Triangle. www.triangle.org.uk/resource-categories/downloads?page_resource-category_downloads=2.

Materials from the BBC showing physical changes associated with puberty. www.bbc.co.uk/science/humanbody/body/index.shtml?lifecycle.

Neela Doležalová, a playwright and teacher, has recently been awarded an UnLtd 'Do It Award' to create a series of drama resources for schools called 'ConveRSE'. These resources, created with young people, will use verbatim theatre to explore key topics within the RSE curriculum. Neela tweets @dolezalova.

Further reading

Woolley, R., and Morris, J. (2008) *Family Diversities Reading Resource* (2nd edn). Lincoln: Bishop Grosseteste University and University of Worcester. A resource of over 150 quality picture books to value a broad range of children's families. http://libguides.bishopg.ac.uk/childrensliterature.

Woolley, R., and Morris, J. (2010) *Transitions Reading Resource*. Lincoln: Bishop Grosseteste University College. A resource of over 100 quality children's picture books exploring a wide variety of changes and transitions in children's lives, including death and bereavement, the birth of sibling, changes to family life. http://libguides.bishopg.ac.uk/ld.php?content_id=2454445 https://www.bera.ac.uk/blog/the-talk-a-play-to-get-adults-talking-about-relationship-and-sex-education.

References

Adams, K., Hyde, B., and Woolley, R. (2008) *The Spiritual Dimension of Childhood*. London: Jessica Kingsley.

Aggleton, P., Baldo, M., and Slutkin, G. (1993) 'Sex Education Leads to Safer Behaviour'. *Global AIDS News*, 4, 1–20.

Barry, P. (2002) *Beginning Theory: An Introduction to Literary and Cultural Theory* (revised edn). Manchester: Manchester University Press.

Department for Education (2014) *National Curriculum*. London: Department for Education.

Department for Education (2018) *Relationships Education, Relationships and Sex Education (RSE) and Health Education: Guidance for Governing Bodies, Proprietors,*

Head Teachers, Principals, Senior Leadership Teams, Teachers. London: Department for Education.

Department for Education and Department for Health (2015) *Special Educational Needs and Disability Code of Practice: 0–25 Years*. London: Department for Education.

Department for Education and Employment (2000) *Sex and Relationship Education Guidance*. Nottingham: DfEE.

Department for Education and Skills (2003) *Working Together: Giving Children and Young People a Say*. London: Department for Education and Skills.

Erriker, C. (2003) 'Against the Protection of Childhood Innocence'. *International Journal of Children's Spirituality*, 8 (1), 3–7.

Greydanus, D., Pratt, H., and Dannison, L. (1995) 'Sexuality Education Programs for Youth: Current State of Affairs and Strategies for the Future'. *Journal of Sex Education and Therapy*, 4, 238–54.

Jewett, C. (1984) *Helping Children Cope with Separation and Loss*. London: Batsford Academic and Educational and British Agencies for Adoption and Fostering.

Mellanby, A. R., Phelps, F. A., Crichton, N. J., and Tripp, J. H. (1995) 'School Sex Education: An Experimental Programme with Educational and Medical Benefit'. *British Medical Journal*, 311, 414–17.

National Healthy School Standard (2004) *Promoting Participation*. London: Department for Education and Skills.

Sandford, T., Hubert, M., Bajos, N., and Bos, H. (1998) 'Sexual Behaviour and HIV Risk', in *Sexual Behaviours and HIV/AIDS in Europe*, ed. M. Hubert, N. Bajos and T. Sandford. London: UCL Press.

Sex Education Forum (2004) *Sex and Relationships Education for Children and Young People with Learning Difficulties*. Forum Factsheet 32. London: National Children's Bureau and Sex Education Forum.

Sweeting, J. (1998) *5–12 years (VI) – Personal and Social Education: Framework and Methodology with Particular Attention to Sex Education*. www.ssc.education.ed.ac.uk/resources/vi&multi/jsweeting98.html (accessed 4 October 2018).

Wellings, K., Wadsworth, J., Johnson, A., Field, J., Whitaker, L., and Field, B. (1995) 'Provision of Sex Education and Early Sexual Experience: The Relation Examined'. *British Medical Journal*, 311, 417–20.

Woolley, R. (2010) *Tackling Controversial Issues in the Primary School: Facing Life's Challenges with Your Learners*. London: Routledge.

6

Children's development and needs

The right to education includes the right to sexual education, which is both a human right in itself and an indispensable means of realising other human rights, such as the right to health, the right to information and sexual and reproductive rights.
– Report to the UN General Assembly, July 2010, item 69, para. 18

Chapter outline

Introduction

This chapter explores notions of age-appropriate Relationships Education and RSE, drawing on areas identified through the 15 Domains of Healthy Sexual Development (developed by the RSE Hub from McKee et al., 2010). It considers the challenges that those working with children in a range of contexts may face in developing a staged approach to Relationships Education and RSE, and how a structured, spiral curriculum of content can be developed from the early years, dovetailing with the curriculum for secondary education. Issues of the need for relevant content within a current context that is rich in media are investigated alongside evidence from research. It discusses the challenges that children and adults face in navigating the internet and particularly aspects of social media.

An aspiration of a twenty-first-century education system, according to the National Curriculum for England (2014), is that it affords children and young people the opportunity to learn the 'essential knowledge' (DfE, 2014: 6) for them to be educated citizens. This aim and aspiration is arguably commonplace across the developed world and is unquestionably one of the core principles for a state education system. The difficulties lie in what is deemed 'essential knowledge' and at what age or stage should children have access and a right to sexual education, as the report to the UN General Assembly, detailed in the vignette at the start of this chapter, outlines. The commitment to RSE concerning the realization of other human rights and the right to information has particular resonance for the issues discussed in this chapter.

A primary concern for many adults working with children and young people is what is developmentally appropriate to teach and discuss with children. This concern is especially so for Relationships Education and RSE and is fundamentally influenced by societal, community, setting, personal values and beliefs. The notion of appropriate discussions with children and young people about sexual matters is a consideration for those who work in formal and informal education settings and the wider sector. This chapter seeks to offer some insight into the issues and decisions that adults face within current and changing contexts. An overriding commitment, as part of this discussion, is that children have a right to sexual education, along with healthy, respectful and fulfilling relationships with self and others.

The context for what is developmentally appropriate

The onset of puberty

According to the BBC (Silver, 2018) the average age for children starting puberty in the UK is ten. Kelly et al. (2017) report that the current expected age for a girl to have her first period is 12.9 years. These averages essentially mean that many children experience significant body changes during their years in primary school. Supplementary advice to the government's SRE guidance outlines that children

> are naturally curious about growing up, how their bodies work and how humans reproduce. Their questions need to be answered honestly, using language and explanations appropriate for their age and maturity, thus avoiding unnecessary mystery, confusion, embarrassment and shame. (Brook, PSHE and SEF, 2014: 8)

The curriculum guidance for RSE (DfE, 2017) recommends that primary schools have a graduated RSE programme for the age, physical and emotional maturity of the children. It is made clear that children who develop earlier than expected need to know about puberty before they experience the onset of physical changes. Therefore, a typical and relevant age to begin to discuss physical changes during puberty is in Key Stage 2, between the ages of eight and eleven (School Years 3–6), in order that 'unnecessary mystery, confusion, embarrassment and shame' (Brook et al., 2014: 8) be avoided.

The human body matures through the biological stages of puberty to enable critical changes to occur physically, cognitively, emotionally and socially (Blakemore et al., 2010). Blakemore et al. argue that this maturation stage sees 'dramatic changes in hormonal levels and physical appearance (including rapid physical growth, changes in facial structure, and the appearance of secondary sexual characteristics)' (p. 926). These do not occur over night; rather the process evolves over a period of years and requires 'a stage of profound psychological transition' (p. 926). Blakemore et al. outline that alongside the body and emotional changes, there is a significant change in the structure and function of the brain. The release of hormones as a function of the human endocrine system during puberty means children experience changes in behaviour and self-image. Changes in behaviour may be related to what Blakemore et al. describe as 'sensation-seeking' and adolescent risk taking (p. 930). These are more likely to be linked to puberty than to age.

Therefore, puberty represents a purposeful and complex biological phase and needs clarity and support for children in order to avoid unnecessary mystery or confusion regarding all aspects of their development. In Chapter 7, a case study is shared where a ten-year-old boy, as part of a 'growing-up talk' in school, asks the teacher, 'Why does the penis go hard, what is that all about?' The boy's confusion was clear regarding what these body changes were for. Talking about a stage of biological change whose purpose is for another biological stage and function could be considered an unnecessary mystery. Halstead and Reiss (2003: 3) argue that sex education

> is about human relationships … it is about the private, intimate life of the learner and is intended to contribute to his or her personal development and sense of well-being and fulfilment. It generally involves intense emotions, to do not only with intimacy, pleasure and affection but also with anxiety, guilt and embarrassment.

The understanding that sex education goes beyond biology to include relationships, sexuality, well-being, fulfilment and pleasure adds a critical dimension to the type of RSE that adults wish to talk to children about, which is deeply rooted in values – implicitly and explicitly. These need to be considered when devising a programme of content for children and young people, whether in or out of school. Where the teaching of content beyond the statutory curriculum (Brook, PSHE, and SEF, 2014) is at the discretion of the adult, this allows for freedom and restriction in content in equal measure as discussed in Chapter 1. In this way, a broader RSE curriculum is arguably dependent on an adult's own personal beliefs and what they feel is appropriate, and this often accounts for why 'topics such as pleasure and desire' remain absent from provision (Abbott et al., 2016). Abbott et al., based on their research, discuss how teachers' own RSE concerns directly affect how they view the needs of children and young people in regard to sex education provision. As Halstead and Reiss (2003) outline, sex education is about human relationships and set firmly in the context of personal, professional, religious, school, community and societal values – explicit or inexplicitly. These different value systems may be aligned or at odds with each other, and within this context, the design of a programme for RSE is problematic and complex.

Media access

A layer of complexity is the role of the media. The ready access to information on the internet presents an important context when considering a developmentally appropriate programme of study for RSE. As discussed in Chapter 2, many children have access to the internet through phones and tablets.

Statista (2014) outline that in the UK 63 per cent of girls and 60 per cent of boys between eight and sixteen years ($n = 1,449$) are using smartphones to browse the internet. Fifty-five per cent of children aged between eight and twelve ($n = 593$), in their primary school years, are browsing the internet (Statista, 2014). The individual usage of a mobile phone makes it challenging for adults to oversee the kinds of websites that children access. The availability and ease of access to sexually explicit material via the internet is a twenty-first-century phenomenon, and the widespread access to this sort of material is compounded by the number of children using their own smartphones, which is a distinct difference in the eighteen years since the first 2000 SRE guidance for schools was issued and, indeed, in the six years since the first edition of this book was published.

Bond (2010: 587) argues that the mobile phone is a modern virtual space and replaces the more traditional physical space of the school 'bike shed' – a place and space for the exploration of intimate relationships and sexuality – and suggests that 'the mobile phone is central to understanding children's sexuality and reflexivity in their construction of self-identity' (p. 589), an important element of change during the stage of puberty. This virtual space allows for direct and private communication between peers and access to wider information beyond the physical and relational sources available, such as libraries, parents, families, teachers, youth workers, etc. From a series of focus groups with young people, Bond outlines that

> the mobile phone provides a new space in contemporary children's lives for developing their sexuality, the sharing of and exploration of sexual material and indeed each other's bodies, all factors still largely concealed from the adult world. (2010: 601)

These behaviours are unsurprising and are not necessarily unusual to the twenty-first-century young person; however, the more global capacity of these relationships and the wider extent of access to pornography suggests that these explorations may leave children and young people more vulnerable to inappropriate material and interactions within these virtual spaces. Bond (2010) presents an interesting critique of the role of the mobile phone in children's exploration of intimacy. She discusses how intimacy is somehow threatened by the capacity of how what would be usually seen as the private sharing of the body, thoughts and feelings can quickly become public through social media beyond the traditional parameters of the relationship. The issues of 'sexting' and the sharing of intimacies can make children and young people feel vulnerable and distressed. This can affect their self-confidence and the development of their sexual identities. So-called 'revenge porn', where intimate pictures are shared via social media and the wider internet without consent, can have long-lasting impact on the victim. Recent media attention (BBC, February 2018) has focused on the increasing rise of 'upskirting' – the act of taking an illicit photograph up someone's skirt. While this term is not acknowledged in law, it is covered as an offence under various prosecution jurisdictions; however, the MP Maria Miller states clearly a need for a stronger legal framework to tackle this behaviour (Topping, 2018). The invasion of a person's privacy and the exposure of personal photographs on the internet can significantly affect their well-being and emotional health. The rapidly shifting world of social media, and its capacities and functions can leave children vulnerable. A broad and comprehensive Relationships Education and RSE programme can address some of these issues, where inter-relationship norms and expectations are explored. It can emphasize how respectful relationships are the same whether real or played out in a virtual world.

Safeguarding and being safe

As discussed in Chapter 1, a key driver in the changed curriculum status for RSE is identified as a societal need to safeguard children. In a policy statement in March 2017, the UK government made clear that with the

> increasing concerns around child sexual abuse and exploitation and the growing risks associated with growing up in a digital world, there is a particularly compelling case to act in relation to pupil safety. (DfE, 2017: 2)

While most societies would advocate the safeguarding of children and young people in all areas of life, it has been disappointing that this appears to be the fundamental concern and the driving force for the new statutory status of Relationships Education (primary) and RSE (secondary). Lobbyists such as the PSHE Association, the Sex Education Forum and Brook have campaigned for years that a comprehensive RSE for children contributes to more than the physical safeguarding of children, it allows for a more robust approach to RSE in supporting physical, emotional and social well-being, resilience, self-respect, respect for others and fulfilment.

The need for a broad content in a twenty-first-century RSE curriculum is indicated in research conducted by Lewis and her colleagues (2017) who undertook a survey analyses of the data from three British National Surveys of Sexual Attitudes and Lifestyles, which reported on the increased diversity in heterosexual practices among young people (n = 45,000) aged 16–24 within the timeframe between 1990 and 2010. This empirical context allows for reflection on policy and Lewis et al. argue for society to provide 'culturally sensitive and appropriate sex education' (p. 702) that focuses on relationships, and specifically communication about sexual desires and personal concerns, that promotes mutual respect. An understanding of shifting behavioural trends allows for greater understanding of the different sexual activities that have become normalized practices for adolescents. Where these are normalized within this demographic of the population and accepted as part of a sexual relationship or encounter, then RSE should rightly include these within the curriculum content in order to support sexual well-being. Lewis et al. (2017) report in the surveys analysed regarding heterosexual behaviours that the surveys have shown an increase in the prevalence of oral and anal sex among those in the 16–18-year-old age band. The evidence outlines that vaginal intercourse remains the most prevalent; however, anal and oral sex have joined this as normalized sexual repertoires. The increase in the prevalence of heterosexual men engaging in anal sex has risen substantially, although less so for women. Interestingly, Lewis et al. suggest that the reasons for these changes in sexual behaviours are complex and cannot be solely attributed to the increased availability to pornography:

> Empirical evidence of a causal relationship between exposure to explicit sexual media and sexual behaviour practices remains equivocal and young people's own accounts of anal sex reveal a complex socio-sexual landscape shaping practice, within which pornography is only one feature. (2017: 701)

The disparity between more men engaging in anal sex than women is considered worthy of note in terms of the gendered expectations within relationships and sexual encounters. This is a critical consideration when working with children and young people at all ages to ensure that an RSE programme explicitly supports mutual respect and the importance of consent without coercion.

Research evidence from Marston and Lewis (2014) indicates that 'prominent cultural discourses among teenagers ... normalise painful, sometimes coercive, anal intercourse'. This is corroborated by research in the United States which reports that women are more likely to engage in repeated behaviours in sexual practices that they dislike (e.g. anal sex) than men. Lewis et al. (2017) also cite research that shows a decline in condom use during anal intercourse between heterosexuals. These issues are important considerations for societal, cultural, educational, and health domains to be included as part of a comprehensive RSE programme that is embedded into the early years and primary school curriculum and provides the critical foundations for continued learning at secondary school and beyond in a developmentally appropriate approach. These domains forefront honest communication, respect for others and keeping emotionally and physically safe as part of all healthy relationships. These essential behaviours and characteristics of human relationships can be openly and purposefully discussed from the early years where it is essential that the values of respect and honesty are developed, in order for subsequent learning to have a solid foundation.

The issues raised in this section are compounded when adults are not prepared, or willing, to accept the virtual and real 'spaces' that children occupy. An unwillingness to acknowledge that children have a natural curiosity as sexual beings that may encompass practices beyond those expected by the previous generation who now need to talk to children about these matters, can lead to a disconnect. Bond (2010: 601) argues for a 'more contemporary debate on sexuality in childhood' that can 'contribute to the consideration of the social and cultural constructions of childhood'. The following section of this chapter outlines a developmental hierarchy of concepts that children 3–11 years can explore as part of a comprehensive, broad RSE programme.

Ages and stages?

The Piagetian notion of age-related learning remains the dominant expectation for children's learning in England as part of the National Curriculum. The identification of age phases for when certain concepts need to be taught is helpful in many ways as these can generally be categorized as normative developmental stages where concepts will generally be built sequentially and viewed as a ladder of learning. However, the hierarchy of concepts for RSE is to be viewed both as interconnected and as relatively fluid. The individual knowledge and understanding of the child, alongside their maturity are key considerations in what needs to be discussed with children and when. This is not essentially different from any other curriculum subject. A key indicator for what children feel ready to know and when is through the conversations held with them, both formally and informally. As a primary school teacher or as a parent, it is always astonishing what children will spontaneously ask as they line up for their lunch in the classroom, or are being driven somewhere in the car. These instances can feel out of context although for the child, there has been a trigger of interest worthy of exploration. These questions to adults provide a purposeful insight to the child's level of development and curiosity. A child's question can allow for a meaningful conversation and a starting point for further exploration.

After school, Jack is changing out of his uniform in his bedroom and his mum starts to fold his clothes. They are chatting about their day, and unconnected to the conversation, Jack asks 'What's sex, Mummy?' His mother, Rachel, is somewhat thrown by this question from her seven-year-old son and enquires where he has heard that word. 'In the playground, some of my friends were laughing and talking about sex.' Rachel decides to say, 'Well, it's the special cuddles that mums and dads have to make babies'. Jack seems content with the answer and nothing more was said. Rachel casually asks around her friends who have similar-aged children whether their offspring are asking the same questions. It does not appear that other children are seeking out this same information. This opens conversations between Rachel and her partner about the developmental readiness of Jack and his apparent curiosity.

A few weeks later Jack enquires again, 'Mum, what is sex?' and Rachel repeats the 'special cuddle' response. 'No, mum, what is sex, I want to know.' Rachel realizes that this is a genuine interest shown by her son and that she feels she wants to share more information with him than previously offered. She buys a book that covers all about menstruation, sexual intercourse, conception and childbirth and is presented in a cartoon style of graphic that she feels comfortable with. She tells Jack she wants to sit with him and to share a book that will help her answer his questions, and once Jack's younger brother is safely in bed, she sits with Jack, and over a period of a few weeks they regularly share the book and have discussions about all the issues it raises. Rachel is able to answer all his questions and she allows Jack to explore the book alone and to keep it on his bookshelf in his bedroom for when he wants to return to it.

This case study represents how significant adults in children's lives can support their understanding and development about sexual matters and how questions can be a stimulus and indicator for what children are ready to know. Crucially, Rachel felt able to provide the information that Jack needed and to answer his questions. Reflecting on the case study of Jack, consider whether:

- it is surprising that Jack, at seven years, is asking these sort of questions and seeking knowledge about sexual activity;
- what is positive and productive about this parent's engagement with their child and how might you respond; and
- how you might support Rachel in her quest for purposeful, good-quality picture books to frame her discussions with Jack.

The type of setting in which an adult is working with the child or young person can depend on how this is managed beyond the family home where children are demonstrating a developmental need for information and discussion about relationships and sexual matters. McKee et al. (2010: 15) make clear that there is limited research into what the components of a healthy sexual development are; rather, there is a 'patchwork history of research … which allows us to recover some sense of normal sexual development of children over the years'. As such, McKee and his colleagues have developed a multidisciplinary framework for understanding healthy sexual development which draws on a variety of experts across a number of related backgrounds (e.g. clinical psychology, early childhood studies, family planning). They identify fifteen key domains which are adopted in this chapter to frame the discussion regarding developmental norms for RSE in so far as this can provide a tentative overview of what children and young people may need to learn and know to support a healthy sexual development. The domains are underpinned by research evidence and have been developed by the RSE Hub to establish statements for a manifesto for practitioners of RSE. These statements are not used wholesale for this chapter as some of the content is not for the age range addressed in this book overall; however, the underpinning foundations for each domain are discussed and viewed as the content for the further statements in each domain. It is also worthy of note that these are for guidance and are foregrounded by a series of distinct principles identified by Halstead and Reiss:

- Physical health
- The development of rational sexual autonomy
- Consideration and respect for others
- Children and young people need to be consulted concerning RSE
- Schools and settings need to take account of parental wishes regarding RSE
- Schools and settings should be mindful, of the formal and informal curriculum and teaching alongside their general ethos
- Adults working with children need to consider carefully their own values and have an awareness of the how these are embodied in resources and their discussions as part of this. (2003: 172)

The 15 Domains of Healthy Sexual Development (n.d.) are seen as interconnected and support considerations of the breadth of content that can, indeed, should be part of a RSE curriculum. These are not presented as linear or in any hierarchical order; rather they are viewed as interconnected:

- Respect and understanding of consent
- Understanding of anatomy, physiology, dysfunction, fertility and sexual response

- Ability to maintain safety (legally, physically and emotionally)
- Understand how to achieve, maintain, and negotiate healthy relationships with peers, family, partners and the wider community
- Openness to exploring sexuality, gaining knowledge and asking for help as part of life-long learning
- Celebrate sexuality, pleasure and the joy of sex and healthy relationships
- Understands own values/beliefs and how they impact on decision making and behaviour
- Ability to comprehend, establish and respect boundaries
- Build resilience to be able to manage any unwanted outcomes
- Developing personal skills: Developing an understanding of agency
- Having an awareness of the diversity of sexual behaviour throughout the lifespan
- Appreciation of the diversity of sexual orientations and gender identities
- Understanding of varying gender roles in culture and societies
- Applying critical analysis to media representations
- Developing a positive attitude to their own concept of self.

Developing a comprehensive programme for RSE

Translating these statements from the fifteen domains into a comprehensive RSE programme for children 3–11 years is more straight forward when understood as part of a spiral curriculum that builds content on from one domain to another in an iterative and cyclical way. The work of Newby and Mathieu-Chartier (2017) provides an overview of programme of content for primary-aged children. The clearly identified duplicated areas of content allow for the revision of concepts and knowledge in a way that continually reinforces but equally provides the foundations for further content at each iteration (see Table 6.1).

Newby and Mathieu-Chartier's framework (2017: 93) was developed in collaboration with schools in Warwickshire County Council (WCC; see Table 6.1). The programme was devised by the WCC Respect Yourself Campaign team and was initiated for all maintained primary schools within the county. The programme was taken from an 'SRE fact-finding visit' to the Netherlands and is called Spring Fever and had originally been developed by Rutgers Group, a Dutch Expert Centre (p. 91). The programme design is for one week across all school years as an encapsulated lesson structure where 'Spring Fever aims to have a positive impact on children's knowledge, attitude and skills concerning sexual health' (p. 93).

Table 6.1 Themes covered across the primary school years (Newby and Mathieu-Chartier, 2017: 93)

Reception (age 4–5 years)	Who am I?	What do I feel?	Being naked	I am a boy you are a girl	We are friends
Year 1 (age 5–6 years)	At home	I really like you	How was I born	What feels nice and what doesn't?	How do I say No?
Year 2 (age 6–7 years)	Who am I?	I am a girl you are a boy	What do I feel?	Being naked	Who is special to me?
Year 3 (age 7–8 years)	At home	I really like you	I am in love	How was I born	What feels nice and what doesn't. and How do I say 'no'?
Year 4 (age 8–9 years)	Who am I?	I am a boy you are a girl	Where do babies come from and how are they born?	Boys and girls about one another	Wanted: a friend
Year 5 (age 9–10 years)	Friendship	Being in love	I change during puberty (girl). and I change during puberty (boy)	My relationships	What feels nice and what doesn't. and How do I say 'yes' or 'no'?
Year 6 (age 10–11 years)	Who am I?	Does bare make you blush?	What is sex?	Men and women in the media	Internet friends

Newby and Mathieu-Chartier (2017) report findings from an evaluative study based on the views of children (*n* = 297) across the primary school range (5–11 years), parents and teachers. The findings show that teachers reported a general excitement about the programme across the children taking part. Teachers across the age phases adapted the lessons in response to their own levels of comfort in how and what they taught. The teachers in Years 5 and 6 (children aged 10–11 years) articulated their feelings regarding the level of challenge due to the increased sensitivity of the content of the sessions with children. However, overall, the teachers felt that the children had responded very positively to the sessions and commented on their surprise by the children's levels of engagement, their capacity to share their views and experiences with the class group. Newby and Mathieu-Chartier (2017: 98) state that the level of challenge and discomfort during these lessons felt by the teachers differed according to 'their values, experiences and perceptions of the children's needs'. The findings suggest that only two of the thirteen sessions were delivered as planned to year six pupils due to the teachers feeling that the content was too sensitive. These views are not uncommon and present a challenge for settings and adults working with children. A key issue may be that when a programme like Spring Fever is taught in isolation as a discrete subject, this may create tensions for adults as there is limited context. Equally, the older children have not had the precursor sessions or benefitted from the experience of working on these in the school in the earlier years. It is important for children to have an open dialogue with adults from an early age, in order to normalize these issues. Indeed, we argue that those working with all children need to feel confident and 'be brave' (Mason, 2010) in their pedagogical approach in order to break down the barriers of systemic avoidance of such content as discussed in Chapter 4.

Does the Spring Fever programme feel to be appropriate for the defined age groups and aligned with the themes from the fifteen domains or the normalized sexual behaviours identified by the NSPCC below? If not, what content would you expect to see or take out based on the session titles? Is there some invitation to challenge the session titles themselves? For example, 'I am a boy, you are a girl' where in its phrasing it is being voiced, spoken by a boy and is patriarchal whereas other titles are neutral. How might you refine or adjust this title to include gender non-conformity?

As discussed earlier in the chapter, it is often challenging to recognize what is appropriate for children in relation to their age and stage of development. The NSPCC provide a useful starting point for this with some indication of normalized sexual behaviours. The NSPCC state that normal sexual behaviours can be seen within these identified age ranges:

0–4 years

- kissing and hugging;
- showing curiosity about private body parts;
- talking about private body parts and using words like poo, willy and bum;
- playing 'house' or 'doctors and nurses'-type games with other children;
- touching, rubbing or showing off their genitals or masturbating as a comforting habit.

5–9 years – As children get a little older they become more aware of the need for privacy while also

- kissing and hugging;
- showing curiosity about private body parts but respecting privacy;
- talking about private body parts and sometimes showing them off;
- trying to shock by using words like poo, willy and bum;
- using swear and sex words they have heard other people say;
- playing 'house' or 'doctors and nurses'-type games with other children;
- touching, rubbing or showing others their private parts.

10–12 years – Children are getting more curious about sex and sexual behaviour through

- kissing, hugging and 'dating' other children;
- being interested in other people's body parts and the changes that happen in puberty;
- asking about relationships and sexual behaviour;
- looking for information about sex, this might lead to finding online porn;
- masturbating in private.

It is important that these be seen as indicators rather than as established norms. As Jack has shown earlier, children's need for information is not necessarily wholly aligned with these. Jack's interest in information for what sex is at seven years does not fully map to the NSPCC's identification of this behaviour at between ten and twelve years.

Navigating the labyrinth: Strategies for support

The fifteen domains that McKee et al. (2010) have devised are a useful framework when viewed alongside the NSPCC developmental statements of normal sexual behaviour. The fifteen domains, while seen as overlapping, have been grouped to share some strategies for how these may be addressed with children in a variety of settings and contexts. The statements in *italics* have been adapted and reworded for specific relevance to the 3–11 years age range, from the work undertaken by the RSE Hub that is originally based on that published by McKee et al. (2010).

Seven domains have been grouped together because we consider they are fundamentally about relationships, the promotion of self-respect, empowerment and autonomy (Halstead and Reiss, 2003: 172). These are not necessarily unique to Relationships Education and RSE and form an essential part of any personal, social, health and emotional programme of study between three and seven years:

- Respect and understanding of consent: *Respect and consent can be taught for the early years through the idea that children's bodies are their own and that they have the right to say no to unwanted touch.*
- Understanding of anatomy, physiology, dysfunction, fertility and sexual response: *From an early age children should know the correct anatomical names for genitalia and about how babies are made. Young people need to understand puberty, masturbation and pregnancy.*
- Ability to maintain safety (legally, physically and emotionally): *Be able to avoid manipulative or exploitative relationships. Developing an ability to communicate with integrity and mutual respect in relationships.*
- Understand how to achieve, maintain, and negotiate healthy relationships with peers, family, partners and the wider community: *Achieving healthy interpersonal relationships in general leads to achieving healthy sexual relationships. An ability to communicate openly and an ability to develop and maintain meaningful relationships are important. This includes the ability to express love and intimacy in appropriate ways.*
- Ability to comprehend, establish and respect boundaries: *It is important to learn to manage boundaries in relation to sexual matters, and the difference between public and private expressions of sexuality. Individuals need to learn to express themselves while respecting the rights of others.*
- Build resilience to be able to manage any unwanted outcomes: *It is important to develop agency, to manage risk, and to have resilience. Individuals must also be able to take responsibility for their own behaviour.*
- Developing personal skills: *Developing an understanding of agency in that individuals are in control of themselves and their bodies. Developing a confidence to resist peer pressure. Learning to communicate effectively, and to develop assertiveness, negotiation and decision-making skills, with an ability to ask for help.*
- Developing a positive attitude to their own concept of self: *Individuals need to be supported in developing a positive attitude towards their own sexual identity.*

They need to be able to appreciate their body, able to accept themselves and feel accepted.

For trans and non-binary children and young people having a positive attitude to their own self-concept can be extremely problematic. At times, teachers and parents may become insistent that what a child feels is neither true, nor acceptable.

The importance of self-respect and those of others is a fundamental part of all relationships whether intimate or not and children can be explicitly taught this from the early years. Self-respect can be about understanding that their bodies are their own and that they have a right to have a say in who sees or touches them. From time immemorial, children across the world are frequently taught to be compliant, to do as they are told. There may be many valid societal reasons for this. However, when it comes to understanding consent, this needs to be sensitively managed with young children where they are empowered to state their wishes regarding their own bodies. In 2016, the NSPCC launched the 'Let's Talk PANTS' campaign to support adults with talking to children about how to stay safe from abuse. It identifies some key messages and provides resources to discuss these with young children:

P = Privates are private
A = Always remember your body belongs to you
N = No means no
T = Talk about secrets that upset you
S = Speak up, someone can help you

These simple messages can support young children to be empowered to challenge adults. Empowerment and agency are linked to rational sexual autonomy that Halstead and Reiss (2003) suggest are where children and young people are permitted to have authority over themselves in this respect and this starts from a young age. Being empowered regarding consent from a young age can allow greater sexual autonomy to support mutual support, as discussed earlier. Self-respect and self-reliance are embedded into the Dutch approach to RSE and these values need to form the bedrock of any Relationships Education and RSE programme to support healthy sexual development.

The understanding of anatomy and physiology are fundamentally interconnected with the first domain as this knowledge underpins what children know of their bodies and its functions. The understandings between privacy and sharing, embarrassment and modesty are complex. Societal norms of our 'privates' being covered and acceptable behaviours in public are difficult to negotiate particularly with young children. Adults need to allow children to celebrate their bodies and to enjoy them without shame or guilt.

Laura takes her children to play in a paddling pool in her friend's private garden during a hot summer day. Her two children (aged three and six) automatically strip off their clothes and play in the paddling pool naked. Laura's friend Sally expresses her unease regarding this and feels unable to allow her own children to be naked in this context. Sally has been brought up that children do not expose themselves in this way. A long conversation is had about Sally's rational for this as Laura questions her reasons. Sally shares with Laura that this was always what her parents insisted on when she was a child. When Sally's children see Laura's children without their swimsuits on, they are resistant to putting on theirs. Sally feels compromised and unable to insist that her children wear their swimsuits without making Laura's children feel uncomfortable.

Reflecting on the experience of Laura and Sally, consider:

- how does this make you feel;
- should children be able to make the choice regarding wearing clothes, or not, in a private garden;
- if not, then what explicit and inexplicit messages are given to them about notions of privacy and modesty; and
- are there other factors such as religion, culture or ethnicity at play here.

Helping children to negotiate social expectation around privacy and shame is challenging alongside personal values and our own experiences. School or wider settings are different from a home environment and these differences need to be explained to children, particularly regarding competing expectations or value systems (Halstead and Reiss, 2003: 113).

Talking to children about their bodies, using the appropriate biological terms, is a means to support their normal development and understanding and it also establishes a suitable, shared vocabulary between children and adults to identify inappropriate education, exposure to sexually explicit material or abuse. Children may well use familial names for their genitals which can be continued alongside understanding the biological terms. Notions of private and public are often challenging for young children to navigate, especially for those in the earliest years (3–4 years), who may find comfort from touching their genitals in situations when they are anxious or tired.

Moses works in an early-years setting in the preschool room. At the end of the day as part of the setting's routine, the children are called to sit on the carpet together to listen to a story that he reads to the group. Moses notices that some of the children will sit cross-legged on the floor and will openly touch their genitals through their clothing. The children are listening to the story although Moses finds these behaviours embarrassing and distracting. He goes to speak to the room leader in the setting who is a more experienced practitioner to discuss this. He asks her whether

1. he should just ignore the behaviour;
2. he should speak to the children directly and openly in front of the class;
3. he should speak to them as individuals;
4. if it is appropriate to talk to the parents,
   - how would you manage this situation as Moses's line manager;
   - how can you respect the child and their emotional well-being;
   - what are the challenges here with parents.

The example given here for Moses is not unusual and how this is managed with children, staff and parents establishes a clear ethos within the setting as to how adults feel and approach these issues with children and their families. The NSPCC's 'Let's Talk PANTS' can be a useful starting point to raise the issues of privacy and public with children. It is important to acknowledge at all ages, children's natural curiosity, pleasure and autonomy within the boundaries of societal and relationship norms regarding private and public behaviours.

The Taxonomy of Relationships, in Chapter 3, can be a useful starting point with children to think about the norms of relationships and boundaries of behaviours at the various stages:

- people we will never meet
- acquaintances
- people who help
- friends
- family members
- best friends
- special friends

Fatima decides she wants to explore these in a reception class (4–5-year-olds) and starts by showing certain examples of different behaviours such as:

- hugging a police officer;
- kissing a baby;
- shaking hands with their brother;
- a child picking their nose;
- punching someone;
- standing beside someone in a queue;

- a child having their hand down their trousers or pants when in a group of friends;
- sitting on an adult's knee;
- saying no to an adult; and
- a child appearing in their underwear during a visit to a doctor with a parent.

Fatima knows the children well as their teacher, and working in small groups, she asks them about what they can see in the pictures and waits to hear how they respond. Fatima challenges the children of different behaviours in different situations; for example, is it appropriate to sit on a stranger's lap on a train? If not, why not? She talks about how the children may not want to behave in that way but also how the stranger may not want that either! She is keen to ascertain how they view the pictures and uses the children's responses to discuss and share different views. Social mores can be explored and discussed as to what is deemed acceptable and unacceptable. Fatima is aware that for some children, awareness will be more acute than for others. Navigating social mores is challenging for adults and children alike, although activities such as this allow adults to sensitively raise issues and assist in helping children to navigate gender-based and power inequalities where relevant. Questions need to be honestly answered and focus on respect for self and those of others; how certain behaviours affect self and others similarly and/or differently. These are often nuanced and situation specific. Children need to be reassured that they have control of their own behaviours and actions. The examples of different behaviours can be extended and widened depending on the age and stage of development.

Consider Fatima's approach to extending the children's learning and understanding. How might she ensure that the learning environment is safe, supporting and secure? How can she enable good-quality discussion without causing concern?

Children are typically well aware of their world and the social mores regarding acceptable and unacceptable behaviours from an early age usually through trial and error from the interactions with their families and wider social experiences, and using these as a starting point for discussion can be very purposeful. Often highlighting what they want to see others doing or experiencing from the behaviours around them can trigger discussions more spontaneously too. Adults can use these incidents to build on what children already know and understand. Teams of staff can discuss and reflect on these to devise activities or strategies that they feel appropriate for the children as in the case with Moses and Fatima. Halstead and Reiss (2003: 182) are clear that these opportunities for discussion are an essential aspect of quality RSE that they demand from the adult 'confidence, a high level of empathy and very good skills in drawing pupils into discussion which while it needs to be serious, should not be without warmth and need not be without humour'. Indeed, humour can be an essential element in connecting with children.

We now address the remaining domains for healthy sexual development (McKee et al., 2010), with one overlapping from those outlined earlier in the chapter and included in its entirety in this section – understanding of anatomy, physiology, dysfunction, fertility and sexual response. While the domains already referred to earlier in the chapter are identified as developmentally appropriate for most children 3–11 years, the domains identified in this section are more relevant for those children 7–11 years. In this phase of childhood, children need to be made aware of the physiological and emotional changes that will be starting in order to be prepared for what lies ahead. As discussed earlier, children will be beginning, during this age phase, to experience and see body changes and feelings that are new and different.

To each of McKee's domains, we have added an indication of what it might involve or mean within a primary school setting:

- *Openness to exploring sexuality, gaining knowledge and asking for help as part of life-long learning:* Curiosity about developing sexuality and sexual feelings is natural. Young people need to feel able to explore these with, and seek information from, supportive and well-informed adults, as well as their peers.
- *Understanding of anatomy, physiology, dysfunction, fertility and sexual response:* From an early age children should know the correct anatomical names for genitalia and about how babies are made. Young people need to understand puberty, masturbation and pregnancy.
- *Celebrate sexuality, pleasure and the joy of sex and healthy relationships:* Developing an awareness of sexual pleasure. Sexual development should not be aggressive, coercive or joyless.
- *Understands own values/beliefs and how they impact on decision making and behaviour:* Individuals need to identify and understand the values and beliefs of families and peers, and to express sexuality in ways that are congruent with their own values.
- *Ability to comprehend, establish and respect boundaries:* It is important to learn to manage boundaries in relation to sexual matters, and the difference between public and private expressions of sexuality. Individuals need to learn to express themselves while respecting the rights of others.

- *Having an awareness of the diversity of sexual behaviour throughout the lifespan:* Developing an understanding of masturbation and delaying sexual involvement with others.
- *Appreciation of the diversity of sexual orientations and gender identities:* Developing an understanding of sexual orientation and gender identities, and especially that these may not be fixed throughout life.
- *Understanding of varying gender roles in culture and societies:* An ability to critically examine biases based on gender, sexual orientation, culture, ethnicity and 'race'.
- *Applying critical analysis to media representations:* Developing an ability to apply critical analysis to media representations of sex, sexual orientation, relationships, body image, gender and sexual expression.

Dealing with pleasure and sexuality

For many adults who work with children, talking about pleasure is frequently deemed as problematic when discussed in the context of sexual pleasure. The concept of childhood innocence is addressed in Chapter 5 and this is central to understanding what children understand and know about in terms of sexual pleasure. Renold (2005: 19) argues that the 'epitome of childhood lies in children's assumed sexual innocence'. Halstead and Reiss (2003: 50) state that children are 'deeply interested in sexual matters' and much of this is due to the context in which the twenty-first-century child exists; one that is steeped in media where a host of issues related to human relationships and sex are constantly streamed into their world. Children learn very quickly what it means to be, for example, 'dating, dumping, or going out' (Epstein et al., 2003: 19) which are some of the behaviours which are often played out and are visible in the primary school playground. In a society where the overarching rationale for a comprehensive RSE is largely justified by government (DfE, 2017) within notions of safeguarding and protection, the complexities of aligning any RSE programme with sexual pleasure is challenging. Educators are encouraged to draw on children's own knowledge (DfEE, 2000) although only with what is deemed age-appropriate which may be at odds with an individual's stage of development. Renold (2005: 22) makes clear from the varied discourses of government, the law and policy agendas, that the 'child' and 'sex/uality' are presented as 'oppositional and incompatible'.

Allen and Carmody (2012: 455) refer to the introduction of pleasure to the debate surrounding RSE programmes as driven by feminism, they argue that 'the effects of the second wave feminist movement had engendered a focus in education on girls, and the pedagogical omissions of their schooling'. The inclusion of pleasure as part of the sex education curriculum is seen as a means to 'recoup power' (p. 455) and agency for women against stereotyped female passivity, sexual objectivity and abuse. Pleasure and desire can be expressed for many things in children's lives; in particular, foods, certain experiences, being with and stroking a pet, going for a walk, being with certain people. Adults should not shy away from talking with children about and sharing their broader interests and pleasures, expressing openly about things that make them happy and that they enjoy. Sexual pleasure may well be a part of that and while we do not advocate open discussion about what adults physically enjoy in their intimate relationships, the concept of pleasure in all relationships as a whole can be discussed. Adults working with children need to 'address the ways in which the adult world treats, recognises, regulates, punishes and ultimately creates children's sexualities' (Renold, 2005: 22). These are frequently visible in playgrounds – 'a multiple territorial site in which children hide, share or display sexuality and sexual relations' (p. 33). She argues for allowing children to be active in the processes for creating their own 'sexual identities, cultures and relations' (p. 22).

Fran works in an afterschool setting for primary-aged children and has recently been aware that Year 5 (9–10-year-olds) are increasingly forming groups where they discuss who is 'going out' with who and who likes which of the children in the setting the most. She is surprised at the content of the conversations, the gendered roles that the children have assumed and the degree of heteronormativity displayed by the groups. The girls occupied passive, permissive roles in the groups while the boys dominated the discussion around the physical attributes of the girls and who 'fancies' who. Reflecting on these behaviours, Fran decides to work with the group to enable them to challenge their objectifying and passive behaviours.

Consider:

- how does the account of Fran's experience make you feel; and
- how can and should you respond to the behaviours, beliefs and values displayed?

Children are constantly navigating the perceived roles and gendered norms presented to them:

> While the playground is deemed the 'official' designated space for children to 'do play' and thus unofficially 'do sexuality', other public and private 'inside' spaces (such as the assembly hall, the classrooms, the toilets, the corridors and the cloakrooms) are just as suffused with an underground sexual economy and a cast of covert and overt sexual performances. (Renold, 2005: 33)

Adults need to recognize their role in supporting children to navigate these, to challenge and to openly discuss with them that there are alternative roles, behaviours and identities in all relationships beyond those assumed. These issues are discussed in more depth in Chapter 8. Allen and Carmody (2012: 460) use the term 'sexual ethics' as way to describe the rules around intimate relationships and is an important consideration as part of a broad and comprehensive RSE programme for children that sees a clear overlap between relationships between friends and the need to be kind, respectful and equal to extend to more intimate relationships that include desire and pleasure.

Critical analysis of media representations

The #MeToo campaign came to the fore in 2018 as a protest against sexual violence against women. This campaign gained currency in the film industry and was actively adopted by female actors who sought to raise media profile concerning the abuse of women in the business. Campaigns such as this can provide the ideal stimulus for discussing with children around issues of consent, gender roles and identities in all relationships. Epstein et al. (2003) discuss how same-sex friendships frequently elicit certain behaviours that 'solidify' friendships and particularly between boys who present objectifying and 'misogynist discourses' (p. 25). These friendships are an important part of the social and emotional development of children although they should be encouraged to use alternative narratives to solidify relationships that do not involve the denigration of anyone else. Children need to feel empowered to challenge norms themselves and this may involve adult encouragement to critically analyse media representations. The need to empower children, and in particular, for girls to have choice, to have their voice heard, to not assume a passivity in relationships is critical in terms of their safety, well-being and health, but also in order to experience a joy in sex and relationships that incorporates pleasure and desire.

Other campaigns, such as Stonewall's 'Get Over It' in 2007, were designed to raise awareness of bullying in schools with a particular focus on LGBT issues. It was a simple message that has been adopted and highlighted by many high profile celebrities across the film industry, in sport and by politicians with the main purpose to change attitudes and perceptions. The media represents certain behaviours that readily become normalized as part of societal culture: the way that people look, what they wear, how they speak and behave in both positive and negative ways. Equally, Stonewall's more recent, first ever, trans-inclusive *School Report 2017* marked a significant publication, as previously Stonewall had not officially included trans people and equality within its remit. In turn, the Church of England's updated

'Valuing All God's Children' publication (2017) overtly articulates that there is no place for trans, bisexual and homophobic bullying in schools. This is worthy of note as many primary schools are Church of England foundations and issues relating to sexual orientation are contentious in some parts of the church.

In the First Dates restaurant, the focus of a popular Channel 4 primetime show, individuals are matched to go for a meal on a blind date. All sexual orientations are represented, all ages and genders. Of particular interest in the paired heterosexual couples is who pays for the meal. The filming frequently surrounds the navigation of the social more that the male pays. For same-sex couples this appears to be less problematic.

Consider:

- what heteronormative behaviours are presented in this example;
- what opportunities can be taken for discussion about the roles that men and women play in relationships; and
- can this be extended to discuss traditional social mores within twenty-first-century diversity.

The media presents how different genders dress and behave through a host of different ways – music video, film, chat shows, reality TV shows, magazines, newspapers and so on – and are discussed in Chapter 7. A broad and comprehensive RSE programme aims to use representations and, indeed, misrepresentations from the media to critically discuss the impact of these on our views and feelings. For example, recent advertising by River Island (and other mainstream 'high street' stores) have included campaigns such as the '100% gender-free' hashtag and the 'labels are for clothes and not for people' campaigns.

Summary of key approaches to support effective practice

In order to develop effective practice it is important to

- develop a staged approach and a structured, graduated curriculum;
- consider both age- and developmentally appropriate approaches to learning;
- appreciate children's natural curiosity, and value their questions;

- help children understand what is going to happen to their bodies, and why changes occur;
- explore appropriate and safe use of a range of media with children;
- Be mindful that issues of pleasure form part of the RSE curriculum;
- Ensure that respect is central to all work with children and especially in RSE, this includes focus on self-respect, autonomy and 'sexual ethics'
- appreciate that common sexual practices and attitudes to sexual practices can change over generations; and
- identify and appraise a range of strategies to support learners.

Conclusion and summary of key points

This chapter has discussed the shifting media and technological context for adults and children to navigate in terms of exposure to different ideas, behaviours and issues. These constantly impact on what children know, want to know and are curious about which is historically no different to today. However, adults are not necessarily feeling able to respond to the ever-changing worlds that children find themselves in and may feel concerned about where their role lies in supporting children's understandings. Schools, nurseries, out of school clubs, youth centres, adults working with children and their families have a responsibility to be aware of the needs of children, their fundamental rights to knowledge about sexual matters (UN General Assembly, July 2010) and the 'essential knowledge' (DfE, 2014) to allow children to be confident, autonomous, healthy and respectful in their relationships and sexual relationships.

Signposts

15 Domains of Healthy Sexual Development (n.d.) www.rsehub.org.uk/resources/15-domains-of-healthy-sexual-development/?page=1&keywords=&area=Policy%20and%20Guidance&schoollevel=&suggesteduse=.
Me Too. https://metoomvmt.org/.
NSPCC: Let's Talk Pants. www.nspcc.org.uk/preventing—abuse/keeping—children—safe/underwear—rule/.
Stonewall. www.stonewall.org.uk/our—work/campaigns/get—over—it.

Further reading

PSHE Association (2018) *Preparing for Statutory Relationships Education. PSHE Education Lead's Pack: Key Stages 1 and 2.* PSHE Association.

www.pshe-association.org.uk/curriculum-and-resources/resources/
preparing-statutory-relationships-education-pshe.

References

Abbott, K. Ellis, S., and Abbott, R. (2016) ' "We've Got a Lack of Family Values": An Examination of How Teachers Formulate and Justify Their Approach to Sex and Relationships Education'. *Sex Education*, 16 (6), 678–91.

Allen, L., and Carmody, M. (2012) ' "Pleasure Has No Passport": Re-visiting the Potential of Pleasure in Sexuality Education'. *Sex Education*, 12 (4), 455–68.

BBC (2018) *Upskirting Should Be Criminal Offence, Campaigners Say*. www.bbc.co.uk/news/uk-43112450 (accessed 4 October 2018).

Blakemore, S.-J., Burnett, S., and Dahl, R. (2010) 'The Role of Puberty in the Developing Adolescent Brain'. *Human Brain Mapping*, 31, 926–33.

Bond, E. (2010) 'The Mobile Phone = Bike Shed? Children, Sex and Mobile Phones'. *New Media and Society*, 13 (4), 587–604.

Brook, PSHE and SEF (2014). *Sex and Relationships Education (SRE) for the Twenty-First Century: Supplementary Advice to the Sex and Relationship Education Guidance*. DfEE (0116/2000).

The Church of England Education Office (2017) *Valuing All God's Children: Guidance for Church of England Schools on Challenging Homophobic, Biphobic and Transphobic Bullying* (2nd edn). www.churchofengland.org/sites/default/files/2017-11/Valuing%20All%20God%27s%20Children%27s%20Report_0.pdf (accessed 4 October 2018).

Department for Education (2014) *National Curriculum in England: Framework for Key Stages 1–4*. www.gov.uk/government/publications/national-curriculum-in-england-framework-for-key-stages-1-to-4/the-national-curriculum-in-england-framework-for-key-stages-1-to-4.

Department for Education (March 2017) 'Policy Statement: Relationships Education, Relationships and Sex Education, and Personal, Social, Health and Economic Education'. Department for Education.

Department for Education and Employment (2000) *Sex and Relationship Education Guidance*. DfEE.

Epstein, D., O'Flynn, S., and Telford, D. (2003) *Silenced Sexualities in Schools and Universities*. Stoke on Trent: Trentham Books.

Halstead, M., and Reiss, M. (2003) *Values in Sex Education: From Principles to Practice*. Oxon: Routledge Falmer.

Kelly, Y., Zilanawala, A., Sacker, A., Hiatt, R., and Viner, R. (2017) 'Early Puberty in 11-Year-Old Girls: Millennium Cohort'. *British Medical Journal*, 102, 232–7.

Lewis, R., Tanton, C., Mercer, C., Mitchell. K., Palmer, M., Macdowall, W., and Wellings, K. (2017) 'Heterosexual Practices Among Young People in Britian: Evidence from

Three National Surveys of Sexual Attitudes and Lifestyles'. *Journal of Adolsecent Health*, 61, 694–702.

Marston, C., and Lewis, R. (2014) 'Anal Heterosex among Young People and the Implications for Health Promotions: A Qualitative Study in the UK'. *British Medical Journal*, 4, 8.

Mason, S. (2010) 'Braving It Out! An Illuminative Evaluation of the Provision of Sex and Relationship Education in Two Primary Schools in England'. *Sex Education: Sexuality, Society and Learning*, 10 (2), 157–69.

McKee, A., Albury, K., Dunne, M., Grieshaber, S., Lumby, C., and Matthews, B. (2010) 'Healthy Sexual Development: A Multidisciplinary Framework for Research'. *International Journal of Sexual Health*, 22, 14–19.

Morris, J., and Woolley. R. (2017) *Family Diversities Reading Resource* (2nd edn). Lincoln: Bishop Grosseteste University. http://libguides.bishopg.ac.uk/childrensliterature (accessed 7 August 2018).

Newby, K., and Mathieu-Chartier, S. (2017) 'Spring Fever: Process Evaluation of a Sex and Relationships Programme for Primary School Pupils'. *Sex Education*, 18 (1), 90–106.

Renold, E. (2005) *Girls, Boys, and Junior Sexualities: Exploring Children's Gender and Sexual Relations in the Primary School*. London: Routledge.

Silver, K. (January 2018) 'Adolescence Now Lasts from 10 to 24'. www.bbc.co.uk/news/health-42732442 (accessed 7 August 2018).

Statista (2014) 'Smartphone Usage Behaviour Among Children in Great Britain 2014, by Age Group'. www.statista.com/statistics/293508/smartphone-usage-behavior-among-children-by-age-great-britain/ (accessed 7 August 2018).

Topping, A. (2018). 'Employers Must Be Forced to Tackle Sexual Harassment, Say MPs: Commons Women's and Equalities Committee Calls for New Laws to Protect Workers'. www.theguardian.com/world/2018/jul/25/employers-must-forced-tackle-sexual-harassment-mps (accessed 7 August 2018).

United Nations (2010) *Report of the United Nations Special Rapporteur on the Right to Education*. https://resourcecentre.savethechildren.net/sites/default/files/documents/2788.pdf (accessed 4 October 2018).

7

Children's difficult questions

Jane is the mother of six-year-old Daniel. Recently she has noticed that Daniel has been playing with a new group of friends, mainly in other houses. Wanting to encourage his friendships, she suggested that he ask his friend round for tea, and after this they have been playing more in his own home. They have been building a den in the garden shed. While Jane was initially delighted that Daniel had made some new friends, particularly as he had found this difficult in the past, she has started to become concerned that their play is regularly out of her sight. Instead of enjoying the garden, the children seem to keep themselves engrossed in play within the shed. On a couple of occasions she has heard laughter and has gone to see what games they are playing. Her arrival has appeared to stop the children's game and it seemed like they were playing a secretive game of which they did not want her to be a part.

Last week she went to the shed and accidentally caught the children by surprise. She found the three boys with their trousers and underpants down, and the two girls were looking at their genitals. All five seemed to be finding the nurses-and-patients game highly amusing, but they were very embarrassed by Jane's presence. Jane asked Daniel about the game later, and he explained that they take turns to be the patients. He said that when he grows up he would like to be a nurse or a doctor and to look after people. She is now considering whether she should speak with the other parents about the game and is not sure who can give her advice about how to speak to Daniel about appropriate behaviour with his friends. At the moment he has not asked any questions about the differences between boys and girls, and she wonders how to help him do this, particularly as he does not have any brothers or sisters to help him to learn about the difference.

Chapter outline

Introduction

As discussed in the previous chapter, Halstead and Reiss (2003: 137) suggest that an appropriate aim of sex education provided by schools 'is to reduce embarrassment, anxiety and inappropriate guilt' and this is especially pertinent when children and young people ask questions. The question of who is the best person to discuss with children and young people issues of a sensitive or private nature may arise in a setting where a spontaneous interest from the children has emerged or where the team is required to teach a programme of RSE. A key factor for any practitioner embarking on a programme of RSE is that they have a comprehensive grasp of the subject and also that they feel comfortable in delivering its content. Children can be highly sensitive to the emotions of others and may detect a sense of the adult's unease which can then disrupt effective learning. The relationships that an adult has with children are pivotal to establishing the context or atmosphere for the lesson. Allen (2009: 33) suggests that in the teacher–learner relationship 'the content of sexuality education positions teacher and student in ways that can disrupt the teacher/pupil binary' and as such, the teacher's role in responding to this 'disruption' requires a careful management of the 'presentation of self [by the teacher], engagement with the pupils [as learners] and general classroom organisation' (p. 33). An open invitation for children to ask questions is essential in order to assess the levels of understanding of the individual children, to plan for future sessions and also to provide a source of biologically accurate and developmentally appropriate information. A sensitive response to children's questions allows for the individual child to feel respected and confident in seeking information on another occasion. As with all aspects of RSE, the practitioner should establish clear ground rules that outline the expectations of behaviour from members of the class or group. These behaviours should include respectful responses from everyone involved in the session – adults and children.

A teacher when beginning a new session in the RSE programme reminds the class of the agreed-upon rules before she begins the lesson:

I am going to remind you of what we agreed at the beginning of the week which is really, really important today. We agreed that we are going to show care and respect to one another. Not just you showing respect to me or me just showing respect to you but to each other all round. We agreed that what we say in the classroom, stays in the classroom apart from the one exception of home. (Mason, 2010: 160)

This reminder to the learners of the need for respectful behaviours includes not laughing at each other's questions. The teacher acknowledged with the class that a more general giggling at some of the content was because of embarrassment, and she reassured the children that this was perfectly normal and to be expected, but that giggling or laughing at each other was not acceptable. This sensitive and honest approach by the teacher gave the children permission to giggle within some agreed parameters. Beyond the initial embarrassment and a few giggles, the children quickly settled.

Strategies for inviting and managing questions

For many practitioners, inviting questions from children may make them feel uncomfortable and reticent to do so for a whole host of reasons. Key reasons for this may be:

- fear that the child or young person may ask an inappropriate question;
- the practitioner may not know how to answer in a way that is appropriate to the age and stage of the child; and
- the practitioner may be embarrassed.

These reasons may possibly contribute to the more common strategy of the teacher opting for a more didactic, exposition-based teaching style. In this way, the teacher is then in control of the content. The danger of not hearing the voice of the child is that the RSE provision may then not meet the needs of the learners. We argue that interacting with children and inviting their contributions is an essential part of any teaching or work with children and young people. A dialogic approach is especially important in RSE, as it enables clear and effective differentiation of content as outlined in Chapter 4. Ofsted (2007: 15) identified that learners need to be able to 'analyse, reflect on, discuss and argue constructively' and to have planned opportunities to develop critical skills.

The process of encouraging children and young people to ask questions can be done in a number of ways. An obvious strategy is to verbally invite questions during an RSE session which some, perhaps more confident children, will find to be a more comfortable way of learning. This approach may lead to discussion with the wider group, developed from a question posed to the whole class or offered by a more confident child. Other strategies may be to invite questions from smaller groups, or from individuals, which enable the less confident children to ask the practitioner. A think–pair–share approach might enable a fuller participation for all children by providing the opportunity to reflect, rehearse ideas with a partner and subsequently share these with a wider audience. However, all of these strategies for inviting questions rely on a level of confidence from the adult in responding.

Feeling vulnerable

Inviting questions from children might concern an adult that they may leave themselves in a vulnerable situation having to respond, often 'in the moment', to questions that they are uncertain of or confused about in knowing the appropriate stance to take. This is an understandable concern, and there are a number of ways to manage this. One solution is to seek the support of a colleague. The collaborating adults may feel comfort from this mutual support although it may inhibit some questions from the children with having a number of adults in the room. An alternative to this can be to use a question box where the children are invited to write their questions anonymously and place them in a box. Such anonymity is helpful for some children as they may feel more inclined to ask a question. The adult can then have the time to think through their responses and discuss these with colleagues. This is a well-used strategy and is valuable in supporting the needs of both the practitioner and the child; however, it can be limited by a child's ability to write.

A key factor in any response from the adult is that a distancing technique is employed. The technique of distancing means that the adult does not refer to their own values and beliefs explicitly or to their own sexual behaviours. An example might be that a child asks a question of the practitioner as to how often they have sex and what frequency is considered normal practice. Here it is essential that the adult thanks the child for their interesting question but explains that their personal life is private and that they cannot speak about themselves. The practitioner may then suggest to the child that when they are older and are ready to enter into a sexual relationship, they too may want to maintain some privacy. However, it is essential to respond to the question. In this instance it may be to explain that the frequency of sex is highly individual: that for some it may be every day and for others it may be once a week, or once a month, once a year, and for some not at all. The question also allows for a discussion about the interpersonal communication in any relationship and can help the child establish an expectation that this would be an instance where the consenting adults in the relationship would discuss their feelings and desires. It may also be an opportunity to share some of the challenges in a mismatch of libido between a couple and how that might be resolved. Parallels can also be drawn to other kinds of relationships where negotiation is necessary to ensure that, for example, a friendship can be maintained. Here one question from a child allows for a wealth of discussion about how a respectful and mutually consenting sexual relationship may be managed.

Managing inappropriate direct questions

To establish whether a direct question from a child is inappropriate or not is dependent on a number of factors: the maturity of the child, the manner and context in which the question is asked, and the knowledge of the child and their relationship. Woolley and Mason (2009) outline that children at all Key Stages will often ask questions to which they know the answer, with the intention of shocking or embarrassing the practitioner, particularly during whole-class discussion, such as 'What is a *blow job*?' This is a common question asked by children; it may be asked specifically to embarrass the adult and perhaps to 'test the water' for further questions. It may also be a term that that child has heard and wants further information about. The practitioner, in instances such as this, needs to ascertain from the response of the rest of the group whether this is a genuine question or not – any laughter or suppressed smiles may indicate that it is not. Children will also giggle as a response to embarrassment and the teacher needs to reassure the class, along with the child asking the question, that it is an open forum for questions regardless of the motive in asking it – to 'test the water', to seek information, or to embarrass. These motives are genuine and purposeful in establishing, or re-establishing, the boundaries during the lesson or discussion, which are:

1 the teacher is a reliable source of information;
2 there is an open opportunity for dialogue; and
3 that respect is reciprocal and established.

Knowledge of the child will be an important measure of the genuineness of the question, as will an appreciation of their level of maturity and developmental stage. A key element in responding to any question, in the first instance, is to assume a calm response and to appear unshocked. When embarrassing questions are asked by children, the practitioner may decide to delay responding and, while thanking the child for their question, the adult may ask for more time to think about a response and that they will answer the question with the child individually. This allows the practitioner some time to consider and decide how best to manage the response. It may be beneficial to seek advice from senior team members about how to answer the question, although it is essential that the question does get some response in order that the child, whether genuine or not in their enquiry, is afforded a respectful answer. Questions – or requests for information – provide an ideal opportunity to encourage the children to refer to the biological or more formal terms (e.g. oral sex) of sexual practices and behaviours, which helps to establish a respectful discussion. It is vital to discuss with the child that oral sex is another way of showing that you love and care for someone, but for some couples this may not be something they choose to do with each other.

Using the vignette at the start of this chapter, consider:

- how Jane might (or indeed should) help Daniel to understand the social norms of personal privacy. There is a view that the secrecy of the children shown by going into the shed suggests that they already are nuanced in such norms. It may be argued that for children this demonstrates a natural curiosity;
- whether Jane needs to speak with the other parents/carers, and why; and
- what age-appropriate means Jane could use to help Daniel to understand the physical differences between boys and girls.

In the Netherlands, emphasis is made in RSE of the 'potential joy and pleasure of sex' (Lewis and Knijn, 2002: 687). They provide an example where the teacher 'tells pupils that "making love takes patience. Your whole body is full of places that want to be caressed, rubbed, licked and bitten softly"' (p. 687). This approach by the Dutch suggests a frankness that explores sex for pleasure and one which some may find uncomfortable to adopt and discuss with children in England. However, perhaps there is a less overt approach that does not necessarily state so explicitly the ways of sharing pleasure; for example, a teacher may talk about exploring each other's bodies as part of intimate relationships and enjoying shared experiences. Some concerns about discussing sexual pleasure with children and young people is that practitioners may feel that they should refer the child to the parent/carer for information such as this. The 2018 RSE guidance outlines a partnership approach where parents are informed as to the content covered in sex education specifically at primary level. Where parents appreciate and understand the breadth of content to be covered, they can then make their choice as to whether they 'excuse' their child from the lesson. It is important to reiterate to the parent considering withdrawing their child, as outlined in Chapter 4, that the child may be left in an information void and may seek inappropriate sources for the answer. Ideally questions should be responded to by the adult to whom they are asked.

In rare cases, inappropriate questions can be an indicator of sexual abuse which require a very careful response. Sexual abuse may be indicated when a child or young person asks a question that suggests inappropriate sexual knowledge for their age and stage of development. Detecting sexual abuse is a challenging aspect of working with children and young people and for many practitioners it can raise some sensitive or difficult personal and emotional responses. The practitioner should respond to the child in the same way as with any inappropriate question by not appearing shocked and suggesting that they will respond personally to them later. This allows time to seek advice and to also implement the setting's child protection procedures following consultation with the staff member responsible for child protection issues. The issue of sexual abuse is dealt with in greater detail in Chapters 2 and 3.

There are occasions when children may not know what they need to know, and this is especially so in RSE. There may be information that the team working with children and young people deem essential, for example, relating to sexual health. The increasing rates of sexually transmitted infections (Boseley, 2010) means that children need to be aware of the risks attached to unprotected sexual practices and of ways in which they may keep themselves healthy and safe. Issues such as these need to be addressed with great care to avoid alarming children and young people. Whole-team decisions about such matters, in collaboration with parents and carers, are essential to ensure a coordinated approach.

Questions that may be asked by children in the primary phase of education

The series of questions addressed in this chapter are used as exemplars of the kinds of questions that primary-aged children may ask. The discussion following each explains how practitioners may manage questions such as these and the issues they raise.

Zenab is five and her mum has just given birth to a baby boy. Zenab is fascinated by breastfeeding, having seen her new brother being fed, and spends time in the home corner of the nursery with the dolls 'feeding' them under her jumper. While queuing up for lunch, she asks the teacher if the chicken breast they are eating is like the breasts with which her mum is feeding her brother. She then asks, 'Will I be able to feed my babies with my breasts?'

Consider:

- how would you feel about a young girl 'breastfeeding her dolls' in the setting; and
- how much detail do you need to explain to Zenab about the difference between a human breast and a chicken breast?

Zenab's curiosity is understandable particularly with the recent addition of a baby brother to her family and having watched her mother feed him. The connections she makes between the word *breast* and the different contexts in which she hears it shows her awareness of its different meanings. Discussion can be focused around the different uses of the word 'breast', for example, pictures of a robin with a red breast, a chicken breast, and doing breaststroke in the swimming pool. This can attribute the muscle at the front of a bird or in a human that is called the breast. Where a distinction can be made with Zenab is the capacity for the human female breast, along with other mammals such as primates, to feed their babies with specially designed milk. A conversation can be had about how when Zenab is old enough and when her body has changed, she may choose to feed her babies in the same way as her mum can.

> Janine has been discussing the changes that the children in her Year 5 class will face as they reach puberty. She is very aware that the children are at different stages of development, and two parents have already questioned her as to how to speak to their children about puberty. After the lesson Sarah, who is ten, stays behind as she has a personal question: 'My "noo–noo" is getting hairy like my Mum's, but she gets rid of hers, why?'
>
> Consider:
>
> - how you would respond to Sarah's use of colloquial language when referring to her body; and
> - how you might respond to Sarah's question either directly or indirectly.

This question raises some interesting tensions between home and the setting regarding the use of terms for body parts. The use of terms such as 'noo–noo' to describe the vulva and vagina is an indication that the family may feel uncomfortable in use of the biological names for genitals. A similar example is that of Simon included in the Introduction to this book, who used the name *Joey* for his penis. The challenge for parents and carers is that to use the biological name with very young children may seem inappropriate and they may be concerned that if the wider community heard a two-year-old referring to her 'vagina', that it may appear indelicate. The adoption of childish terms to name genitalia is common practice for this reason and can create difficulties for the practitioner in managing the shift from these to biological terms. Respect for the family's approach is essential in maintaining an effective relationship with parents/carers and the inclusion of parents in planning for RSE is good practice. The response to the child may be that you refer her to lessons she has had where the biological term 'vulva' has been used, to which she refers with 'noo–noo'. It is important to avoid confusing the child by using the term 'vagina', as the correct biological term should be used to indicate where pubic hair grows. The question provides the opportunity to use pictures and diagrams to identify the female anatomy and to introduce the correct terminology associated with it. Further discussion can revolve around the evolutionary purpose of hair on the genitals and other parts of the body where hair is evident, for example, eye brows, legs, ears, nose, etc., and why this occurs. Focus can be made on how personal preference regarding hair removal is individual. The girl should be encouraged to understand that she chooses whatever is acceptable for her body. Other discussions may concern religious reasons for pubic hair modification or for health reasons beyond personal preference.

Following a lesson on RSE, a ten-year-old boy approached his teacher to ask, 'Why does the penis go hard, what's that all about?' The boy had been in a 'Growing-up Talk' that had addressed the changes during puberty. This question arose when the boys had been moved away from the girls into a separate room to talk about wet dreams and erections, while the girls talked about menstruation and sanitary products (Mason, 2010). The boy looked genuinely confused and seemed to not understand what erections were for.

Consider:

- how you would respond to this question and what the question suggests about the boy's understanding; and
- how the lesson might have included the opportunity to allow questions and to check for miscomprehension.

The question asked by the boy raises some interesting issues – for example, when the RSE content omits the biological reasons for the changes during puberty, that is, sexual pleasure, intercourse and reproduction. The danger of this is that children can become unnecessarily confused. The questions asked by children also indicate that they require, and are seeking, more information than is offered to them. In the first instance, the practitioners need to consider how they might respond to the child – with either a whole class or an individual response. In this particular question it concerns sexual pleasure and arousal, along with the logistics of sexual intercourse and can be responded to by outlining that unless the penis is erect, then it cannot be inserted into the woman's vagina. The practitioner can discuss how clever the body is in how it does this. Many boys have erections from birth and so they will probably be aware of how it feels. It is vital to explore with the group, or the individual, that this is a normal and healthy response by their bodies either from arousal or spontaneously which is more common in younger boys and men. It is also an opportunity to talk about how sometimes erections happen at inappropriate times, especially when they are going through puberty, and that while they cannot help this, they may feel embarrassed. The adult should explain that mornings are a time when erections are very common, or during the night-time, and can explore the practical management of having wet dreams in the same way that girls may begin to explore how to manage the logistics of menstruation and sanitary products. An important aspect of discussing the changes during puberty is that they are all normal and to be celebrated as a signification of maturity and another phase in the child's life rather than shame. It should be explained that each body is different in terms of size, shape and times for changes and that all of these are very normal. The use of images that show real bodies is helpful in establishing the differences in body shape and size.

> During playtime, Alice, who is in the School Year 6 (aged eleven), approaches her class teacher who is on duty on the schoolyard. After some initial conversation she raises a question that has clearly been developing in her mind since a discussion in an RSE lesson earlier in the week. She asks, 'How does intercourse happen if the man has a large penis? Does sex then hurt the woman?'
>
> Consider:
>
> • the context, outside in the school yard, in which the question is asked and whether this affects the teacher's opportunity to answer; and
> • how you might respond to the question, or what other response or strategy you might employ.

Alice's question provides an insightful consideration of logistics of an intimate sexual relationship and how these may be managed. She demonstrates some understanding of the possible differences in bodies and genitals and as such maturity in how the mechanics of sexual intercourse can be managed. The teacher should thank Alice for her question and explain the importance of negotiation and interpersonal communication in relationships. The notion that the man and the woman would talk about this and ensure that each were comfortable and happy in trying different ways of having sex in order for it to be comfortable for both of them should be discussed with the child. The concept that a physically intimate relationship also includes an emotionally intimate dimension is essential for the child to explore and understand. That the individual logistics of a sexual relationship are unique to the relationship and established through honest and open communication are key features of an emotionally healthy relationship.

There are increasing concerns, highlighted by the government in 2009 (HM Government, 2009), of violence by young men towards young women in sexual relationships. The Family Planning Association (FPA, 2015) outlines the distinctions between coercion and consent, what is appropriate and inappropriate, and what is legal and illegal in the context of sexual relationships. In 2010 a TV prime-time advertising campaign highlighted the issue of male violence towards women through a scene of a boyfriend and girlfriend cuddling on a bed, where the boy presses the girl to have sex with him, which she declines. This leads to a violent episode where the boy hits the girl. Observing this behaviour is the boy's alter ego thumping on the window telling himself to stop. It is a powerful message and seeks to raise awareness of violence becoming a 'normal' aspect of a sexual relationship. RSE has the potential to challenge these emerging (or enduring) masculine stereotypes, often highly visible in pornography, and to develop realistic expectations for what a mutually respectful sexual relationship entails. The SEF (2009: 4) advocates the teaching of communication skills that 'promotes the ability to express needs, feelings and emotions and to negotiate within relationships. Skills development should specifically support communication between boys and girls.' This may be developed through a cross-curricula approach, particularly using examples from the media and literature to develop discussions. Emphasis also needs to be made on developing assertiveness in young girls, and the SEF suggests strategies for this can be implemented:

> Learning about relationships should explore what a healthy relationship is and help young people to understand what violence is and that it is not acceptable. This could include exploring definitions of domestic violence, sexual bullying and exploitation. Stories, scenarios and role-plays can be used as starting points for discussion. (2009: 4)

Mandatory Relationships Education (DfE, 2018) as part of the curriculum can raise these issues and provide an ideal opportunity for addressing the complexities of all relationships. The need to provide opportunities to discuss issues of negotiation and interpersonal communication is critical for children and young people to explore in relation to, particularly, those illustrated in the media. This is necessary when children and young people have the opportunity to seek information about sexual relationships from other sources, such as pornography, where the messages of availability and female submissiveness are evident. Notions of masculine aggression and female submission can be challenged and discussed through RSE with emphasis on respectful and mutually consenting relationships from a young age. The question asked by Alice allows for a wealth of issues about sexual intimacy, logistics and gender roles within sexual relationships to be addressed. It is important that these issues are not limited solely to heterosexual relationships.

Children in Year 6 have been discussing gender stereotyping in both print and broadcast media as a part of a series of lessons in PSHE. Discussions have included how people dress, the work and family roles in which they engage and how some media products use images to appeal particularly to men or to women. During one lesson Sunita asked, 'All the ladies in the music videos I see have big boobs, what if a girl doesn't, will they still be attractive to men?'

Consider:

- the impact of images portrayed in the media on children's understanding of their gender identity and developing sexuality;
- how media representations may pressure children and young people or introduce unrealistic expectations; and
- how you would begin to respond to Sunita's question.

Sunita's question gives opportunity to develop understanding of both body image and perceptions. Messages given through music videos identify the female physique as slender, tall, tanned, large-breasted and scantily clad. These women are invariably dancing in a sexual manner and around the males in the video which explicitly portray a specific female body image and behaviours that are attractive to the opposite sex. These examples provide opportunities to discuss with children and young people the reality of these images. A careful critique of whether these images are realistic is important in redressing the balance of what is, in reality, a 'normal' body shape. The notion of difference and the celebration of this is vital to ensure that children are aware that attraction is unique and that not all possible partners are attracted to the same image. The messages from the media about celebrities and body shape are powerful and potentially misleading, creating an unobtainable aspiration.

Select a range of magazines available in your own location, and ask the children to cut out pictures of those who they think look beautiful or attractive. Ask them to explain why they think that. This will evoke discussion of stereotypes and differences which can be a valuable opportunity to explore issues of body shape and image. A key point that can be addressed in using these examples is the manipulation of the images through digital enhancement and airbrushing which shows an unrealistic picture of the celebrities. An interesting comparison can be made through the use of a selection of photos collected from a non-published source, for example, family holiday pictures or pictures from a party (anonymity or permission should be ensured), that would provide a more 'normal' range of body images. Emphasis can be made with male and female learners on being healthy and confident with their bodies with a realistic body image.

An important aspect in addressing this question will be in reassuring the child that who they are – and not only what they look like – is an essential part of being attractive to a partner.

Jamelia is in Year 5 and comes from a family with strong religious convictions. Her teacher has recently been speaking with her parents as they were concerned about whether the planned programme of materials on RSE would sit comfortably with their beliefs about both marriage and the use of contraception. During one lesson in the RSE programme Jamelia tells her teacher, 'My mum says that having sex before you are married is disgusting and sinful . . . what do you think?'

Consider:

- how you could respond to Jamelia's question;
- how you would take into account the views of her parents while also acknowledging that the question has arisen within the context of a lesson with the whole class; and
- how you might respond and what further responses you could make.

In Chapter 1 we raised the notion that all education, across all curriculum areas, is values based. This question raises some of the possible tensions that emerge from differing values systems. For many families, sexual activities should be conducted only within the institution of marriage which may present an outdated value base for other families. The sanctity of sex within heterosexual marriage is a value that has been established from religion and although, in some religions remains, in an increasing secular country is a declining viewpoint. However, for this child's family it is clearly a strong moral point and as such, the practitioner should be careful in responding to this question in order to not discredit the family view. In directly opposing the views of the family, the practitioner may be placing the child in an uncompromising position with their family. In order to address the question, the practitioner can introduce other possible viewpoints for discussion. A possible strategy in the first instance is to ask the child what they think about the idea of sex before marriage. This will allow for the practitioner to ascertain the perspective of the child and decide how to manage the topic. It is important that the child is helped to explore a range of viewpoints regarding sex and marriage in order that they can be empowered to make their own decisions about themselves and their bodies. The notion of self-reliance and self-respect is promoted in the Dutch approach (Lewis and Knijn, 2002) where children are encouraged to be responsible for themselves and their own behaviour. Here, self-respect is the overriding value, where as long as behaviours are within the boundaries of the law then individuals can have consensual sexual relationships however and whenever they choose, as Lewis and Knijn comment, 'The Dutch approach to the subject [RSE] has been to encourage self-reliance, respect for self and respect for others. The approach has been positive, emphasizing sex as part of everyday life and to be celebrated' (2002: 685). The idea of celebrating sex outside the context of a marriage is an interesting one in relation to the question posed. Children's rights (see Chapter 4) suggest that children have the right to make choices and to have access to information that is age and stage appropriate which indicates that there is currency in exploring a range of value frameworks in response to this child in order that they may make their own decisions when they are ready. A critical feature of this strategy is that the practitioner does not adhere to a particular value framework. A distancing technique can be adopted such as, 'Some people who are not married might feel that having sex is something that they want to do and that they don't feel that it is disgusting or sinful.' A further example is provided in Chapter 5, when Maria and Stuart express the tensions between the delivery of RSE and their personal religious beliefs.

Self-esteem and identity are key features to making choices about sexual relationships and issues about inappropriate guilt have relevance in developing these. Having the right to make decisions for themselves, and to not be judged, will clearly be challenging within the family's views identified in the question. However, the child may choose to adhere to the religious framework and have a healthy, fulfilling sexual relationship as a married person. The practitioner should stress to the child that these are deeply personal decisions and that they have the right to choose.

Summary of key approaches to support effective practice

In order to develop effective practice it is important to consider the following:

- how practitioners can reduce children's embarrassment, anxiety and guilt when addressing issues relating to relationships, sex and sexuality;

- strategies to develop clear and effective ground rules that establishes mutual respect;
- ways of addressing inappropriate questions from children;
- distancing techniques to support discussions about sensitive or difficult issues;
- ways of being open to genuine questions from children;
- how to explore children's fears about difference;
- strategies to tackle heteronormativity and heterosexism;
- ways of developing subject knowledge to support professional practice;
- strategies to avoid awkwardness or embarrassment; and
- how to promote children's physical and emotional well-being.

Conclusion and summary of key learning points

In England the primary school teacher is responsible for teaching the majority of curriculum areas and programmes of initial teacher education are designed to support this. In some instances other adults, such as the school nurse or another healthcare professional, may take responsibility for a programme of RSE in a school setting. Based on research conducted in Australia, Allen (2009) reveals that young people consider peer educators as the most effective for RSE, with teachers ranked second and health professionals ranked third. The participants involved in this research were of secondary school age and peer educators may have more resonance. Stephenson et al. (2008: 4) formed the team for the RIPPLE study which explored the benefits of peer-led sex education and place some caveats on the effectiveness of peer-led strategies. A comprehensive multi-method study was undertaken with control groups where learners were not taught through a peer led approach. They suggest,

> The outcome results by age 16 showed that the peer led approach improved some knowledge outcomes; increased satisfaction with sex education; and reduced intercourse and increased confidence about the use of condoms in girls. Girls in the peer led arm reported lower confidence about refusing unwanted sexual activity (borderline significance). The incidence of intercourse before age 16 in boys and of unprotected first sex, regretted first intercourse (or other quality measure of sexual experiences or relationships), confidence about discussing sex or contraception, and some knowledge outcomes for both girls and boys were not affected.

In considering primary-aged children, there may be some currency in supporting learning through a peer educator approach due to the earlier exploration of issues that may built on learners' knowledge and understanding. Children from the secondary phase of education may provide a valuable resource for those in the primary phase. This is a somewhat unconventional teaching strategy, however, with careful management it may elicit purposeful learning, particularly when children can ask questions of their peers that they may not wish to ask of an adult. Research suggests that children and young people prefer an interactive classroom pedagogy (Allen, 2009) which identifies opportunities for questioning and discussion as an important aspect of any RSE programme.

The role of the educator is a critical feature in an effective RSE programme along with their gender. In the primary phase there is often a dearth of male teachers and this may present issues for boys in being able to feel at ease when discussing changes to their bodies, or sexual matters, with a female member of staff. Allen (2009: 46) refers to her research in establishing that the gender of the educator for RSE is not necessarily of relevance, more important are the 'qualities' or 'characteristics' of the person. These specific characteristics indicate that 'being knowledgeable', 'able to relate to young people' and 'relating to a sense of professionalism' (p. 46) are essential qualities. The notion of professionalism outlines the standards and values that are embodied in the management of any aspect of the primary curriculum. This is especially so in RSE where the learners' entitlement to information about sexual matters may require bravery from the professional which is a vital component to the kind of professionalism we advocate.

In order to develop practice, it is essential to invite questions from children and young people as a key aspect of effective RSE. The DfE guidance (2018) outlines that teachers may need specific training to help them to know when to respond to a question in a whole-class or individual situation. Fundamentally, questions from children:

1 should be managed sensitively to ensure that the emotional well-being of the adult and the child is maintained;
2 can provide an ideal opportunity to explore issues about intimate relationships and effective interpersonal communication; and
3 can promote an understanding about trust, self-respect and respect for others within relationships.

Signposts

Family Planning Association: a range of advice, resources and training opportunities. http://www.fpa.org.uk/.

Further reading

Aggleton, P., and Crewe, M. (2005) 'Effects and Effectiveness in Sex and Relationships Education'. *Sex Education*, 5 (4), 303–6.

Allen, L. (2009) ' "It's Not *Who* They Are It's *What They Are Like*": Re-conceptualising Sexuality Education's "Best Educator" Debate'. *Sex Education*, 9 (1), 33–49.

Mason, S. (2010) 'Braving It Out! An Illuminative Evaluation of the Provision of Sex and Relationship Education in Two Primary Schools in England'. *Sex Education*, 10 (2), 157–69.

References

Allen, L. (2009) ' "It's Not *Who* They Are It's *What They Are Like*": Re-conceptualising Sexuality Education's "Best Educator" Debate'. *Sex Education*, 9 (1), 33–49.

Boseley, S. (2010) 'Young at Risk as Sexually Transmitted Infections Reach Record Levels'. *Guardian*. www.guardian.co.uk/society/2010/aug/25/sexually-transmitted-infections-hit-record-high (accessed 7 August 2018).

Department for Education (2018) *Relationships Education, Relationships and Sex Education (RSE) and Health Education: Guidance for Governing Bodies, Proprietors, Head Teachers, Principals, Senior Leadership Teams, Teachers*. London: Department for Education.

Family Planning Association (2015) *The Law on Sex Factsheet*. www.fpa.org.uk/factsheets/law-on-sex (accessed 4 October 2018).

Halstead, M., and Reiss, M. (2003) *Values in Sex Education: From Principles to Practice*. London: RoutledgeFalmer.

HM Government (2009) *Together We Can End Violence Against Women and Girls: A Strategy*. http://webarchive.nationalarchives.gov.uk/20100408115933/http://www.homeoffice.gov.uk/documents/vawg-strategy-2009/index.html (accessed 4 October 2018)

Lewis, J., and Knijn, T. (2002) 'The Politics of Sex Education in England and Wales and the Netherlands since the 1980s'. *Journal of Social Politics*, 31 (4), 669–94.

Mason, S. (2010) 'Braving It Out! An Illuminative Evaluation of the Provision of Sex and Relationship Education in Two Primary Schools in England'. *Sex Education*, 10 (2), 157–69.

Ofsted (2007) *Time for Change? Personal, Social and Health Education*. London: Ofsted.

Sex Education Forum (2009) *Together We Can End Violence Against Women and Girls Consultation*. Sex Education Forum Response.

Stephenson, J., Strange, V., Allen, E., Copas, A., Johnson, A., Babiker, A., and Oakley, A. (2008) 'The Long Term Effects of Peer-Led Sex Education Programme (RIPPLE): A Cluster Randomised Trial in Schools in England'. *Lancet*, 364 (9431), 338–46.

Woolley, R., and Mason, S. (2009) 'Sex and Relationships Education', in *Education Studies: An Issues-Based Approach* (revised edn), ed. J. Sharp, S. Ward and L. Hankin. Exeter: Learning Matters.

8

Developing inclusive Relationships Education

Neil has just started working in his second school, three years into his teaching career. Although he had a boyfriend during his time at university, he has been single since graduating, and as he becomes increasingly busy with work he has not been dating for several months. Colleagues in his new school have variously asked about his wife, whether he has children that needed to settle into new schools, and whether he would like to join in the monthly staff night out, where colleagues often bring their partners.

Chapter outline

Introduction

This chapter considers the nature of inclusion, its scope and breadth. While some professionals use the term to mean special educational needs and disabilities (and these areas are explored in Chapter 5), others (including those contributing to Woolley, 2018) use the breadth of the protected characteristics from the Equality Act (Legislation.gov.uk, 2010) and additional elements (e.g. social disadvantage, social class). This chapter explores how Relationships Education can be inclusive in primary schools. It considers gender inclusion including cis and trans identities, and considers some of the key vocabulary relating to gender and sexual identities. It acknowledges the range of patterns of family life from which children come, and the different ways of being family and relating to one another. It addresses strategies for the development of inclusive and anti-bullying approaches, including homophobic bullying, drawing on original research with student teachers in England, and a case study example from practice in primary education.

Gender permeates many of the ways in which we interpret other ways of identifying ourselves. For example, if we identify as gay, questions are asked such as 'so are you the man or the woman in the relationship', which at different times might be expressed as being 'top or bottom' or 'butch or fem'. Such questions belie an assumption that gay relationships mirror heterosexual relationships, with one partner taking a lead or being more assertive. Indeed they assume such an imbalance in straight relationships, and may presume some kind of traditional gender-role stereotyping. Such ideas stem from an outdated and misconceived understanding of gender identity. However, they are not uncommon. Some would argue that this binary approach to gender is highly problematic with other gender identities, 'strung out between them, like laundry drying on the line, or circling around them in orbit like some kind of errant Sputnik' (Wilkins, 2014: 82). This chapter considers different gendered identities and resources to combat stereotyping and gender-based assumptions.

In recent years public awareness of gender identities and their diversity has grown in the UK, as well as in other contexts. This is reflected in the comments from student teachers outlined later in this chapter, but also in public discussions about accessible toilets and changing facilities and media features about gender identities of public and other figures. This raises the profile of such matters and, at least potentially, provides opportunities to develop discussions about promoting inclusion and celebrating difference.

Consider your own gender identity:

- What key terms do you use when thinking about this part of your identity?
- How many of these terms are positive, negative or neutral?

- Are any of the terms comparative, expressing who you are in relation to others?
- How strongly do you feel your gender identity has an impact on you in personal or professional spheres?
- Can you recall the age at which you began to have a sense of gender identity? Has this evolved over time? When did you feel you were who you say you are?

Terms and terminology

One area that practitioners find sensitive is the use of terms and terminology. In order to feel confident when talking about gender, sex and sexuality, it is important to feel confident in the use of language. Language is always evolving, and its use and interpretation develop over time.

Consider the following brief definitions of terms relating to gender, sex and sexuality.

With which terms are you most familiar? Are there any that you have not come across before, and might want to learn about? Which of these terms and concepts do you anticipate to encounter (i) when working with children in schools or settings and (ii) when liaising with parents, carers and other stakeholders in schools and settings?

Abstinence: choosing to refrain from sexual activity, sometimes for reasons of religious belief; self-enforced restraint.

Androgynous: having both male and female characteristics.

Asexual: a person who does not experience sexual attraction. They may engage in sexual acts; it is not a synonym for abstinence or celibacy. An asexual person may or may not experience romantic attraction.

Biphobia: an aversion to bisexuality or bisexual people, including negative stereotyping or denying the validity of bisexuality.

Bisexual: sexual attraction, sexual behaviour or romantic attraction towards both men and women.

Celibacy: voluntarily being sexually abstinent or choosing not to marry, often for religious reasons; it usually involves taking sexual activity out of your life to commit to a larger purpose.

Cisgender: identifying with the gender you were assigned at birth.

Demisexual: a person who does not form a sexual attraction until they have made an emotional connection.

Gay: attracted to a person of the same sex, often used to refer to a man who is romantically and/or sexually attracted to another man.

Gender: socially constructed identity, often associated with terms like masculine and feminine.

Gender fluidity: having an identity where gender identity is evolving and changing over time.

Genderqueer: an inclusive term for those not identifying within a gender binary; this may include identifying with some traits that are masculine, feminine or neither.

Heteronormative: a view of the world that presents being heterosexual as the norm.

Heterosexism: a presumption that heterosexuality is the norm.

Heterosexual: someone sexually attracted to a person of the opposite sex.

Homosexual: someone attracted to a person of the same sex. The Greek word *homos* means same (not to be confused for the Latin word *homo* meaning man). It was a term used to identify a medical disorder by the World Health Organization until 1990, and as such is avoided by some people because of such negative associations. See also *gay.*

Homophobia: prejudice against homosexual or gay people.

Intersex: a variety of different characteristics that do not fit the traditional characteristics of female or male physical identity. It should be noted that intersex people have sometimes been physically 'erased' at birth when well-intentioned medical professionals advise parents/carers on surgical options. There are arguments that individuals should be enabled to make such choices for themselves at an age and stage when they are able to express their identity and their wishes.

Lesbian: a woman who is romantically and/or sexually attracted to another woman.

LGBT: lesbian, gay, bisexual and trans. An acronym often used to group together people. Sometimes expressed as LGBT+ to include wider groups, or with additional letters, for example, Q for questioning, Q for queer, C for curious, I for intersex, TS for two-spirited, A for asexual and P for pansexual.

Non-binary: a gender or sexual identity that is not defined in terms of binary opposites, for example, homosexual–heterosexual, male–female.

Pansexual: not restricted by gender identity, gender or biological sex.

Pronouns: she/he/they/them/theirs. Others include ze and zir which are not associated with gender identity. Some people prefer to use their name in place of a pronoun.

Queer: an overarching term for people who are not heterosexual and/or not cisgender. Some view this as slang, others as an empowering term to express their identity. It is sometimes used as an insult; it is also a well-established term in academia (e.g. Queer Studies).

Questioning: seeking to understand your own identity, gender or sexual orientation.

Sex: an identification based on biological features, often male or female.

Sexual orientation: sexual identity in terms of who one is sexually attracted to.

Sexuality: the way of expressing your sexual orientation. This may be emotional, physical, sensual, spiritual or erotic.

Straight: a heterosexual person; someone attracted to a person of the opposite sex.

Trans: having a gender identity different to the one assigned at birth. Trans people can be asexual, bi, gay, straight or choose not to label their sexual orientation. It is important not to confuse gender identity with sexual orientation.

Transition: the journey of moving to live according to your inner sense of gender identity. This may or may not include therapies or surgery.

Two-spirited: a person with both masculine and feminine 'spirit'; traditionally used as a third gender in some indigenous North American communities.

Consider:

- with which of these terms do you identify;
- how do you feel these could impact your role working in schools or settings; and
- how can you avoid making assumptions about the ways in which colleagues and other stakeholders identify?

Consider the account of Neil in the vignette at the start of this chapter. What advice might you give to Neil about what personal information he shares with colleagues or other stakeholders in the school? What positives and what risks might Neil consider when sharing personal information. What should his workplace do to ensure that it provides a supportive, inclusive and welcoming environment for all its staff?

Anti-bullying and promoting positive relationships

Homophobic bullying can affect anyone regardless of sexual orientation. Anyone who is thought to be gay, or just through to be 'different' can be called 'gay' or experience homophobic abuse. (DCSF, 2007: 71)

This assertion is interesting as it comes three years before the Equality Act (Legislation. gov.uk, 2010) brought into law the ideas of being bullied due to actuality, perception or association. Indeed by 1990 Harry (cited in Hellen, 2009) was suggesting that behaviour was a better indicator than actual sexual orientation in predicting incidences of homophobia. As Hellen (2009: 95) reinforced,

> It may be reasonable to argue that homophobic bullying in schools, especially primary schools, is a result, not of a child's sexual orientation, but of a child's appearance or mannerisms in relation to gender.

Developing inclusive classrooms

Hellen's point that it is often gendered behaviours and not sexual orientation itself that leads to homophobic bullying is interesting, and warrants further discussion. It is essential to consider how to tackle homophobic, transphobic and indeed any bullying, and how to develop inclusive school environments where individuals are valued and respect, care and mutual appreciation are fostered in order to prevent bullying occurring in the first place.

Hellen (2009: 97) provides an example of embedding acceptance and inclusion within the ethos of a school or classroom, ensuring that values are addressed in a proactive way rather than in response to need. He argues that there is a precedent in the UK for developing transgender-friendly classrooms, even if it is not known that there are any transgendered children in a school:

> Teachers [are] instructed to have a 'dyslexia-friendly' classroom despite the fact that there may be no diagnosed dyslexic children in the class. In this way any transgendered children will receive the message that their gender identity is not a problem and that they may not need to conceal their gender identity, at least in school.

This is an interesting approach to developing inclusive classrooms, and can be applied to any matter relating to diversity and equality. It provides an effective counterargument for situations where school leaders claim that resources showing diverse families (or for that matter ethnicities, disabilities or other protected characteristics) are not relevant to their setting because their school population is claimed to be homogenous.

Hellen's research indicates that 'the majority of transgendered people were aware that they were transgendered well before puberty' (2009: 88). This contrasts with his suggestion that sexual orientation is more likely to become apparent to an individual when they reach puberty. For example, Hellen cites a survey suggesting that 21 per cent of ten-year-olds were aware of their sexuality, and only 2 per cent had accepted the fact (p. 85); however, 'the majority of non-transgendered boys and girls do not wait until puberty until they begin to adopt gender-specific behaviour' (p. 89). This suggests that gender identity develops earlier than an awareness of one's own sexual orientation. Readers may wish to consider whether this was the case in their own experience (see also the discussion of gender stability in Chapter 2). Clearly the two are separate and distinctive, yet also interlinked along with many other facets of who we are and how we identify.

The conclusions from Hellen's research indicate that most children will be aware of their different gender identities (i.e. being cis or trans gender) by the time they leave primary school; this has particular implications for those working in secondary schools and for transition between phases of schooling. Thus it is important that schools acknowledge that gender is more complex than a simple binary in order to foster inclusion, encourage mutual respect and acceptance, and to ensure that an invisible minority is not excluded by the omission of any resources, language or acknowledgement of their existence. Notably, a survey undertaken by the Terence Higgins Trust (2016: 31) found that only 24 out of 818 respondents had been taught about gender identity and 98.8 per cent (161 out of 163) of non-cisgendered young people 'were not taught about issues related to trans people in school'. Furthermore, the physical environments of schools can compound the lack of education and support to trans children and young people:

> Gender binary facilities force individuals to misgender themselves or feel invalidated as they are forced to use facilities that do not align with their gender identity. For gender diverse learners, this may present a source of confusion, apprehension and discomfort. Consequently, this has a wider impact on the learner's educational experience. (Hewston, 2018: 109)

While moving from a sense of gender binary (female and male) to a spectrum of gender(s) brings greater complexity to our understanding and appreciation of diverse identities, the latter still infers a range with two ends and classifies all points in between as being shades. This gender binary has more to do with physical attributes (i.e. one's genitals) than with the behaviours and self-expression that are gender: for those who feel that their gendered identity is different from the sex they were assigned at birth, when medical staff made a decision based on genitals.

Persisting with a sense of binary gender is an interesting concept, particularly in the evolving twenty-first century. While many people may continue to live quite comfortably within a conventional gender binary, the presence and visibility of trans and non-binary identities provides a gift in questioning such traditionally gendered role behaviours. Maintaining traditional role behaviours based on physical characteristics denies the socially constructed nature of gender:

> We expect men and women to behave in slightly different ways. We expect men to be 'masculine' and women to be 'feminine', but really there's no real reason for this. Women can be masculine if they want, and men can be feminine. People can be an even mix of the two, or something completely different. That's because 'man' and 'woman' are genders. They are social ideas about how people who have vulvas and

vaginas, and people who have penises and testicles should behave, but it doesn't really work like that. (Brook, 2017: 2)

One school in Guernsey has moved from having a head girl and a head boy to having a chair and vice-chairperson, the intention being to avoid inferring that gender is the reason why an appointment is made, and to move away from gender-stereotyped roles (Woolcock, 2018).

Children's picture books provide an ideal way to explore gender identity and to challenge gender stereotyping, using a 'one-step-removed' method of discussing characters and stories. The *Family Diversities Reading Resource* (Morris and Woolley, 2017) includes over 150 books exploring diverse families and also gender identity and role stereotyping. The resource itself includes detailed reviews of the books, and a summary of some of the key publications in this area is included here:

10,000 Dresses *(Ewert, 2008)*

Bailey dreams about dresses every night: each one is different, and there are ten thousand of them. They are made of precious stones and the light bounces off the crystals causing rainbows to jump out. When he shares his dreams with his mum, dad and then his brother, they do not understand what he is speaking about. They all tell him that he is a boy, and boys do not wear dresses. When Bailey meets Lauren, a girl who lives down his street, they find a way of sharing their talents to create a dress that literally reflects their identities.

Are You a Boy or Are You a Girl? *(Savage, 2015)*

When Tiny starts a new school there are discussions about gender roles, and one child is particularly unpleasant about these and about Tiny. Finally his friend Mia asks whether Tiny is a boy or a girl, to which Tiny responds, 'I am me!' This book will be useful when discussing gender with children, when considering their assumptions and preconceptions about gender, and when supporting children who do not identify on a traditional binary scale.

I Am Jazz *(Herthel and Jennings, 2014)*

Jazz was born with a girl brain but a boy body. She explains that this is called transgender. Jazz tells the story of her gender identity and how early on it was not appreciated by those around her. She describes how she felt like she was living a lie when she had to wear boy's clothes. After a while her parents took her to a doctor, who clarified that Jazz was transgender. This led to her parents encouraging her to be herself and expressing their unconditional love for her. The book is based on real life experience.

Introducing Teddy (Wolton, 2016)

Thomas the Teddy and Errol play together every day. One day Teddy is not happy, and is concerned that Errol may stop being a friend. Teddy explains that she has always known she is a girl teddy and wishes her name was Tilly. Errol is very supportive. The main focus of the story is about being yourself, and being a good friend. Addressing the issues through a non-human character (Thomas/Tilly) may help discussion with children and enable adults to discuss understandings of gender identity more easily.

Made by Raffi (Pomranz, 2014)

Raffi lives with his mum, dad and dog. He likes to ask lots of questions, including why he feels different from other children. Is it because of his appearance, his choice of clothes, or something else? He likes to sit by himself, and this brings him to sit with a teacher who is knitting. He learns the skill and embarks upon a scarf for his father's birthday. His parents support the new hobby, although there is some teasing from other children at school. Raffi chats with his mum about why he is different. He wonders if there might be something called a *Tomgirl*. Mum affirms their love for him and how proud they are of him and his interests. Later, when the class put on a play, Raffi designs and makes a cloak for a main character, to general acclaim. Maybe he could become a famous designer one day?

Morris Micklewhite and the Tangerine Dress (Baldacchino, 2014)

Morris Micklewhite lives with his mother Moira and their cat named Moo. Morris likes to visit the dressing-up area in his classroom at school, where the tangerine dress is his favourite attire. He likes the noise it makes, its feel, and the colour is a reminder of many special things. Perhaps this is a story about a boy who has well-developed or acute senses, and appreciates vibrant colours, sounds, textures and sensations.

Sometimes other boys and girls make fun of him when he wears the dress. While he pretends that he cannot hear their comments, he can. Sometimes other children don't sit with him, and by Friday Morris has a tummy ache and spends the day at home in bed reading. This gives him the chance to gather his thoughts and prepare for the days ahead. This book is essentially about a boy who likes to wear a dress. It may be about gender identity, traditional expectations, or pressure to conform. Perhaps this story is really about having the choice to express yourself in the way that you wish, and about developing resilience.

Rosie Revere, Engineer (Beaty, 2013)

Rosie Revere is inspired by the junk that she finds around her. Where others may see rubbish, she sees the opportunity to be creative, to design and to make. Rosie makes things secretly, although when she was younger she had been braver making hot dog dispensers and helium pants for her uncles and aunts. Rosie has positive role models from other generations who have challenged gender stereotypes. Her aunt teaches her that failure is a part of the learning process and a platform on which to build future success.

William's Doll (Zolowtow, 1972)

William's Doll takes a look at gender stereotypes and the pressures these can place on children. William is a boy struggling with the stigma attached to his wanting a doll, and the negative reaction he receives from his family and neighbours. Through his father's attempts to encourage William's masculinity and 'boyishness' we see that he is good at basketball and enjoys his train set. The conclusion to the story shows William's grandma buying him a doll and explaining to his dad why she has done so. Her explanation (that William needs it so that when he is a dad he will know how to take care of his baby) is a nice touch that also serves to highlight the irrationality of gender stereotypes. This ending makes an assumption about William's future life, and could reinforce a different expectation or stereotype. However, it provides an interesting discussion starter for the consideration of gender stereotyping.

Consider how you would use carefully chosen picture books with children.

Might you use them as a discussion starter, or would you include them in a varied diet of books chosen to reflect the rich diversity of society without needing to highlight or to comment on particular issues? An example of how a school has used such picture books to develop awareness of and celebrate diversity is included later in this chapter.

Supporting inclusive Relationships Education

At one point it was suggested that the Equality Act (Legislation.gov.uk, 2010) did not relate to schools in England by the then Secretary of State for Education Michael Gove:

> The education provisions of the Equality Act which prohibit discrimination against individuals based on their protected characteristics (including their sexual orientation) do not extend to the content of the curriculum. (Tehan, 2012)

This was later clarified and aspects of the protected characteristics of individual persons named in the Act were included in the revised National Curriculum for England (DfE, 2014), namely,

> Teachers should take account of their duties under equal opportunities legislation that covers race, disability, sex, religion or belief, sexual orientation, pregnancy and maternity, and gender reassignment. (section 4.2)

The National Curriculum for England also states that, 'all schools should make provision for personal, social, health and economic education (PSHE), drawing on good practice' (DfE, 2014, section 2.5), although the scope and content for this are not specified. This provides a legal underpinning for taking an inclusive approach to Relationships Education.

In England, part of the statutory inspection framework for schools (specifically for Early Years provision) includes that inspectors will consider children's

> respect [for] each other's differences and build their understanding and respect for different families, people and communities beyond their immediate experience. (Ofsted, 2015: 60)

This is reflected in a focus on respect in later years although direct mention of families is not included. Ofsted also considers the effectiveness of the overall leadership and management in a school with regard to

> how well leaders and governors promote all forms of equality and foster greater understanding of and respect for people of all faiths (and those of no faith), races, genders, ages, disability and sexual orientations (and other groups with protected characteristics [as defined in the Equality Act]), through their words, actions and influence within the school and more widely in the community. (2015: 39)

This underlines the requirement within the National Curriculum (DfE, 2014) to address matters relating to relationships, and reinforces through statutory inspection the importance of valuing diverse family relationships. These two statements from Ofsted indicate how schools are expected to both promote and value the notion of family, both those of the children within the school, and models of family found within the wider community. It must be noted that promoting a diverse understanding of ways of being 'family' in primary schools is often both sensitive and contentious (Woolley, 2010; Smolkin and Young, 2011; Kelly, 2012; DePalma, 2016). It was a theme that emerged from research undertaken with student teachers in England exploring the potentially difficult and controversial issues they may encounter with their pupils.

Research undertaken with final year student teachers in England sought to explore the issues that they felt would be most difficult to address in their first teaching post. An online questionnaire was circulated to course leaders of initial teacher training courses in universities (often referred to as 'centre-based' training) for distribution to students during the late spring and early summer terms of 2016. Courses were identified through practitioner networks and institutional websites, with permission being sought from a gatekeeper (usually the Head of Education or Course Leader), and additional permissions gained at a more senior level depending on organizational policy. A link to the questionnaire was then passed to the gatekeeper, along with an introduction to the project to give explanation to the students. All institutions and participants were anonymous, and no university, course or student is identifiable within the data. Ethical approval was gained from the researcher's home university; all participants gave informed consent at the initial stage of completing the questionnaire and had the right to withdraw at any stage during the data collection process. This followed the pattern used in 2008 for a similar survey (Woolley, 2010) in order to enable comparison.

The survey was structured using initial questions to identify the age range for which each student was training to teach, their regional location, the type of course being undertaken and their gender. Initial questions used a sliding scale to identify: issues that had been addressed during the training course; the importance the students placed on each issue; and how often they expected to encounter the issues in their first year of teaching, with each being given in response to a list of issues prepopulated by the researcher. They were then asked, *Which three issues do you anticipate finding most difficult to address in school?* drawing on those provided in earlier questions, or adding their own, with the opportunity for free-flow responses to give reasons. The particular data from this survey on issues relating to families, relationships and children's home lives are addressed in this chapter.

Initially, data were coded using themes identified from a similar research project of 2008 (Woolley, 2010), and reviewed and revised as new themes emerged, detecting frequencies of terms with shared meanings. Subsequent readings refined and clustered codes extrapolating themes and meta-themes (Krippendorp, 2004). This process was repeated several times to minimize the risk of researcher bias or inconsistency.

Participants were asked which three issues they anticipated finding most difficult to address in school in their first teaching post. Of the 105 open responses to this question, the most frequent concerns expressed were the following:

- death and bereavement 33.3 per cent
- homophobia 27.6 per cent

- anti-racist/multicultural issues 26.4 per cent
- sex and relationship issues 20.7 per cent

It is interesting that each of these areas relates to the broad area of Relationships Education, whether with peers, family members or others in the community or wider society. Overall, 91 per cent of respondents identified one or more issues relating to relationships and the ways in which relationship issues impact on wellbeing (e.g. sexual orientation, growing up, families, and homophobia). Student teachers were also asked about the issues that had been covered during their course. Clearly this is a matter of student perception or recall, but 47.6 per cent indicated that issues relating to families had been covered: this compares to 57.3 per cent of the 160 respondents to the 2008 survey (Woolley, 2010: 7). While it is not possible to undertake a detailed comparison of the two surveys (2008 and 2016) here, this comparison is worthy of brief note and provides an area for monitoring through future research. These data suggest that students have concerns about issues within families, changes that occur in children's home experience, and issues within the community between families, but that more than half do not recall exploring these issues during their course in order to prepare strategies to use in the classroom. In terms of family diversities, the three main themes that emerged from the data, namely family, identity and sexual orientation form elements for consideration in the next sections of this chapter.

Family

In free-flow explanations of their responses to the questionnaire, students identified in some detail the basis of their apprehensions. One was already working as an unqualified teacher:

> I have been in post for nearly four weeks and have already had to deal with four individual family issues. I did not receive adequate training or advice for these situations e.g. divorce and one parent not being [allowed] to pick up a child but turning up at the door, a child with no mother and a father with MND [motor neurone disease] and the impact it has on the child, a child with a life threatening illness and trying to manage parent expectations and ensure the wellbeing of a whole class and other safeguarding issues with families.
>
> (Undergraduate student, West Midlands)

Another student acknowledged the diversity she anticipated encountering in her first classroom, and the need to take this into account when addressing children's pastoral needs:

> Children will come from diverse backgrounds and their needs [relating to family issues] will be greatly different so I have to be aware of these and adapt them accordingly.
>
> (Undergraduate student, West Midlands)

Some of the students were aware of the changes that children may be facing in their home lives. On addressing family separation, one student commented,

> It seems so common that it is the elephant in the room and tricky to acknowledge the difficulties that may arise as everyone 'copes'.
>
> (Undergraduate student, north-west)

It is interesting that this student has gained a perception that family separation is an issue that is not spoken about within the classroom, and one wonders how this has come about. It may be that a focus on curriculum and attainment has lessened the opportunity for practitioners to address pastoral and personal needs, but such an assumption would do a disservice to the dedication and care offered by many teachers. It may be that as a new entrant to the profession the student has not received sufficient training in such areas, and that the intensity of teacher training courses and the focus on subject knowledge and core subjects has not allowed the opportunity for learning that will come subsequently through experience early in their career. This sentiment is reflected by another student:

> [Family separation] is something a lot of children go through and I feel I don't have the skills to support children within this region [*sic*] effectively.
>
> (Undergraduate student, West Midlands)

Another student teacher reflects on additional pastoral issues, which again may benefit later from experience gained through further practice. However, early preparation for significant changes in a child's life is important if those new to the profession are to be effective in their first post:

> I worry about addressing bereavement that children may be going through, what to say and how to address this. Particularly at times such as Mother's day, Father's day, Christmas etc. I want to do best by the child and therefore, want to make sure that they are able to deal with the bereavement and achieve their potential.
>
> (Undergraduate student, East Midlands)

A further student has clearly thought about their approach to difficult issues faced with their learners, and has a positive intention, and an awareness that others in their class will need to be empathetic and begin to understand about changes in life:

> I think it is important to discuss [difficult family situations, for example divorce or the death of a family member] with the whole class; how we can support a child through these difficult times. I would discuss the issue sensitively.
>
> (Postgraduate student, London and south-east)

These examples indicate a willingness on the part of the student teachers to address issues with their learners, but some degree of apprehension about doing this effectively, having appropriate strategies to hand, and discussing sensitive issues. The issues reinforce those chosen for coverage in the *Family Diversities Reading Resource* (Morris and Woolley, 2017) and suggest it can provide readily available resources to support the early career teachers. Elements of this resource are outlined later in this chapter.

Consider your response to these views from final year student teachers.

- Have you encountered issues relating to diverse families in your own practice in schools or settings?
- What issues do you anticipate finding challenging or do you feel apprehensive about facing?
- How have you prepared to support children through their (and their peers') life-changing experiences?

Identity

Other students were concerned about issues relating to identity, and in particular sexual orientation whether relating to a child or a member of their family:

> I wouldn't have a problem teaching [about homophobia] but I feel that it is an issue that many parents may have strong feelings about towards the teaching of it and I think this is where the main difficulties would lie.
>
> (Undergraduate student, West Midlands)

This reflects some of the issues raised in the research in 2008, when concerns about parental views formed a significant part of student responses. One very clear example was provided by an undergraduate student from the north-east of England:

> It is really that classic thing of children going home having listened to their teacher and repeating it to the parent and the parent replying. 'I don't care what your teacher says this ... is the way it is!' (Woolley, 2010: 7)

Homophobia may arise from differences between children, from real or perceived differences concerning families, or through association with others. In England each of these areas is covered by the Equality Act (Legislation.gov.uk, 2010). Allied to this is an understanding of gender identity, which research suggests is becoming increasingly understood by young people in a more fluid and flexible way (Dahlgreen and Shakespeare, 2015; Marsh, 2016; Olchawski, 2016):

I think that there are so many instances where gender stereotypes are present in the schools and they are not noticed and considered normal. This is also something that children encounter a lot at home and if this is something that children are struggling with then this is really going to affect their progress in their education. As a teacher, it is a subject that is really hard to get children to think about what it means to be a particular gender as they are so ingrained in our society and there is not a lot of awareness within schools themselves. I don't expect that there would be a great deal of support in a school for teachers should a situation arise.

(Postgraduate student, north-east)

This student later elaborated,

There has been focus placed on the fact that our role as teachers is to develop the 'whole child' but there has been little [content during my training course] about what that actually means and ways of practically achieving this.

Whatever the reality of levels of support within school, it is important to note that at this point the student is not confident that it exists. This suggests that it may be beneficial for training programmes to include information about accessing school policies, the responsibilities of school leaders including governors, and support networks external to schools that can be called upon if needs arise. It may also be beneficial to consider whether schools with different foundations (e.g. church schools) have different approaches, although all maintained schools in England are covered by the same equality legislation. While it cannot be ascertained whether such materials were included in this student's course (or may have been included at a later date), what is clear is that had this been the case they have not assimilated or internalized them at this point. This contrasts with the response from another student, who states:

By having in depth inclusion sessions, I feel I am prepared going into my first teaching post with a deep understanding of the many sensitive issues that can arise within primary school. However I do not think you really can be prepared until a situation arises.

(Undergraduate student, East Midlands)

While it could be inferred from these two students that the one on a longer course of study (four years as opposed to one) may have received a broader range of coverage due to the extended timescale of their training, it was not only students on one year postgraduate courses that noted a lack of some aspects of content within their course. This suggests that course design plays a significant part, not only course duration:

I do not think some issues which are becoming of increasing importance such as transgender children and homophobic bullying are dealt with in teacher training as it is presumed that students will know how to deal with these when they arise. I think that more should be done to address how to deal with such issues identified and how it can be integrated into the curriculum.

– Undergraduate student, north-west (King-Hill and Woolley, 2018: 133)

This apparent omission from the course is interesting. In Ofsted's definition of the requirements of a 'good' school it is stated that

teachers and other adults are quick to tackle the rare use of derogatory or aggressive language and always challenge stereotyping. (2015: 53)

This includes the range of issues detailed by the student, as well as those identified in earlier quotes from participants in the survey. The need to challenge inappropriate language and to always challenge stereotyping is a strongly stated expectation of the requirement for a 'good' school and could be expected to be reflected as such within a student's course of training. One respondent gives a view on why such an omission may occur:

I don't believe that enough training is given on developing children as a whole person. I feel that my training has focused almost entirely on their academic development to the detriment of helping to prepare children for life. Preparing children for life is important, especially in a world of ever-increasing problems, and it is this that I think will be hard to deal with.

(Undergraduate, East Midlands)

Another student suggests that gender stereotyping may be so engrained within society that it may be possible for a teacher to miss its occurrence by being so used to experiencing it:

[Gender stereotyping] is frequent at a low level (you can't do that because you're a girl) and almost excepted [sic] so will be hard to know when to confront it.

(Postgraduate student, London and south-east)

Tackling instances of stereotyping or prejudice is important, but the *Family Diversities Reading Resource* provides the means to take a proactive approach, by including books in the school library, classroom bookcases and in lessons which promote an understanding or diversity and inclusion rather than reacting to a deficit.

Finally, with regard to gender identity, the 2016 survey highlighted some concerns about addressing trans issues. This was an area that did not appear in the results of the 2008 survey:

I feel that the world is becoming more accepting [of trans people] and people are allowed to be different however I feel that working with primary aged children this is an issue that they may find hard to understand and it is quite abstract to imagine not feeling right within your own body.

(Undergraduate student, north-west)

This is an area that has been addressed in the revised edition of the *Family Diversities Reading Resource* (2017), with responses to the student teacher survey reinforcing the need for the inclusion of additional picture books relating to gender identity and non-binary understandings of gender. As was noted earlier in this chapter, books including *Are You a Boy or Are You a Girl?* (Savage, 2015), *I Am Jazz* (Herthel and Jennings, 2014), *Introducing Teddy: A Story about Being Yourself* (Wolton, 2016), *10,000 Dresses* (Ewert, 2008) and *Morris Micklewhite and the Tangerine Dress* (Baldacchino, 2014) all provide high-quality stories and illustrations appropriate for learners in primary schools. The original resource (2007) included classifications of 'gender stereotyping' and 'difference' but not gender identity in such an overt way.

Consider:

- what factors might impact on a parent, carer or teacher's views on how trans and cis identities are discussed in school;
- how aware are you of gender stereotyping or gender-specific expectations manifesting themselves in schools or classrooms; and
- how important do you consider gender identity is in the development of someone's personal, unique identity? Might it be centrally important for some people, and more peripheral for others?

Sexual orientation

Intergenerational concerns are highlighted by the student teachers' responses to the questionnaire, which anticipate a tension between what they feel able to discuss with children, the views of the children themselves, and attitudes held within families. This reflects the concerns expressed by the student teachers in the research undertaken in 2008, an example of which was noted earlier (Woolley, 2010). In 2016 students indicated that

> I feel [homophobia] will be a difficult issue to tackle with children often following parents' views on the matter.
>
> (Undergraduate student, Yorkshire and Humber)

> Throw away comments such as 'you're gay' need to be tackled and understood that this is homophobic language, however the children might not realise they have done anything wrong.
>
> Undergraduate student, East Midlands (King-Hill and Woolley, 2018: 133)

At primary age I have found that children may display non-heteronormative behaviours and mannerisms however they tend to be too young to identify as LGBT, making it difficult to address homophobia as children may not realise that specific bullying is homophobic if they do not know they are gay etc or if another child is.

(Postgraduate student, north-east)

The developing sexual identity of children or young people is discussed in Chapter 6, and was touched on briefly early in this chapter. What is evident here is that they are aware of a range of ways of expressing that identity through being family, from their peers, members of their community and the characters they see portrayed on the television. Children are therefore aware of families with two male parents, those with parents separated by divorce or work, and many other models of family life. Promoting acceptance and an appreciation of diversity is thus not raising new issues for them, but rather bringing their knowledge into the safe space of a school classroom in order to discuss difference, diversity, respect and mutual understanding. As one student notes, there is still progress to be made in this area:

Because we are still in a society where heterosexuality is the 'norm' and other sexualities are outside of that 'norm'. This is shown when we discretely teach sexualities rather than having one lesson where we talk about possible relationships – that could include m–f, m–m, f–f etc. (including family structure). By secluding [sic] out sexualities and difference (rather than simply acknowledging and celebrating all possible differences) we are still inferring that heterosexuality is the 'norm' and that we have to make the others explicit. Therefore, tackling negative views of sexualities.

(Undergraduate student, East Midlands)

Another student expresses some caution at how to address such issues of diversity, and how to do this in an appropriate manner:

Again, the 'correct' approach to this. How far would you go into detail with primary age children to address [homophobia]? How would you deal with staff/ families/ pupil families who were inappropriate?

(Female undergraduate student, West Midlands)

These comments suggest that the trainee teachers are nervous about addressing homophobia due to caution about parental views, a perceived sensitivity to the subject, and wanting to use appropriate strategies. Each of these suggests a need for additional training to enable critical reflection on practice in this area (e.g. through resources from Stonewall, Schools Out or Gendered Intelligence signposted in this book). This will support them in meeting and maintaining the Teachers' Standards, which state that a teacher must

- establish a safe and stimulating environment for pupils, rooted in mutual respect;
- demonstrate consistently the positive attitudes, values and behaviour which are expected of pupils. (DfE, 2011: 10)

Further, these standards also state that teacher must 'have a secure understanding of how a range of factors can inhibit pupils' ability to learn, and how best to overcome these' (DfE, 2011: 11). Such factors must include areas of difference that may lead to bullying, and appreciating and valuing the diverse backgrounds of children, including the families and homes from which they come.

Consider the extent to which you feel heteronormativity (the assumption that everyone is straight) to be prevalent within society and the communities in which you live and work.
- How might this impact on those who do not identify as heterosexual?
- Reflect on Neil's experience from the vignette at the start of this chapter. Should school policies identify the need to avoid heterosexism? How could Neil's colleagues, and indeed Neil himself, be encouraged to avoid making assumptions about members of the school community?

Following the use of the *Family Diversities Reading Resource* (Morris and Woolley, 2007) and the sharing of the research with student teachers from 2008 (Woolley, 2010) with undergraduate trainee teachers, student representatives fed back on the effectiveness of this input to their course during its management committee. A head teacher who was present at this meeting took the picture book resource back to his school and set up a Pupil Focus Group to decide which of the books might make a positive addition to the school library. Having audited the school's resources, children accessed the picture books in the local library and evaluated them according to their own criteria to judge which might have an impact on others within their school: 'Focus centred on issues such as divorce, separation, disability and different types of families (single parents, same sex parents, children in care, fostering)' (Intuition, 2014). These children (aged 9–11 years) then set up a diversity reading club, where they shared the books with peers aged 6–8 years. The head teacher observed,

Children leading these sessions have reported that their peers have responded positively to these texts. Younger children are posing lots of questions and in doing so are challenging their predetermined perceptions and broadening their comprehension of diversity. The lead group of children reported that their peers had also learned to respect differences. They had recognised that everyone was different and that they understood how everyone deserves to be treated the same, irrespective of their circumstances. (Intuition, 2014)

This reflection of the use of the resources in a school was an unexpected addition to the review of the *Family Diversities Reading Resource* and helped to provide an indication that a new edition was a worthwhile enterprise. Far more extensively, the No Outsiders Project (a twenty-eight-month project funded by the Economic and Social Research Council from 2006) provided schools with packs of books relating specifically to LGBT issues and evaluated their effectiveness (No Outsiders, 2010) with significant reach and impact. The Family Diversities project, which emerged at a similar time, has focused on the needs of student teachers, and on providing pre-service and in-service training for teachers, with a broader focus on a variety of issues relating to difference and families. Unlike No Outsiders it did not research the impact of the use of the picture books in schools, although a small number of students have explored their use through their research projects during undergraduate and postgraduate courses.

One question we are often asked when teaching about inclusive RSE is whether approaches should differ in church schools. The Church of England addressed this to some degree in 2017 through the publication of the second edition of *Valuing All God's Children*, which specifically addressed LGBT matters in schools:

> In creating a school environment that promotes dignity for all and a call to live fulfilled lives as uniquely gifted individuals, pupils will be equipped to accept difference of all varieties and be supported to accept their own gender identity or sexual orientation and that of others. In order to do this it will be essential to provide curriculum opportunities where difference is explored, same-sex relationships, same-sex parenting and transgender issues may be mentioned as a fact in some people's lives. For children of same-sex or transgender parents or with close LGBT relatives this will be a signal of recognition that will encourage self-esteem and belonging. (Church of England, 2017: 20)

This is a welcome clarification of approach, and provides a firm basis for schools to develop policies for anti-bullying and RSE.

Summary of key approaches to support effective practice

In order to develop effective practice in developing inclusive Relationships Education it is important to

- consider our use of language, including gendered language and language about families, and parents/carers;

- evaluate the resources available in schools and to consider not only what is presented but also what is currently omitted;
- develop a full appreciation of the implications of equality legislation, and strategies for its implementation; and
- develop conceptions of how diversity and equality issues can be addressed in classrooms, in order to ensure that children feel safe, valued and appreciated whatever their background, identity or maturity.

While these sentiments may be reflected in both legislation and statutory documentation in England, it would appear from participant responses to the research outlined in this chapter that the issues have become less of a priority in training settings (at least according to student perception) over the past decade. While this research is relatively small-scale, and the students self-selecting, this is an area of concern that requires careful monitoring.

Conclusion and summary of key points

Research into student teacher concerns about the issues they will face in their first post indicate that relationship issues, including family relationships, are of significant concern. This includes working with children who have one, two or more parents/carers, have family members absent for a variety of reasons, or live in a family pattern different to some of their peers. The three main themes highlighted from that research, namely family, identity and sexual orientation (outlined earlier in this chapter) each relate directly to the broad area of relationships and are highlighted by student teachers both as areas for apprehension, and of importance. The *Family Diversities Reading Resource* provides materials that can support children in these areas, representing their home lives in positive ways which seek to ensure that they are included in the core resources in a school or classroom library, and providing role models in literature that might otherwise be absent. These resources reflect the areas of concern identified by the student teachers.

Learning from the Family Diversities project suggests that the focus must be on high-quality resources, and that professional staff in schools need to ensure that the purchases they make avoid stereotypes, inappropriate language and books that are well intentioned but lacking in an inclusive focus. The student teachers' needs suggest that either initial teacher training courses need to provide an induction to high-quality resources that the students can evaluate and choose to employ in their classroom practice, or that the delivery of training in this area needs to be more effective. This requires not only an evaluation of the family backgrounds of the children in a class, but also how wider society is portrayed. Whatever the current experience of pupils, their lives may be subject to change, and sometimes unexpected change. It would be interesting to identify through further research whether the perceptions of these student teachers changed in the early stages of their career.

The concerns of one parent who was considering the possibility of their child identifying as trans or gay provide one indication of the need to develop inclusive Relationships Education in primary schools:

> I don't want my child to be the one to pave the way. It might be selfish, but because of that risk ... Who knows where we will have come in another ten years, but right now with the amount of issues that they will come up against in terms of social pressure, teachers not understanding, registering or supporting ...

Ensuring that we do not presume or assume, being thoughtful about the resources we use, and considering the power of language each provides the opportunity to work increasingly towards inclusive Relationships Education, and indeed inclusive schools.

Signposts

Gendered Intelligence: a not-for-profit community interest company seeking to increase understanding of diverse gender identity; it works particularly with young trans people aged 8–25 years. http://genderedintelligence.co.uk/.

Mermaids: support for trans and gender-diverse children and young people. www. mermaidsuk.org.uk/.

Morris, J., and Woolley. R. (2017) *Family Diversities Reading Resource* (2nd edn). Lincoln: Bishop Grosseteste University and University of Worcester. http://libguides. bishopg.ac.uk/childrensliterature.

Schools Out: an educational charity seeking to help schools to become safe spaces for all, with a particular focus on support for LGBT students and staff. www.schools—out. org.uk/.

Think2Speak: empowering young people to speak out; a youth group for gender-diverse young people. www.think2speak.com/.

Two websites that offer particular support and information about and for intersex people are Intersex Human Rights Australia (https://ihra.org.au) and Intersex Day (https://intersexday.org/en/).

Further reading

Church of England (2017) *Valuing All God's Children: Guidance for Church of England Schools on Challenging Homophobic, Biphobic and Transphobic Bullying*. London: Church of England Education Office.

Terence Higgins Trust (2016) *SHH … No Talking: LGBT-Inclusive Sex and Relationships Education in the UK*. London: Terrence Higgins Trust.

References

Baldacchino, C. (2014) *Morris Micklewhite and the Tangerine Dress*. Toronto: Groundwood Books/House of Anasi Press.

Beaty, A. (2013) *Rosie Revere, Engineer*. New York: Abrams Books for Young Readers.

Brook (2017) *Gender*. www.brook.org.uk/your—life/category/gender (accessed 5 August 2018).

Church of England (2017) *Valuing All God's Children: Guidance for Church of England Schools on Challenging Homophobic, Biphobic and Transphobic Bullying*. London: Church of England Education Office.

Dahlgreen, W., and Shakespeare, A. E. (2015) *1 in 2 Young People Say They Are Not 100% Heterosexual*. https://yougov.co.uk/news/2015/08/16/half-young-not-heterosexual/ (accessed 7 August 2018).

DCSF (2007) *Homophobic Bullying: Safe to Learn–Embedding Anti-bullying Work in Schools*. London: DCSF.

DePalma, R. (2016) 'Gay Penguins, Sissy Ducklings … and Beyond? Exploring Gender and Sexuality Diversity Through Children's Literature'. *Discourse: Studies in the Cultural Politics of Education*, 37 (6), 828–45.

DfE (2011) *Teachers' Standards: Guidance for School Leaders, School Staff and Governing Bodies*. www.gov.uk/government/publications/teachers-standards (accessed 7 August 2018).

DfE (2014) *National Curriculum in England: Framework for Key Stages 1–4*. www.gov.uk/government/publications/national-curriculum-in-england-framework-for-key-stages-1-to-4/ (accessed 7 August 2018).

Ewert, M. (2008) *10,000 Dresses*. New York: Seven Stories Press.

Hellen, M (2009) 'Transgender Children in Schools'. *Liminalis: Journal of Sex/Gender Emancipation and Resistance*, 81–99. http://eprints.gold.ad.uk/3531/ (accessed 5 August 2018).

Herthel, J., and Jennings, J. (2014) *I Am Jazz*. New York: Dial Books for Young Readers.

Hewston, R. (2018) 'Gender Diversity', in *Understanding Inclusion*, ed. R. Woolley. London: Routledge.

Intuition (2014) *Intuition: A Newsletter for Students by Students – Primary BA QTS, Edition 2, 2014: Interdisciplinary Learning: Respecting Diversity in Professional Practice*. Worcester: University of Worcester.

Kelly, J. (2012) 'Two Daddy Tigers and a Baby Tiger: Promoting Understandings about Same Gender Parented Families Using Picture Books'. *Early Years*, 32 (3), 288–300.

King-Hill, S., and Woolley, R. (2018) 'Sexual Behaviours and Development', in *Understanding Inclusion: Core Concepts, Policy and Practice*, ed. R. Woolley. London: Routledge.

Krippendorp, K. (2004) *Content Analysis: An Introduction to Its Methodology*. Thousand Oaks, CA: Sage.

Legislation.gov.uk (2010) *Equality Act 2010*. www.legislation.gov.uk/ukpga/2010/15/contents (accessed 7 August 2018).

Marsh, S. (2016) 'The Gender-Fluid Generation: Young People on Being Male, Female or Non-binary'. *The Guardian*. www.theguardian.com/commentisfree/2016/mar/23/gender-fluid-generation-young-people-male-female-trans (accessed 31 March 2018).

Morris, J., and Woolley. R. (2007) *Family Diversities Reading Resource*. Lincoln: Bishop Grosseteste University.

Morris, J., and Woolley. R. (2017) *Family Diversities Reading Resource* (2nd edn). Lincoln: Bishop Grosseteste University. http://libguides.bishopg.ac.uk/childrensliterature (accessed 7 August 2018).

No Outsiders (2010) www.researchcatalogue.esrc.ac.uk/grants/RES-062-23-0095/read (accessed 7 August 2018).

Ofsted (2015) *School Inspection Handbook*. www.gov.uk/government/publications/school-inspection-handbook-from-september-2015 (accessed 7 August 2018).

Olchawski, J. (2016) *Sex Equality: State of the Nation 2016*. London: Fawcett Society.

Pomranz, C. (2014) *Made by Raffi*. London: Frances Lincoln Children's Books.

Savage, S. (2015) *Are You a Boy or Are You a Girl?* Sine loco: Print Ninja.

Smolkin, L., and Young, C. (2011) 'Missing Mirrors, Missing Windows: Children's Literature Textbooks and LGBT Topics'. *Language Arts*, 88 (3), 217–25.

Tehan, M. (2012) 'Gove Rejects Plan to Ban Catholic Booklet from Schools'. *Catholic Herald*, 23 February. www.catholicherald.co.uk/news/2012/02/23/gove-rejects-call-to-ban-catholic-booklet-from-schools/ (accessed 7 August 2018).

Terence Higgins Trust (2016) *SHH … No Talking: LGBT-Inclusive Sex and Relationships Education in the UK*. London: Terrence Higgins Trust.

Wilkins, R. (2014) *Queer Theory, Gender Theory*. New York: Magnus Books.

Wolton, J. (2016) *Introducing Teddy: A Story about Being Yourself*. London: Bloomsbury.

Woolcock, N. (2018) 'Head Boys and Girls Outdated Says Guernsey Grammar School'. *Times*, 18 April. www.thetimes.co.uk/article/head-boys-and-girls-outdated-says-guernsey-grammar-school-29djwddtb (accessed 5 August 2018).

Woolley, R. (2010) *Tackling Controversial Issues in the Primary School: Facing Life's Challenges with Your Learners*. London: Routledge.

Woolley, R. (ed.) (2018) *Understanding Inclusion: Core Concepts, Policy and Practice*. London: Routledge.

Zolotow, C. (1972) *William's Doll*. New York: Harper Trophy.

Where next?

Hadriana, a head teacher of a primary school, explains her concerns about the next steps in developing an effective approach to RSE in her school:

> *As a head, it is difficult to know where to start in moving a potentially sensitive and controversial area of the curriculum like RSE forward. I know that what we are doing at the moment is probably not really meeting the needs of the children but I don't want to create any problems with my staff or parents ... it's really difficult. We have a policy but it is pretty minimal. I need to look carefully at how we can do this.*

Chapter outline

Introduction

This final chapter explores the possible next steps for professionals working with children and young people in developing policy and practice in their settings or school. It addresses the design of a policy for RSE in a primary setting, particularly in terms of age-appropriate content and how decision making by a whole team is an essential element of an effective RSE programme. It also considers how to develop partnerships with parents/carers, the wider community and links with secondary schools as a part of policy making. Issues concerning professional confidence and child protection/safeguarding are addressed which, we consider, are key elements in establishing best practice.

Developing a policy for RSE

The chapters in this book have discussed the wider government policy agendas which impact on schools and settings, and this chapter addresses the issues that inform the development of a clear school/setting policy that reflects an appropriate pedagogical approach to RSE. Blake (2008: 34) states that learning about sex 'is a core part of school life' through 'daily playground education' along with three other areas within schools: the formal curriculum, pastoral care and health services. An awareness of the importance of the pastoral care of children within both formal and informal settings continues to grow. Blake draws upon the Sex Education Forum's confirmation of what an effective RSE educational entitlement provides:

- *Information about the law and public policy*, so that children and young people know, understand and claim their rights as citizens.
- *Information about religious and secular values*, including those values and practices enshrined in scripture and the everyday reality of diverse lives, so that young people respect the right of others to have different views and beliefs, and acquire the skills to live in a diverse world.
- *Health education* to ensure that young people understand emotional and physical health and the skills and confidence to maintain and look after their health. (2008: 34)

The issues outlined above offer some structure for the development of a policy although these, it may be viewed, overlap with other areas of the curriculum. Chapter 4 addressed the transference of content within RSE into other curriculum areas and this interrelatedness strengthens the overall RSE programme.

It is a requirement that all primary schools in England have a written policy for Relationships Education. This must be freely available to those who request a copy, and be made available on the school website (DfE, 2018: 9). This policy should

- define Relationships Education;
- set out the content and how it is taught;
- describe how the subject is monitored and evaluated; and
- include information about why parents/carers do not have a right to withdraw their child. (p. 9)

Where a primary school chooses to teach sex education beyond the content of the mandatory science curriculum, a policy should outline both the content and information about a parent/carer's right to withdraw their child. Importantly, from 2019, guidance indicates that the curriculum should reflect the views of teachers and pupils: 'Listening and responding to the views of young people will strengthen the policy, ensuring that it meets the needs of all pupils' (DfE, 2018: 10).

A separate policy ensures that the appropriate skills and knowledge about relationships and sex are not compromised by the already burgeoning curriculum. We have argued in this book that the RSE policy document should reflect the subject's interrelatedness to all areas of the curriculum, and we advocate that a holistic, cross-curricular design is necessary for all aspects of relationships and sex to be addressed. We have also argued that choosing to omit sex education (apart from the mandatory aspects of the science curriculum) leaves children asking 'why' when taught about the physical changes that occur during puberty. Not providing any context or further explanation to explain why their bodies change is similar to providing a partial learning experience, which does a disservice to their maturity and intellectual ability. This is one reason why we believe that sex education must be fully integrated within policy design in primary schools.

Getting started

A useful starting point for any team of adults working with children and young people is to consider existing practice and programmes for RSE. Schools and settings offer a wide variety of provision, and it is helpful to think about what the provision offers in order to identify future directions.

A team leader gathers staff together to discuss the development of the RSE policy. Oliver recounts,

As part of our regular reviews of elements of the curriculum, the team leader wanted us to talk about the RSE policy. I was a bit out of my depth because I had never taught it, had never watched the programme being taught and was unsure what I could contribute to developing it. I don't really know what primary school children should be learning about in Relationship Education. We started by looking at the current policy and it seemed very

> *limited and generic. We were also given the RSE policy from another school and an outline of their content and it was easier to compare and contrast the two documents. It was a really useful exercise and we talked in depth about what we felt we could and could not cover in our school.*

Based on Oliver's experience of developing his school policy, some key observations are the following:

- it should be a whole-team/school approach, including consultation with pupils;
- it should offer other examples of practice which can be sought through networking with other schools and agencies;
- it should be within the remit of the law (see Chapter 1); and
- it should ensure that professional confidence is maintained.

The value of a whole-team approach in developing an RSE policy is the establishment of a shared ethos that reflects the needs of the children in the setting and is therefore specific to the staff involved in planning, children and the wider community. A school's culture 'is a continual process in which attitudes, values and skills continually reinforce each other' (Senge, 2000); this suggests that these 'skills' lie within a school, or setting, and are determined by the people working within it. MacGilchrist et al. (2004: 27) refer to Sammons et al. (1995: 8) who identified twelve characteristics of an effective school, one of which is 'shared vision and goals'. This implies a vision that has been agreed between those working within it and extends to the implementation of the goals. In order to have a vision that is *shared*, the attitudes and values of the professional community, which make up the school, or setting, must contribute to the culture. Furthermore, the 'skills' must reflect the needs of staff, learners and the wider community. In the eleventh characteristic, focus on teachers taking responsibility for their continued professional development is stated in order to develop and sustain the desired skills. While each setting can customize its RSE policy to meet its specific needs, culture and ethos, the learners' entitlement to appropriate content and a flexible pedagogy should be maintained. This can be established through professional development in PSHE/RSE in order that the wider context beyond the setting's gates be reflected to reduce the polarization of the programme. A tool to support policy development is provided by the PSHE Association and is included in the Signposts at the end of this chapter.

The need for trained staff in RSE is a well-recognized strategy to support colleagues as well as meet the needs of the children (SEF, 2005; UK Youth Parliament, 2007; Macdonald, 2009). Piercy and Haynes (2006) suggest that for an effective delivery of RSE, teachers require formal training, in particular in the primary school sector. In 2001 the DfES launched a pilot scheme to address the professional development of teachers responsible for the teaching of RSE. The Professional Development and the Accreditation of the Teaching of Sex and Relationships Education scheme aimed to improve the quality of RSE within the context of PSHE in schools. The scheme was closely linked with the National Healthy School Standard, making explicit connections between health and education and, therefore, was part of a ten-year programme to reduce teenage pregnancy rates in the UK. Around thirty teachers volunteered to take part in the national pilot scheme, from a range of settings.

The evaluation of the pilot was intended to inform areas for revision and to identify the strengths of the programme, with a possible extension to the wider national availability of the programme in 2002–3. Among the main strengths of the pilot programme was the formation of partnerships between teachers and health professionals. During the training provided by this programme, opportunities for networking allowed teachers to enter into professional dialogue to reflect on their policies and practices regarding RSE/PSHE. Warwick et al. (2005: 241) make the point that the majority of teachers volunteering to take part in the pilot were experienced RSE teachers and acknowledge that these teachers noticed most improvement in their classroom practice. It could be claimed that the under-confident and inexperienced teachers for whom the programme was designed to assist were not targeted sufficiently. A further and possibly more significant point from the evaluation of the pilot programme is that, although enhanced professional practice was considered to be a strength, Warwick et al. (2005) recognize that the impact on children's learning was not assessed and stress that assumptions about this cannot be drawn from the pilot evaluation alone. The wider availability of the official programme in 2002–3 recruited fifty local authorities who expressed an interest in taking part, and increased funding was provided to allow 750 teachers, nationally, to participate. Furthermore, Vincent (2007) comments that high teacher workloads result in potential conflicts with other curriculum responsibilities and the non-statutory status of RSE diminishing its entitlement within the wider primary curriculum. A lack of time to plan, consult and develop specialist knowledge means that RSE may not be given the priority it deserves within the curriculum. The move to make Relationships Education mandatory in primary schools addresses this to some degree, but still leaves sex education at risk where schools choose either to not address it or to under-resource it.

Networking with other primary schools or settings can be a useful way for practitioners to compare RSE policies and programmes. Through awareness of the wider provision in RSE reassurance can be sought for team members who may feel uncertain or anxious about making decisions regarding an RSE programme and policy. This is especially so for head teachers or team leaders who may feel uncomfortable about RSE. RSE is one of the most challenging areas of the curriculum according to Walker et al. (2003); the research outlined in both the Introduction and Chapter 8 in this book indicates that this challenge remains.

Other research evidence (Mason, 2008) suggests that some teachers feel that their course of initial teacher education did not sufficiently prepare them for teaching RSE, although having many years of teaching experience does increase confidence. Research evidence collected by Walker et al. (2003: 325) suggests that where whole teams are involved in professional development for RSE, PSHE coordinators or curriculum leaders feel less isolated and that the team's overall capacity to deliver high-quality RSE is improved. When teams have a shared vision or purpose for the outcomes of a programme of RSE, designing a policy becomes a more cohesive process. Through working collaboratively, and through the involvement of members of the senior management and possibly governors, increased confidence in developing RSE programmes and policy, particularly concerning the development of resources, may be felt. Piercy and Haynes (2006: 13) report on a case study of a primary school embarking on a new whole school approach to RSE that involves all teachers and teaching assistants in the implementation of the programme. They describe how the staff, in the early stages of designing and delivering the new RSE programme, engaged in some focus groups that centred around exploring the level of experience in teaching RSE, their feelings about a whole school approach to RSE, staff concerns about the programme and any staff training needs. The findings from the focus groups identify three key concerns:

1 Content of the material in the new programme
2 The teachers' knowledge levels
3 Management of the teaching. (Piercy and Haynes, 2006: 13)

The new programme proposed the use of new resources consisting of three videos to be introduced at varied stages in the primary phase. Staff, in the focus groups, shared concerns that some of the material may be inappropriate for the younger-aged children. These concerns regarding resources are corroborated by Mason (2008). The staff commented that the 'naming of body parts using correct terminology was considered particularly problematic' (Piercy and Haynes, 2006: 13). In their groups staff shared their embarrassment and feelings of being ill-prepared to discuss with children matters of a sexual nature. Piercy and Haynes make the point that the focus groups provided an opportunity for staff to reveal vulnerability and to feel reassured that some of their colleagues also shared these concerns. Also, conversations were undertaken about how the programme could be delivered, for example, in single-sex groupings with same gendered teachers. In providing these opportunities to discuss and explore the concerns of staff, this primary school offers a model for others engaged in the development of a policy and RSE programme. Staff members were afforded the opportunity to share, and resolve, issues while maintaining a sense of shared purpose and commitment to their role in providing a comprehensive programme of RSE. In this instance, the collaboration of the staff provided a source of support and confidence for the whole staff. Kippax and Stephenson (2005) suggest that effective RSE offers young people opportunities for 'agency' which depict the ability to take action, power and operation. We propose that where whole teams work collaboratively, they too are afforded 'agency'.

Key elements of a policy

In the design of a policy and then a programme for RSE a number of key elements should be considered; aims and objectives; ways of learning and teaching.

Within the legal framework, the aims and objectives of the policy define the ethos for RSE in the setting. Blake and Muttock (2004) suggest the following six steps to support those involved in the formulation of an RSE policy and programme, which remain valid when considering the implementation of revised guidance in England:

- Step 1: identifying need
- Step 2: responding to need
- Step 3: delivering RSE
- Step 4: assessment of learning
- Step 5: evaluation of teaching programme
- Step 6: reporting and recording process

Many educational programmes contain these steps and RSE is, in many ways, no different, although the considerations of the planning, delivery and assessment cycle are important aspects of an RSE programme. We have addressed steps 1, 2 and 3 in Chapters 4, 5 and 7 and the assessment of learning will be focused on later in this chapter. The process of the evaluation of a policy and a programme is necessary in order that the programme maintains its relevance in the setting and the wider community and the process of review remains key. The policy should also consider how children's progress is recorded and reported. The communication of the outcomes of learning in any curriculum area is important to both the learner and their parent or carer. Clear consultation with parents and carers on progress should be carefully considered in the establishing of an RSE policy and programme.

The pedagogy of being brave in teaching matters of relationships and sex has been a theme underpinning the content of this book and we firmly support this approach. Although an agreed and clear pedagogical approach is essential, it is also necessary to explore what concepts and content should be addressed at each stage (see also the discussion in Chapter 6). Chapter 7 explored some of the questions that primary school children may ask and which reveal their levels of understanding. We have identified the need to begin RSE before puberty in order that children are prepared for the physical and emotional changes involved in physical maturation. Piercy and Haynes (2006) suggest that a 'structured and integrated approach' to RSE content between the ages of five and eleven assures that children have the opportunity to consolidate knowledge and a secure reinforcement 'of key theoretical principles while simultaneously addressing the variability in cognitive ability and maturational development within each class' (p. 13). The idea that curriculum content revisited in order to develop knowledge and understanding by building on earlier experiences is a valuable model to adopt. Piercy and Haynes are clear that it is crucial for programme content to be revisited with children throughout the primary phase in order that it is differentiated appropriately and that any misconceptions are resolved.

As we noted in the Introduction to this book, the RSE guidance (DfEE, 2000) identified that the three main elements of RSE were:

- attitudes and skills;
- personal and social skills; and
- knowledge and understanding.

These areas still provide relevant foci when designing the curriculum. Vincent (2007) makes clear that by addressing each of these elements any tendency for knowledge and understanding to dominate the RSE programme can be avoided. It is important that personal attitudes and attributes are the focus of the curriculum.

In preparation for a meeting of a full governing body in a medium-sized primary school, Andrea, a community governor, has been reviewing a range of policy documents including one for RSE. She comments,

I have been a school governor for three years and I think that I have developed a good understanding of how the school works. As governors, we discuss a range of policies every year in order to make sure that they are current and relevant. Sometimes I feel that my lack of experience of working in a primary school – I am the manager of a local supermarket – hampers my understanding of how the policies will be implemented. I joined the governing body as a part of the contribution of our business to the local community and feel that I can offer a range of skills in people management, health and safety issues and finance. However, I do not have any particular understanding of child development and my own memory of education about relationships during my own schooling is scant. I am concerned that this means that I rely too heavily on the views of the head teacher and other teachers on the governing body, when my role is meant to be that of a critical friend.

Consider:

- how the school might support Andrea so that she feels more confident when scrutinizing policy documents;

- what sources of additional information and advice Andrea might access to prepare herself to undertake the task; and
- whether the school can provide opportunities for Andrea to see the school's RSE programme in action, and what issues this might raise for children or those delivering the programme.

Developing progression through the primary phase and beyond

Progression is a key element of any RSE programme if it is to be effective (Piercy and Haynes, 2006). It is important that there is an emphasis on developing knowledge, skills and attitudes and appropriate teaching methods that provide clear progression of content. Earlier, in Chapter 4, we identified the need to seek the views of learners which should inform the design of a programme of study. It is, therefore, necessary to be clear in the writing of an RSE policy and programme that any proposed content is flexibly placed to accommodate the needs of the individual and group.

As many children begin puberty at eight (for girls) or nine years of age (for boys), we strongly recommend that sex education be included alongside Relationships Education in Key Stage 2, and probably before the prescription in the science curriculum. This will build on the learning undertaken through effective Relationships Education throughout a child's schooling, particularly focusing on attitudes, social and personal skills. The Sex Education Forum has long suggested that aspects of emotional development should be taught and that children should be provided with opportunities to practice 'managing emotions confidently, developing empathy for others, building emotional resilience and resourcefulness, developing independence of thought and behaviour' (2005: 3). Likewise for social skills, children should be taught about how to develop and maintain relationships with others and to take responsibility for their own and others' emotional health. These skills apply to a wealth of different relationships beyond those of a sexual nature and have been addressed in Chapter 3.

Planned progression through the primary phase of education allows for clarity between teams and parents/carers. Repetition can be avoided by planning RSE in a coordinated way across primary and secondary phases of education. Piercy and Haynes (2006: 12) define this progression as 'coherent, comprehensive and continuous'. The notion of coherence is also identified in the Macdonald review of RSE (2009). It recommends one 'coherent' guidance document for the PSHE curriculum, to ensure that practitioners are clear about the common principles underpinning effective PSHE education. In turn this will enable a clear progression between phases and stages of education and stages of development, which new guidance terms a graduated approach (DfE, 2018). Developments in Relationships Education have brought an additional mandatory Health element (DfE, 2018) but not integrated the whole of PSHE. Coordination between primary and secondary school teams is a necessary element in devising an RSE policy and programme.

Who should teach RSE?

Throughout the design of an RSE policy and programme, the team should consider which of its members are most suited to implement it. Guidance (DfE, 2018) indicates that the school policy should indicate who would deliver the curriculum (by which we suggest role, rather than named persons). In a primary school where individual class teachers have responsibility for teaching and planning all aspects of PSHE, it may be relevant for the whole team to play a part in delivering the programme. However, specific topics may be dealt with by designated team members or representatives of outside agencies. The benefits of using outside agencies or other visitors can be that they offer other perspectives to children and young people about issues of a sexual nature, or are more prepared to answer more sensitive or probing questions (Corteen, 2006: 83) because of their more distant relationships with children. This is contrary to the often-cited value of the developed relationships between the primary class teacher and their learners. There are, therefore, opportunities that exist in RSE to provide for a range of different adults to implement the programme to ensure that the needs of different children are to be met. For example, for some children the comfort of a familiar adult is helpful and for others it might lead to embarrassment. The Macdonald review (2009: 25) suggested that at the primary phase this is the preferred mode of teaching as 'typically, the primary teacher understands the pupils' individual needs very well and uses this in planning'. This, however, is not as necessary at secondary level where learners are taught by a range of adults. Corteen (2006) states that some teachers in her study preferred school nurses to deliver more sensitive content such as issues relating to sexual orientation. If responsibility is allocated to different people, gaps in the content can emerge (Corteen, 2006) which can prohibit the 'continuous' model of an RSE programme advocated by Piercy and Haynes (2006). The careful construction of assigned content along with shared or observed sessions with children may lead to assurance that the programme is being comprehensively covered. This may, however, lead to a reticence by the children to explore issues of a sexual nature when there is a roomful of adults. In these instances, a careful debrief following each practitioner's input may prove to be a solution.

A key component of a successful RSE programme relates to the confidence and knowledge of the teacher. As the Macdonald review (2009: 27), from research conducted by Ofsted (2005: 6), notes, 'a teacher's lack of knowledge and/or enthusiasm are quickly apparent to the pupils, who react negatively, or are simply embarrassed by their tutor's reluctance to teach the subject'. Teacher confidence appears as a critical element in RSE programmes and should be a considered aspect of the whole school decisions taken when designing the policy and programme content.

Ways of teaching

We have outlined throughout this book the need for a dialogic and discursive approach to RSE, and this pedagogical approach should underpin the ways of teaching. The 'normalizing' of RSE into other curriculum areas to ensure a holistic approach ensures that RSE does not become a 'standalone' subject. The embedding of PSHE and RSE into daily activities and tasks ensures its importance in the primary curriculum. Some generic strategies were outlined in the Introduction to this book. We now develop the consideration of some of these, using focused examples.

Common teaching strategies that can be used to achieve this are:

- circle time;
- children's literature;
- role play;
- debates and philosophy for children; and
- visualization

Circle time

Circle time is a valuable strategy for exploring views and understanding both in large and small groups. Mosley (2005a, 2005b, 2006) outlines that it is a tool that can be used with children at all ages, and also that it can be used effectively with a staff team. For children, circle time can provide the opportunity to engage with a range of emotions and complex relationships in a safe way that is supported by the adult.

The practitioner wants to explore the emotional aspect of puberty, having already introduced the children to some of the bodily changes that occur during this time. A small group of children aged ten are sitting around a table as the adult outlines the session:

'Today we are going to think about being a grown up; what do you think it might feel like? If you feel that you would like to say something when our special circle time shell comes round to you then you can, but

remember that you can pass the shell on if you are still thinking about your contribution, or don't want to say anything ... that is fine. Sophie, I shall pass the shell to you first but I will help to get us thinking by talking about when I was a little girl and what I thought it must be like to be a grown up! When I was about the same age as you, I thought that my mum and dad were really lucky because they seemed to know all the answers to things!' The teacher passes the shell to Sophie who begins the circle time, 'I think it must be fun being a grown up because you can go to bed whenever you like!' Then Peter decides to pass the shell on and not to contribute at this time. For Jack's turn, he comments, 'I think it must be good to be a grown up because you don't have to eat your vegetables if you don't want!' The discussion moves around the small group of eight children until the shell returns to the adult. She wants to begin to talk about how the children feel about being a grown up and the changes they will experience during puberty. She says, 'I enjoyed that, thank you. Now what makes us a grown up then?' Sophie takes the shell. 'Well, our bodies change and we just grow up.' Peter wants to contribute this time and says, 'My brother is at the secondary school and he has got really grumpy all the time and he has grown really tall.' Other children contribute to the discussion about their older siblings' bodily and emotional changes. The teacher is able to use these comments to explore what makes these changes and the emotional responses that can occur during puberty.

The use of the focused time with children to build on the more biological changes during puberty to explore the emotional aspects of those changes allows the children to challenge their assumptions and feel some confidence that this is a natural and expected part of becoming an adult. Other starting points for circle time can be

- special friendships that they have and that they see in their families such as school friends, best friends, their parents, their grandparents, etc. The continuum of friends might be explored (as outlined in Chapter 3); and
- what makes a family? This circle time provides the opportunity to explore the compositions of different families (as outlined in Chapter 5).

Children's literature and media

Books can be an invaluable tool for supporting discussion and tasks at all ages; picture books can play an essential starting point for RSE with children of all ages in the primary phase of education. As noted in Chapter 5, celebrated children's author Babette Cole, among others, has embraced issues of where babies come from. *Mummy Laid an Egg!* (1995) explores some of the myths associated with conception and childbirth and allows for the misconceptions of children to be discussed and corrected. The book is humorous, with cartoon illustrations that are typical of Cole's other publications and so do not stand alone due to their subject matter. Other authors such as Harris and Emberley (1999, 2007, 2010) have published a series of books, each version is updated and revised and become increasingly candid with each version. Other books raise opportunities to discuss diversity in families, such as Valentine (1994), Parnell and Richardson (2005) and Carter (2006), which includes families with same-sex parents. It is important that agreement between the staff team is sought for the use any resource in order that its content is sufficiently familiar to everyone. In this way, staff members are not placed in situations where they feel uncomfortable when using these resources with children. An example may be that a particular illustration or piece of text in a book may not be felt to be suitable and therefore should only be used if agreed by the team. Teams should ensure the provision of a range of books that reflect sexual diversity and not be exclusively heterosexual (more signposts to children's literature are provided in Chapter 2). A range of media can provide useful starting points to introduce issues regarding relationships and sex. One local authority in the East Midlands has commissioned a local youth theatre to create an educational DVD to address issues such as alcohol and risky behaviours and smoking. These are intended to be used as a resource in every secondary school within the county and this innovative peer-educated focus could be used as a strategy at primary level to explore relationship issues and the emotional changes during puberty.

Role play

Role play provides a valuable strategy for children and young people to explore some of the issues raised through RSE. For example, conflict resolution and negotiation in relationships can be successfully addressed through role play.

A group of children had been arguing in the playground for a number of days. The group of eleven year olds, comprising of three boys and two girls, were frequently demonstrating gender-stereotyped behaviours that resulted in the boys being aggressive towards the girls. The teacher, having observed this during playground duty, wanted to support the children in managing their disputes in positive ways. He decided to use the strategy of role play to explore some of the children's perceptions of their behaviour. The following afternoon the teacher, Rob, gathered the whole class together and asked the children to work in small mixed-gender groups. He asked them to play the roles of friends. Rob asked the children to mime actions that showed different feelings such as kindness, anger, friendliness and aggression. He asked different groups to perform their mimes to the rest of the class and began to discuss what each emotion looked like. Rob then asked the groups to act out these emotions using their voices this time. Again, he asked for performances and discussed these with the children. He finally asked the children who were the receivers of the emotional responses; both mimed and not mimed how it felt to be on the receiving end of the behaviours. Rob encouraged contributions from members of the class and spoke about verbal and non-verbal behaviours and how they made each other feel. This short session with the children provided the opportunity to reinforce positive behaviours in the classroom with reminders of how it feels to be the recipient of aggressive behaviour. Rob devised further sessions where he asked the groups to act out the solutions to some friendship problems that he posed. The groups explored different scenarios and discussed the emotional impact of each. These were so successful that Rob devised some activities to use with other year groups within the school.

Bullying, and particularly homophobic bullying, can be sensitively managed through role play (see Chapter 3 for a discussion of homophobic and other bullying). Drama groups and theatre companies can be a valuable resource to explore some of the issues related to bullying of any kind.

Debates and philosophy for children

The strategy of inviting children and young people to engage in debates supports our view that listening to the views of children (Chapter 4) is a vital aspect of all education, and especially so in RSE. Where children can openly raise points, question and share views between themselves with adult support, misconceptions and difference can be investigated.

Paul is a lead practitioner working in an after school club where a range of children of differing ages (5–13) and faiths attend. Frequent disputes have arisen between some of the older children which have left the younger children confused and influenced by the views of the older groups about a recent storyline in a soap opera that depicts the personal anguish of an Asian man who is gay but who is married to a woman. He begins a sexual relationship with a man. Some of the older children at the club have discussed the storyline and openly condemn the man. The younger children have heard about the programme and are asking questions about the complex relationships being presented and about the response of the older children. Paul feels unsure about how he may support the children's need to explore these issues but decides to invite the children to undertake a debate. He organizes the older children into two groups: one to represent the feelings and views of the man and the other to debate the view of his family. He allows for those younger children who want to, to observe the discussion. Paul chairs the debate and begins the activity by ensuring that all the children understand the need for clear ground rules so that all those involved show respectful and appropriate behaviours to each other. Paul then begins the debate by explaining the storyline:

As grown-ups, there are times when things may change, such as feelings and special friendships. In the programme there is an man whose marriage was arranged for him and he did not want to make his parents cross with him so he got married to the woman who his family chose for him. He now has two children but he begins to feel unhappy. He begins to realise that he loves his wife like a good friend but that he is not sure that he loves her as a special friend. He wants to be the special friend of someone else but he knows that his family will be angry and upset with him.

Paul then allows the groups who are debating three minutes each to present their cases. A further five minutes is offered to allow for questioning and answering. A range of viewpoints are explored and the children offer some valuable insights into their thinking. Paul rounds off the debate with a summary that focuses on the need for respect for difference and diversity within relationships. The children have found the activity interesting and have engaged with the process well. Paul congratulates the children on their mature approach to the issues.

This short, focused opportunity to engage in debate about issues related to family values, religion, sexuality and interpersonal relationships supports children's curiosities about complex relationships and the range of opinions that people may have about these. Analogies can be made to the difficulties that children themselves may have in their friendship groups that are similar; for example, parents not wanting them to play with certain friends and how they might feel about that. Paul uses the debate as an opportunity to introduce other ways of thinking about the issues raised, while emphasizing those related to self-respect and diversity. Further information about philosophy for children can be found at www.philosophy4children.co.uk/.

Visualization

Visualization is a useful strategy within RSE as it offers a framework to explore the views of children and to challenge stereotypes where appropriate.

Sue, an experienced Year 5 teacher, is increasingly concerned about the girls' interest in celebrity cultures. She overhears the girls in the toilets commenting on their own body shapes and sizes negatively and decides to undertake an activity with the class to discuss some of these perceptions. She gives the learners a non-gendered outline of a person and asks the children to imagine what they would like to look like when they are twenty years old. She places the children in pairs to discuss these images and opens a whole class discussion on what they have drawn. She uses this discussion to explore body image and to stress the 'beauty' in every body. Sue discusses different body shapes and sizes, while emphasizing how special each person is.

Such visualization of *what could be* is a useful tool for discussion about wider issues.

Assessment and recording learning in RSE

In 2002 Ofsted published a report, *Sex and Relationships*, suggesting, as part of wider recommendations, that schools should broaden their definition of achievement in RSE to include the development of learners' values, attitudes and personal skills. These elements are included in our recommendations for curriculum design outlined earlier in this chapter. While the assessment of these is commendable, they are also complex and difficult to measure, and have remained so over the years. We would argue that they are also potentially subjective judgements on ability and competencies. Although many curriculum assessments suggest an element of subjectivity on the part of the practitioner, it is important that this be reduced through the selection of appropriate tools for assessment. Department for Education (2018) guidance includes a brief focus on assessment, indicating that it should be aligned with high expectations of pupil achievement ensuring progression in learning. Assessment can occur during planned opportunities and also those that are unplanned. Blake and Muttock (2004: 17) suggest that there are different approaches to assessment which can encompass:

Private reflection: This can involve a logbook or diary. A learner may be given frequent opportunities to draw or write their reflections which can form a personal account of their learning following a discussion, or activity.

Self-assessment: Children may be asked to assess their understanding against the objectives of the session and to rate this through a traffic light system.

Peer assessment: Learners may assess through constructive feedback on the work or contributions of others. The practitioner should keep a record of this to inform a developing picture of achievement.

Structured informal assessments such as observations: These can be used to inform records and to track progress.

Formal assessment: This could take the form of a piece of writing or artwork in response to a task.

It is important for a range of assessments to be undertaken in order to monitor the progress of learners and for the reporting of this to parents/carers. In turn as part of the overall assessment process, careful evaluation of the RSE programme should be undertaken regularly at individual and whole staff levels to ensure the appropriateness and efficacy of the delivery and content.

Conclusion and summary of key learning points

This chapter has addressed the importance of the involvement of whole staff teams in establishing a setting/school policy and programme for RSE in order that staff can feel confident in their role in its delivery. The need for consultation with parents, carers, the governors and children in the process of writing a programme and policy has been explored, along with teaching strategies, assessment processes and continuous evaluation. Staff teams should engage regularly with other schools, particularly where children move to a secondary school, to assist with continuity of content. The notion of empowerment in RSE (Spencer et al., 2008) for children and young people is a key element in a programme's efficacy. Empowerment offers a more inclusive and comprehensive approach to education where children are actively and collectively participating in their learning, where course content is negotiated according to children's interests and needs and ensures that that no one set of values or behaviours are dominant or promoted.

Final thoughts

Our ambition in writing this book has been to provide a text that is accessible to a range of adults working with children and young people in the primary phase of their education. The book is intended to provide a clear pedagogical approach that can be adopted and which supports staff in devising a policy framework for RSE and an appropriate programme that will offer children the sexual competencies (Hirst,

2008) that they need for adulthood. Hirst (2008: 404) cites Wellings et al. (2001) in establishing a meaning and constructed measure for 'sexual competence' derived from variables on the reasons for and circumstances surrounding first intercourse:

- absence of regret;
- willingness (not under duress);
- autonomy of decision (a natural follow on in the relationship, being in love, curiosity), as opposed to non-autonomous (being drunk or peer pressure); and
- reliable use of contraception.

Hirst (2008) is clear that these competencies are lacking the inclusion of 'nuanced and complex' aspects of sexual activity such as pleasure and enjoyment. While the sexual competencies outlined by Wellings et al. (2001) define some of the expected outcomes for RSE, we would advocate that issues of intimacy, pleasure, enjoyment and respect for self and others be taught as fundamental and explicit aspects of any RSE programme. In order to facilitate this, adults working with children do need to be brave (as discussed in Chapter 1) in their approach to helping children to achieve sexual competence. Blake (2008: 39) outlines,

> We need to accept that young people are [usually] sexual beings, have sexual feelings, and need support on their journey through puberty, adolescence and into adulthood.

The need for the wider context, such as parents/carers and the media, to understand and acknowledge their role and responsibility in supporting children on their journey to adulthood (Chapter 2) is interrelated with the efficacy of an RSE programme. Blake also comments that it is for adults to accept that children and young people will make mistakes in all aspects of their lives, including sex, and this is an important part of growing and developing. We outlined in Chapter 3 the value of assisting children in developing a wealth of different relationships which are fundamental in offering networks of emotional support for mental and physical well-being, along with the interpersonal skills required to successfully maintain these. Chapter 4 discussed the value of hearing the views of children when devising programme content for RSE and how these provide a vital strategy for the appropriate differentiation of content. Where children are provided with opportunities to be listened to by adults with whom they can discuss matters of a sexual nature, research suggests that first sexual experiences are delayed. In turn, this may predict fewer propensities for regret as actions and behaviours from a more mature young person may be more considered. Issues of childhood innocence and religious concerns have been addressed in Chapter 5, where practical suggestions are made for managing the differing views about these. A key theme of the book, and particularly Chapter 5, is that of educational entitlement. We outline that children and young people should be offered the right to information about sexual matters and the opportunity to develop life skills related to their future relationships. Blake (2008: 40) outlines that RSE is defined as comprehensive; anything less is not RSE, 'describing what we understand as comprehensive RSE suggests that there is an alternative to a comprehensive programme'. While Blake's view has resonance, and is a preferred outcome of any RSE programme, we are realistic that staff and settings are working on a continuum of what can be defined as 'comprehensive' and as such this book has sought to help adults with practical pedagogical strategies for managing this sensitive curriculum area. Chapter 6 considered how to ensure that RSE is age-appropriate, and the need for a spiral curriculum to support ongoing and evolving learning. Chapter 7 explored such strategies in establishing ways that adults can respond to difficult questions from children. Chapter 8 considered the breadth of diversity in society and approaches to supporting inclusive and empathetic RSE.

It is important to note that the ambition of developing the sexual competence of all children within the context of high-quality relationships is a worthy and purposeful outcome: the processes for its achievement are not without challenge, many of which we have discussed. Hirst (2008: 411) refers to sexual competence as being the 'gold standard' however, is clear that

> sexual competence is not something one has or does not have, all of the time. Rather it is something one might have in one sexual situation or relationship but not another, and the quest is to work towards feeling competent *more of the time.*

The exploration of realistic expectations in RSE programmes can ensure that children and young people are adequately prepared because relationships of all kinds have their own challenges. Hirst concludes that

> issues such as the place of control, active decision-making and pleasure, and their [the children's] role within a diversity of relationships, signals recognition of young people's sexuality and their capacity to experience it. (2008: 411)

It is our hope that the materials developed within this book provide support in order to enable practitioners to facilitate children and young people in facing such challenges.

Signposts and further reading

PSHE Association (2018) *Preparing for Statutory Relationships Education. PSHE Education Lead's Pack: Key Stages 1 and 2.* PSHE Association. www.pshe-association.org.uk/curriculum-and-resources/resources/ preparing-statutory-relationships-education-pshe.

References

Blake, S. (2008) 'There's a Hole in the Bucket: The Politics, Policy and Practice of Sex and Relationships Education'. *Pastoral Care in Education*, 26 (1), 33–41.

Blake, S., and Muttock, S. (2004) *Assessment, Evaluation and Sex and Relationships Education: A Practical Toolkit for Education, Health and Community Settings*. London: National Children's Bureau.

Carter, V. (2006) *If I Had a Hundred Mummies*. London: Onlywomen Press.

Cole, B. (1995) *Mummy Laid an Egg*. London: Red Fox.

Corteen, K. (2006) 'Schools' Fulfilment of Sex and Relationship Education Documentation: Three School-Based Case Studies'. *Sex Education*, 6 (1), 77–99.

Department for Education and Employment (2000) *Sex and Relationship Education Guidance*. Nottingham: DfEE.

DfE (2018) *Relationships Education, Relationships and Sex Education (RSE) and Health Education: Guidance for Governing Bodies, Proprietors, Head Teachers, Principals, Senior Leadership Teams, Teachers*. London: Department for Education.

Harris, R., and Emberley, M. (1999) *Let's Talk about Where Babies Come From*. London: Walker Books.

Harris, R., and Emberley, M. (2007) *Let's Talk about Girls, Boys, Babies, Bodies, Families and Friends*. London: Walker Books.

Harris, R., and Emberley, M. (2010) *Let's Talk about Sex: Changing Bodies, Growing Up, Sex and Sexual Health*. London: Walker Books.

Hirst, J. (2008) 'Developing Sexual Competence? Exploring Strategies for the Provision of Effective Sexualities and Relationships Education'. *Sex Education*, 8 (4), 399–413.

Kippax, S., and Stephenson, N. (2005) 'Meaningful Evaluation of Sex and Relationship Education'. *Sex Education*, 5 (4), 359–73.

Macdonald, A. (2009) *Independent Review of the Proposal to Make Personal, Social, Health and Economic (PSHE) Education Statutory*. London: Department for Children, Schools and Families.

MacGilchrist, B., Myers, K., and Read, J. (2004) *The Intelligent School* (revised edn). London: Sage.

Mason, S. (2008) *Braving It Out! An Illuminative Evaluation of the Provision of Sex and Relationship Education in Two Primary Schools in England* (unpublished). Lincoln: Bishop Grosseteste University College Lincoln.

Mosley, J. (2005a) *Circle Time: Ages 5–11*. Leamington Spa: Scholastic.

Mosley, J. (2005b) *Circle Time for Young Children*. London: Taylor and Francis.

Mosley, J. (2006) *Step-by-Step Guide to Circle Time*. Trowbridge: Positive Press.

Ofsted (2005) *Personal, Social and Health Education in Secondary Schools*. HMI 3211. London: Ofsted.

Parnell, P., and Richardson, J. (2005) *And Tango Makes Three*. London: Simon and Schuster Books for Young Readers.

Piercy, H., and Haynes, G. (2006) 'Coherant, Comprehensive and Continuous: Developing a Curriculum for Effective Sex and Relationship Education in an English Primary School'. *Education and Health*, 25 (1), 12–15.

Sammons, P., Hillamn, J., and Mortimore, P. (1995) *Key Characteristics of Effective Schools: A Review of School Effectiveness Research*. London: Office for Standards.

Senge, P., Cambron-McCabe, N., Lucas, T., Smith, B., Dutton, J., and Kleiner, A. (2000) *Schools That Learn*. London: Nicholas Brealey.

Sex Education Forum (2005) *Sex and Relationships Education Framework*. Forum Factsheet 30. London: National Children's Bureau and Sex Education Forum.

Spencer, G., Maxwell, C., and Aggleton, P. (2008) 'What Does "Empowerment" Mean in School-Based Sex and Relationships Education?' *Sex Education*, 8 (3), 345–56.

UK Youth Parliament (2007) *Sex and Relationships Education: Are You Getting It?* London: UK Youth Parliament.

Valentine, J. (1994) *One Dad, Two Dads, Brown Dads, Blue Dads*. Los Angeles: Alyson Wonderland.

Vincent, K. (2007) 'Teenage Pregnancy and Sex and Relationship Education: Myths and (Mis)conceptions'. *Pastoral Care*, 25 (3), 16–23.

Walker, J., Green, J., and Tilford, S. (2003) 'An Evaluation of School Sex Education Team Training'. *Health Education*, 103 (6), 320–29.

Warwick, I., Aggleton, P., and Rivers, I. (2005) 'Accrediting Success: Evaluation of a Pilot Professional Development Scheme for Teachers of Sex and Relationship Education'. *Sex Education*, 5 (3), 235–52.

Wellings, K., Nanchahal, K., Macdowall, W., McManus, S., Erens, B., and Mercer, C. (2001) 'Sexual Behaviour in Britain: Early Heterosexual Experience'. *Sex Education*, 8 (4), 399–413.

Index